COMMUNICATION

AND

WOMEN'S

FRIENDSHIPS

Communication and Women's Friendships:
Parallels and Intersections in Literature and Life

Edited by

Janet Doubler Ward
JoAnna Stephens Mink

Bowling Green State University Popular Press
Bowling Green, OH 43403

Women's Studies Series
General Editor
Jane Bakerman

Other books in the series:

Child Brides and Intruders
Carol Wershoven

Alice and Eleanor: A Contrast in Style and Purpose
Sandra R. Curtis

PN
471
.C66
1993

For LaVahn and Roberta

ACKNOWLEDGEMENTS

In addition to the scholars whose work comprises the following chapters, we thank others whose ideas helped us to shape the focus of this anthology: Brinda Bose, Joan Kuczma Costello, Lillian Faderman, Lori Schroeder Haslem, Sarah R. Morrison, Caryl K. Sills, Lisa Tyler and Angela Vietto. We thank the many who responded to our calls for papers and who otherwise indicated an interest in our work.

We thank Dan Ward and Roland Nord for helping with computer-oriented tasks.

We thank Pat Browne and her staff at the Bowling Green State University Popular Press for their splendid help and encouragement.

For typing envelopes and other clerical tasks, we thank the secretarial support staff of the Mankato State University Department of English, particularly Christopher Harbo for compiling the list of Primary Works Discussed or Mentioned, which appears at the end of this book. For incidental postage expenses, we thank the MSU Department of English.

We thank Elizabeth G. Peck and Susan Koppelman for including us on their panel on feminist collaboration at the 1991 Midwest Modern Language Association Conference—and providing us with the opportunity to think not only about our own collaborative efforts but, more important, about our friendship.

And for child-minding when we needed "quality" work time, we thank Dan Ward.

Most of all, we thank the contributors to this anthology—without whose ideas, energy and cooperation our task would have been insurmountable.

J.D.W. and J.S.M.

CONTENTS

INTRODUCTION

The subject of women's friendships and communication has long held both personal and professional interest for us.

We were friends first. Actually, we were graduate school officemates in 1983, sharing a desk, class notes, cigarettes. Something happened, we don't recall exactly what—some crisis about a seminar paper deadline or some man—but, as a result, we became good friends. Our friendship has continued to evolve and to strengthen, in spite of the long distances between us, in spite of changes in both of our lifestyles and in spite of the various professional challenges which we have faced. As we were working together on a paper on feminist collaboration, which we presented at the 1991 Midwest Modern Language Association Conference, we had the opportunity to evaluate for ourselves, to discuss with each other and then to articulate to an audience the many parallels and intersections of which our friendship is comprised. We decided that the single factor which has strengthened our friendship (and our professional collaboration on three anthologies of essays as well as several conference sessions) is our ability to communicate—not too surprising, considering that we are both professors of English. But it's more than that.

Within the last few years, much has been written in popular and scholarly literature about the changing role of women and how women have expanded and redefined their "place" in our society through their friendships and mentoring. Indeed, the paperback and magazine displays at any mall bookstore bear witness to the increasing emphasis on the shift in roles which women play, as well as on our analysis of the effects of these changes. For several reasons, we, as individuals and as members of our society, have become more aware of the significance and vitality of women's friendships, an interest which quite naturally has been addressed by literary scholars as well—and which publishers' catalogs and articles in scholarly journals attest.

Like much else, the ways in which women (and men, for that matter) develop and maintain friendships go back to our mothers.

2 Communication and Women's Friendships

Some mothers, for example, don't seem to have close or significant friendships with other women, a situation perhaps resulting from their relative isolation, perhaps living on the outskirts of town and staying in the home or to their natural reticence about feelings and emotions. But if young women have no model from their mothers upon which to base their adult relationships with women, they may tend to see them as competitors—for attention, for affection, for professional success. Some mothers, on the other hand, have several women friends. Daughters remember their mothers' friends coming over to the house for coffee and talking about whatever their concerns were at that time. In cases such as these, the role models are more positive resulting, it is to be hoped, in supportive adult friendships between women. Although the types of friendships may differ, female friends are an important part in many women's lives—perhaps now more than ever.

We certainly are not arguing for the limitation of women's lives to the private sphere as defined by the Cult of True Womanhood in the eighteenth and early nineteenth centuries. The idea of separate spheres for men and women—whereby men would dominate in the "public" world of business, politics and the professions, and women would reign in the private domestic sphere, becoming the moral touchstone for hearth, husband and children—served mostly to keep women in their place, angels emprisoned in the house. Women developed relationships with female relatives and other women, a network upon which they relied for advice and friendship. This domestic network became less significant at the turn of the century as increasing numbers of women entered the public, male world. In fact, to a certain extent, to be considered "successful," a woman needed to sever her ties to other women, to be "like a man."

Neither case—the almost complete reliance on only women's separate sphere or the rejection of female friendships for the more powerful male associations—is, in our opinion, an acceptable state of affairs. However, we recognize that today, women need once again to develop the bonds of "sisterhood" which can provide the support which our families, our "significant other" relationships and our social institutions have left void. One important way of doing this, of course, is to turn to examples of literary friendships. By looking at various *types* of friendships and by examining how they either lapse or develop into strong relationships, we may better understand ourselves and our relationships.

This anthology, our third, is the culmination of a two-year process. Once our idea took shape and we sent out announcements and calls for papers, we received over 50 abstracts submitted by scholars from the United States and abroad, a clear indication that the topic is of interest to many. After much reflection—individual and collaborative—we determined that a valuable approach was to frame discussion of the discourse communities and the literary texts against a background of the historical and multi-cultural aspects of women's friendships. We believe that the 11 essays which comprise this book demonstrate the changing ways in which women have been viewed and how contemporary eyes view women's friendships differently than those of the past. This anthology suggests that women's friendships are to be greatly valued—indeed treasured—as very significant parts of women's lives, perhaps even more significant and fulfilling than their male friendships.

The chapters which form our discussion in this anthology offer a variety of perspectives, which necessarily overlap and defy distinct categories, just as the relationships which they depict interconnect individuals and the facets of their lives. We begin with diaries, journals and letters, probably the most personal forms of communication; the inherent intimacy of these modes of discourse can also affect the fiction which women authors write. Our second section illustrates ways in which women's friendships are important images in canonical nineteenth- and twentieth-century novels by women. The role of female friendships, beginning in the eighteenth century and continuing into the twentieth century, took on political overtones, as the chapters in our third section discuss. Our final section focuses on ways in which female friendship is depicted in novels and stories from non-Anglo cultures.

* * * * *

Suzanne Bunkers explains in "'Faithful Friends': Diaries and the Dynamics of Women's Friendships" the ways in which women's diaries functioned as confidantes and friends for their writers. She uses three "pairs" as examples: Emily and Sarah Gillespie, mother and daughter; Ada James and Ada Briggs, cousins; and Caroline Seabury and Emily Quiner, teachers during the Civil War. Her pairs illustrate some important concepts about these nineteenth-century women and their diaries: relations between women which are based on kinship can, with the catalyst of an intimate medium of communication, transcend those familial ties and develop into true friendships between the women. Sharing their diaries, an act based on trust, is characteristic of women's kinship and friendship networks. Furthermore, during particularly trying times in such women's lives, the diary itself becomes a confidante and, as Bunkers concludes, takes on the role of a beloved sister or a constant, faithful friend.

Our next chapter extends Bunkers' discussion of nineteenth-century diaries and journals by analyzing the intense and intimate way that journals are used by contemporary authors. In her chapter, "Linking Women Across Generations: The Journals and Letters of Lessing and Sarton," Barbara Frey Waxman demonstrates how Doris Lessing and May Sarton create a discourse, by means of fictional and authentic journals, that describes old age and youth and that provides contexts in which older and younger women communicate physically, psychologically and philosophically. For example, Jane Somers, in Lessing's *The Diary of a Good Neighbor*, uses the first-person diary in order to better understand her attachment to an elderly woman. Likewise, Caro Spencer in Sarton's *As We Are Now* often uses her notebook to speculate on the nature of friendships between women and, in particular, as a way of better understanding her relationship with Anna; the journal is more freeing than other forms of communication, letters, for instance. Finally, Waxman explains how Sarton's own journal, *At Seventy*, celebrates her female friendships within the context of her own aging process.

Pamela J. Olano's essay, "'Women Alone Stir my Imagination': Intertextual Eroticism in the Friendships/Relationships Created by Virginia Woolf," brings together two important aspects of our general topic of women's friendships and communication. Olano shows the connection between an author's journals and letters and her fiction, and she puts that discussion within the framework of lesbian relationships. Olano investigates the intricate psychological constructions of Woolf as female friend, lesbian lover, incestuous sister and woman who craved from other women that which for her only women could provide—the stimulus to create and the security to seek health. Using Woolf's letters and journals as the text, Olano reconstructs the relationship between the writer's life and her fictional characters. The relationships between women in *To the Lighthouse* and *Mrs. Dalloway* reinforce Woolf's strongest desire in her associations with Vita Sackville-West and Dame Ethel Smythe— to communicate with other women.

Elizabeth Cooley's chapter "'The Medicine She Trusted To': Women, Friendship and Communication in *The Voyage Out* and *Night and Day*," continues the discussion on Woolf by exploring female friendship in Woolf's earliest novels. These novels are often viewed as apprentice works, more as Victorian romances than modern innovations. But, Cooley explains, they are more: In each novel the protagonist learns essential lessons about communication and human relations which help her to grow psychologically and emotionally. These early novels, though not presenting the complex characterizations of Woolf's later works, are important in showing how Rachel and Katherine each develop after experiencing her first adult friendship with a woman and engaging in the "good medicine" of "woman-talk."

Laurie Buchanan's essay, "'Islands' of Peace: Female Friendships in Victorian Women's Fiction," shows how nineteenth-century novels by women not only provide a text for women's lives and friendships, but also illustrate how women's friendships stand as an "'island' of peace and understanding" within that text and how the text becomes a discourse that allows women to communicate their experiences to each other. Thus the novel, itself, serves as a mode of communication—a network and a text—between the woman writer and her reader. Using the work of Tess Cosslett and Nancy Chodorow as the basis of her discussion, Buchanan explores the importance of female friendships as a way of replacing and circumventing unsatisfying mother-daughter relations.

When women do not or cannot communicate, the results can be disastrous. This lack of communication is often a socio-political, rather than an individual, construct. In "'I can step out of myself a little': Feminine Virtue and Female Friendship in Hannah Foster's *The Coquette*," John Paul Tassoni connects the views of the women characters in this late-eighteenth-century novel to their social and political milieu. Feminine virtue was one of the most important cornerstones in the Cult of True Womanhood, an image that had its beginnings in the political arena of post-Revolutionary America. Although the new republic was based on ideals of personal liberty and morality, the social and political arena was clearly patriarchal. Seeking to find a "place" for women within this male-ordered world, the Cult of True Womanhood was developed and supported by both men and women, an ideology whereby women became the embodiment of the morality and virtue necessary for the continuation of the new republic. Tassoni examines *The Coquette*, one of the most popular novels of its time, against this political and social framework, focusing on the rhetoric of virtue in the context of late-eighteenth-century American female friendships. He finds that the way in which the women characters "read" Eliza Wharton illustrates the cultural—and patriarchal—concerns which determined perceptions of women in the new republic, and shows the intersection between life and literature.

Susan Yadlon's essay parallels Tassoni's in that "The Bluestocking Circle: The Negotiation of 'Reasonable' Women" focuses on the cult of domesticity in eighteenth-century England. Her chapter focuses on Elizabeth Montagu, Hester Chapone, Lady Mary Harley, Elizabeth Carter and Catherine Talbot—women in the Bluestocking circle, a group of middle-and upper-class women who from 1750 to 1790 lobbied for an expansion of female education. Their friendships had epistolary origins due to the geographically isolating conditions under which these women lived. Tracing the development of their friendships and their ideas on female education by looking at their letters, Yadlon argues that the women in the Bluestocking circle should be recognized for their success in championing female education within the acknowledged limitations implicit in the realm of domesticity.

Nora Ruth Roberts' chapter, "Three Generations of Radical Women's Man-Talk," also focuses on politically-defined communities of women. By examining the ways in which women talk about men in three novels by women radicals, she shows how "man-talk" among radical women has served to redefine both women's friendships with each other and women's particular relationship to radical politics. Her analysis of Meridel Le Sueur's *The Girl*, Doris Lessing's *The Golden Notebook*, and Marge Piercy's *Small Changes* is useful in several ways. Firstly, Roberts explicates the medium—the form—of communication between women. Secondly, she analyzes how that medium is affected by their subject matter, specifically when it is about men but also concerning politics, families, sexuality. Finally, she finds that by exchanging confidences about the men in their lives, women find their own communality and bonding and, in fact, form a sisterhood that functions at a more real plane than the rhetoric of class unity that bombards them from the men in their political spheres.

Katherine B. Payant's chapter is the bridge into what we have loosely identified as our final section of this anthology. In "Female Friendship in the Contemporary *Bildungsroman*," Payant explores three novels which illustrate the role of female friendship in novels of initiation involving female protagonists. *During the Reign of the Queen of Persia* by Joan Chase shows four adolescent girls, who are sisters and cousins, living together in a female-dominated household in rural Ohio. Their relationship is important not only because it goes beyond the bonds of kinship into true friendship, but also because the novel shows how women's friendships between generations (the girls' mothers, aunts and grandmother) develop. *Rumors of Peace* by Ella Leffland confronts several themes important to three girls approaching adolescence during World War II. The relationship between Suse, the novel's protagonist, and her two friends, sisters and foils, focuses on an important theme—racism, the fear and hatred inflicted on Japanese-Americans in the girls' California town. The change in Suse is depicted by her changing friendships with the other girls, just as the change in Celie, Alice Walker's protagonist in *The Color Purple*, is highlighted by her female friendships. Payant's chapter explores three different types of female friendships involving both adolescents and adults to illustrate her point that contemporary novels are less apt to portray women as rivals, as has historically been the case, and more likely to emphasize the gifts which women give each other and their enduring bonds of friendship.

These bonds of female friendship are important in novels about Native American women, as Julie Tharp shows in "Women's Community and Survival in the Novels of Louise Erdrich." *The Beet Queen* presents female friendship outside of both traditional Native culture and heterosexual marriage. In *Love Medicine* and *Tracks* Erdrich develops a view of women's friendships complicated by tribal politics, familial feuds and sexual infidelity, but their strong relationships help them to survive. Tharp's discussion focuses on the ways in which Native American women in Erdrich's novels must deal with institutionalized control of women which the Anglo culture has imposed upon their traditional cultures. Thus, Tharp's chapter, by focusing on different Native American women and their friendships, points out that while the form and political context of friendships may differ, the importance of female bonding transcends racial and ethnic distinctions.

Continuing our section on multi-cultural literature and completing our discussion of the various forms of female friendships is Renee Larrier's study, "Inscriptions of Orality and Silence: Representations of Female Friendship in Francophone Africa and the Caribbean." Her investigation begins with how women's friendships are represented in oral narratives. She shows how different forms of discourse inform women's friendships by a close reading of four novels and one short story by twentieth-century male and female writers from Senegal, Guadeloupe and Martinique. Heretofore, an examination of female friendship in francophone African or Caribbean narratives has not been done. Larrier's chapter lays the groundwork in answer to this need; her examination shows that women writers especially are concerned with communication as their narratives are informed by oral, written and silence discourses that characterize women's communication.

* * * * *

In planning and reflecting during the early stages of putting together this book, we learned a number of things. One was the high value we place on our own friendship and communication with each other. Another was the vital purpose that women's friendships and communication have in all women's lives. As our contributors discuss the fundamental values of women's friendships and communication in the studies which form this collection, we can identify and understand the many parallels and intersections between literature and life. May the essays provided herein give impetus to our continuing appreciation for the many types of women's friendships.

JoAnna Stephens Mink
and
Janet Doubler Ward

"Faithful Friends":
Diaries and the Dynamics
of Women's Friendships

SUZANNE L. BUNKERS

For there is no friend like a sister
In calm or stormy weather;
To cheer one on the tedious way,
To fetch one if one goes astray,
To lift one if one totters down,
To strengthen whilst one stands.
—from "Goblin Market" (1862)

These lines, taken from one of Christina Rossetti's best-known poems, express sentiments echoed by many nineteenth-century American women in their private writings. Scholars such as Carroll Smith-Rosenberg, Marilyn Ferris Motz and Lillian Faderman have demonstrated the importance of women's memoirs, letters and diaries as channels for establishing and strengthening ties of kinship and friendship. My own research has borne out their belief: women's diaries enact stories that embody the dynamics and conditions of women's friendship. Like other kinds of women's stories, women's diaries locate women's culture, transforming experience into ways of knowing. As Bettina Aptheker writes: "Women's stories locate women's cultures, women's ways of seeing; they designate meaning, make women's consciousness visible to us. Stories transform our experiences into ways of knowing—about ourselves as women and about ourselves as women looking at the world" (43).

In this essay, I wish to explore that transformation. My observations are based on my eight-year study of diaries by nineteenth-century Midwestern American women, most of whom did not consider themselves writers and many of whose lives passed without public recognition or acclaim. My sample includes over 200 unpublished manuscript diaries written by Minnesota, Iowa and

Wisconsin women during the period from approximately 1840-1900 and housed in state and local historical society archives.

For these women, as for many of their contemporaries, the diary was an especially useful medium for developing and sustaining close friendships because it embodied the trust and security characteristic of women's kinship and friendship networks. In many women's cases, the diary itself took on the role of a beloved sister or a constant, faithful friend.

Commenting on the issue of audience in women's diaries, Margo Culley explains that some "are intended for real audiences but in many more the audience is implied. In some instances, the diary itself takes on this role as it is personified. 'Dear diary' is a direct address to an ideal audience: always available, always listening, always sympathetic" (11). In her discussion of the roles played by diaries in women's lives, Jane Dupree Begos writes that keeping a diary "is a conversation with the self, a personal laboratory for making observations and examining feelings" (ii). "For many," Begos explains, "the diary/journal is the non-judgmental confidante, the friend to whom one can 'tell all' without fear of criticism" (ii).

Penelope Franklin describes the diary as "a 'safe place' where new roles can be tried out, protected from censure; a sounding board for ideas or emotions that may not be acceptable to friends or family; a testing ground where creative experiments of all kinds can be tried, with no one to laugh if they fizzle; a means of regaining balance when caught by conflicting emotions; a valuable record of progress and growth; a place where past, present and future live together—and all under one's control" (xix). Franklin continues: "The diary often evolves into a friend, a confidante, the first place to run with an exciting secret and a last refuge when other people can't or won't listen. This has been especially important to women, who are often isolated physically by the conditions of their lives or psychically by restraints placed on the expression of their feelings" (xix).

Like the work of Elizabeth Baer, Virginia Beauchamp, Margo Culley, Dure Jo Gillikin, Minrose Gwin, Rebecca Hogan, Cynthia Huff, Judy Nolte Lensink, Laurel Thatcher Ulrich and other scholars who have studied women's diaries, my own research has confirmed the belief that the diary cannot easily be pigeon-holed as either a "public" or a "private" text. Contrary to popular mythology about diary-keeping, diarists generally have a keen sense of audience. As Margo Culley notes,

The importance of the audience, real or imagined, conscious or unconscious, of what is usually thought of as a private genre cannot be overstated. The presence of a sense of audience, in this form of writing as in all others, has a crucial influence over what is said and how it is said. Friend, lover, mother, God, a future self—whatever role the audience assumes for the writer— that presence becomes a powerful "thou" to the "I" of the diarist. It shapes the selection and arrangement of detail within the journal and determines more than anything else the kind of self-construction that diarist presents. (11-12)

Unlike today, a hundred years ago the diary was not generally considered a highly secretive, carefully guarded text, intended only for its writer's eyes. My research has not uncovered a single nineteenth-century woman's diary that has a lock and key. The notion of the "private" diary appears to be a distinctly post-Freudian phenomenon. Caroline Seabury's and Ada James's diaries, for example, were collaborative texts, with entries planned and/or written by two or more women. Emily and Sarah Gillespie's diaries were chronicles of family life, initiated with the intention of creating a group document spanning generations. Many women's diaries fulfilled the role of trusted allies; in fact, Emily Quiner called her diary her "faithful friend." All of these texts amply demonstrate the centrality of women's diaries in defining and nurturing relationships among women.

In this essay, I will consider some ways in which nineteenth-century American women's diaries functioned as trusted friends and confidantes and ways in which friendships between women were explored and cemented in their diaries. I am going to draw on diary entries made by six women: Emily and Sarah Gillespie, a mother and daughter living in rural Iowa; Ada James and Ada Briggs, cousins growing up in Wisconsin during the late 1800s; and Caroline Seabury and Emily Quiner, Midwestern teachers, each of whom kept a diary during the Civil War. My intention is to illustrate ways in which the diary functioned as a mode of discourse that generated, cemented and strengthened friendships between women in nineteenth-century America.

Keep well this book and bear in mind
A constant friend is hard to find.

On January 1, 1877, Sarah Gillespie wrote these lines on the cover page of her diary. Like many girls, Sarah Gillespie started keeping a diary shortly after she learned to write. Along with her older brother Henry, Sarah grew up on her parents' farm near Manchester, Iowa. As a girl, Sarah first attended country school; but, with her mother's support, she eventually began attending the Manchester Academy, a mile from the Gillespie farm.

Sarah's mother, Emily Gillespie, had begun keeping a diary in 1858 at the age of 20, and she wrote regularly in it for 30 years. Her marriage to James Gillespie was contentious and abusive; Emily's unhappiness was soon recorded in her diary. Sarah observed her parents' relationship, and her own diary became a trusted friend in whom she could confide her feelings. Emily and Sarah Gillespie read and wrote in one another's diaries, a fact which makes possible a fascinating longitudinal study of rural women's daily activities, family relationships and socio-economic support networks. Most importantly, in terms of this essay, these texts show how the diary functioned as a friend for each of its writers and as a means of fostering a friendship between mother and daughter.

Like many nineteenth-century women's diaries, Emily and Sarah Gillespie's diaries cannot be easily classified as either private or public. Both Emily and Sarah Gillespie played central roles in creating and preserving their diaries. Their diaries were apparently not intended for publication; however, before her death, Emily gave her diaries to her daughter. In later years Sarah painstakingly recopied Emily's first five diaries into notebooks and then donated all ten volumes of her mother's diary, numbering over 2,000 pages, to the State Historical Society of Iowa in 1948. At the front of each volume, Sarah wrote brief biographical information about Emily, and Sarah pasted family photographs inside the diaries' front covers. Sarah's decision to preserve the family papers has insured that her and her mother's diaries are extant today.

Sarah's earliest diary, a tiny volume hand-sewn by her mother, was given to Sarah when she was five. It contains handwriting exercises such as "I am a good girl" and "Learn your lessons well." A second early diary is filled with sentences such as "Be gentle, Ever be kind" and "Sarah is a nice girl in school." Subsequent diaries mark Sarah's development as a writer; her entries include descriptions of school work, daily chores, weather patterns and visits to friends as well as highly introspective passages about family relationships. Sarah's last diary (1951 to 1952) is filled with entries about her failing health and her efforts to type biographical information on her mother and herself for the State Historical Society archives. All told, Sarah's 17-volume diary numbers over 3,500 pages.

She had, of course, learned the role of diarist from her mother, who encouraged her daughter's early attempts to keep a journal and who modeled the process by keeping one herself. Based on Judy Lensink's and my intensive study of both women's diaries over the past ten years, it has become clear that Sarah and her mother read and on occasion wrote in one another's diaries. As their mother-daughter relationship grew closer, their diaries became their mutual confidantes. Emily wrote about her daily chores, her visits with friends and her fear of her husband's abusive outbursts. Sarah described her daily chores, her budding career as a teacher, her mother's unhappiness and her father's abusive behavior. As early as March 5, 1881, at age 15, she wrote: "Ma & Pa went to town. they had a '*spat*' I guess. ma told me about it." On October 9 of that year, she expressed her fears following one of her father's outbursts: "Its no use to repeat here what he said. But it was a great deel. He almost despises the ground that Ma walks on & its too bad, I was afraid of her dear life last night...."

In 1883, Sarah began teaching at a country school a few miles from the family farm. She boarded with relatives and students' parents on weeknights, then returned to the Gillespie farm on most weekends. At several points in her diary, Sarah questioned how long she would be able to continue teaching, given her father's continuing attempts to undermine her mother's declining health.

A series of entries during February and March 1886 illustrates the nature of the mother-daughter diaries. At the time, Sarah was teaching in a country school several miles from home and boarding with her pupils' families. She left her diary in her bureau drawer at home, and she wrote daily diary entries in another notebook, later copying them into her diary. On February 16, 1886, Sarah wrote in her diary about feeling lonesome and discouraged as a teacher. On March 1, Emily responded by writing this entry in her daughter's diary:

> Sarah, you said last night, "Ma write in my Journal. *I* can't." I just thought I would write a line as I saw it in the Drawer. I tried to not read a word, but Sarah my eyes do take in so much that the above could not quite escape. I get lonesome every day— only that I think of Henry & you. how you are getting along so

well. his letters and your sunday visits I should almost give up. I am so thankful that you are both all my heart could wish and can I really appreciate the blessing. You must never get discouraged with the annoyance which some pupils are ever ready to give. do only the best you can and their cutting words and misdemeanor will give them the most inconvenience. *they* will *not* forget. There is no use for us to worry or be made unhappy at the folly of others. just let them pass....

These and other entries in both Emily's and Sarah's diaries amply demonstrate that this mother and daughter included one another in their intended audiences and that their diaries served as confidantes. Their "private" writings both shaped and reflected the nature of their mother-daughter bond.

During her final years, Emily Gillespie became too disabled to write in her diary, and she asked Sarah to do it for her. On May 26, 1886, after Emily had been disabled by a stroke, she dictated a diary entry to Sarah, who recorded it in her mother's diary: "Ma cant write in her journal & wants me to. She is feeling some better is able to sit up awhile. She came very near dyeing. It seems almost impossible to keep her alive every night...." Sarah continued writing many diary entries for her mother; these entries offer additional evidence of the extent to which Sarah knew what was in her mother's diary.

Emily Gillespie died on March 24, 1888, at the age of 49. Although Sarah Gillespie eventually married, she continued to teach, which was highly unusual for a married woman at the turn of the century. In January 1913, at the age of 47, Sarah was elected to a term as Superintendent of Schools in Page County, Iowa. Following her husband's death in January 1914 and her failure to win re-election to another term as county superintendent the following year, Sarah returned to the family farm to keep house for her brother Henry, a lifelong bachelor.

Not surprisingly, Sarah and Henry began to repeat the dysfunctional pattern long before established by their parents. Henry verbally abused his sister; she confided in her diary about the abuse and apparently suffered in silence, a way of coping that ultimately did not serve her well. On April 14, 1916, Sarah wrote:

I am so sorry I came. and that I allowed my things to be brought here. I hope never to misjudge and ill treat anyone. He [Henry] seems revengeful and to harbor prejudice and bitterness of real

or imagined wrongs. Is resentful and crushing...I only wish that I
had them [my things] in a little home of my own somewhere *to
night.*

As this entry demonstrates, Sarah's diary continued to be her
"constant friend" throughout this trying time in her life.

By June 1917, Sarah's health had broken, and she spent five
weeks at Hinsdale Sanitarium near Chicago. In August 1917 she left
the farm to supervise new teachers. Over the next 20 years she
became a highly respected voice in the movement to train teachers
to develop effective curricula for country schools. She earned
bachelor's and master's degrees, and she continued to train new
teachers until 1935, when she faced mandatory retirement at the
age of 70. Once more she returned to the family farm to keep house
for her brother. Subsequent diary entries reveal that Sarah continued
to confide in her diary during nearly 20 more miserable years on the
farm with Henry, where the siblings remained locked in a love/hate
relationship. Henry died in 1954 and Sarah in 1955.

The diaries of Emily and Sarah Gillespie reveal the outline of
their close relationship, one which illustrates the complexity of the
mother-daughter bond, examined in depth by contemporary
theorists such as Nancy Chodorow, Adrienne Rich, Judith Arcana
and Sara Ruddick. Adrienne Rich's analysis of motherhood within
patriarchal culture is especially relevant to the lives of Emily and
Sarah Gillespie because it helps to account for the complexity and
paradoxes inherent in the mother-daughter relationship, defined to a
great extent by the institutionalization and idealization of
motherhood in nineteenth-century America. At the same time,
Emily's and Sarah's diaries show how the women became friends
and allies. They used their diaries to name familial abuse and
validate one another's feelings. Their patterns of interaction were
embodied in their diaries' pages, and Sarah's preservation of their
diaries was part of this interaction. For mother and daughter, the
diary became a confidante in whom family secrets could be
entrusted—and a safe place where they could be preserved. These
women's diaries are rich in texture and detail, interweaving love
and trust between mother and daughter. The diary, for both Emily
and Sarah Gillespie, was a "constant friend"—and, as Sarah
observed, such constant friends *were* hard to find.

Like these women's diaries, the diaries kept by Ada L. James of
Richland Center, Wisconsin, illustrate the ways in which the diary
can foster and nourish friendship between women and the ways in

which the diary itself can function as a friend. Ada James was born in 1876; she began keeping a diary as an adolescent and continued until shortly before her death in 1952. As a young woman, Ada James trained to become a teacher. In later years she became a central figure in the women's suffrage and child welfare movements in her home state.

Ada James's diaries for 1895-96 reveal the importance she attached to her friendships with other young women. At the time she was being courted by Charles Cornwall, whom she often identified as "C.C." in diary entries. Ada worried about the negative effects that the courtship might have on her relationships with her good friends Elsie and Irene, and especially on her relationship with her closest friend and confidante, her cousin Ada Briggs. Many of Ada James' diary entries centered on herself and her cousin. The "two Adas," as they often referred to themselves, were devoted friends who read and wrote in one another's diaries. As it turned out, they were being courted by the same young man—"C.C." This became apparent to Ada James in April 1895. On April 9, she wrote in her diary:

> I went to Shakespeare. Ada was there. I am very much afraid that we girls are permitting an indescribable feeling to spring up between us, sometimes it is hard to choke the tears back, but I don't know what I can do to help it. I am only afraid of making things worse.

The next several diary entries continue in this vein until April 16, 1895, when Ada James wrote that she had had a long talk with her cousin: "I told her all I felt I ought." Shortly thereafter, the "two Adas" apparently resolved their differences over "C.C." They remained close friends; perhaps not coincidentally, Ada James wrote in her diary of reading Eliot's *Daniel Deronda* aloud with her cousin and emphasized their discussion of tangled love relationships in that novel. On June 22, 1895, Ada Briggs and Ada James met for a visit.

On July 8, 1895, Ada James noted that she had been chosen for a teaching position for the coming fall, and she commented: "It will be such a satisfaction to be able to at least *prove* myself a failure. But I am so anxious to teach that I don't feel as though I could do anything else than succeed." Later that month, the "two Adas" spent time together again. Writing in her cousin's diary, Ada Briggs outlined what she called her "prophecy" for Ada James:

A fair young teacher, after a year of most successful work in the schoolroom, steps out into the world once more, followed by loving thoughts and dearest wishes of the little flock who will long for the return of Sept. because it may bring with it the bright presence of the girl who loved everyone of them. The girl who never tired of studying them, while she taught. Will she return to the school-room in Sept. 1896? Yes, I think she will, but her determination to make teaching a life work—or rather to confine her efforts principally to giving instruction in our public schools—is not quite so strong as it was when she told her coz. that she meant to become a fixture in the schoolroom. What has modified her determination? Well, ask that tall, athletic young gentleman who so cleverly sends the balls across the net to his fair opponent, for, methinks, *he* it is who should receive the blame for what our schools have lost...

Upon reading her cousin's prophecy, Ada James wrote this reply in her diary:

...I have been wondering what young man Ada B. had reference to. My anticipations for the next year are so great. I hope the realizations can be as much. It seems so strange to think how little I used to look forward to the future. I feel so confident that Ada doesn't care for C.C. yet I am afraid she doesn't want me to. She would like to have him for a friend & I hope she always may, as I feel sure she will.

The following year, on July 22, 1896, Ada Briggs wrote another prophecy in Ada James' diary:

To-night my Ada and I sit, as we did just one year ago, at 1545 10th Street, writing and talking, not by mere coincidence, but by appointment, and each has begged the other to open the diary of "the other Ada" with a prophecy for the coming year. These two pledging themselves to meet on the evening of July 22nd, '97 for the same purpose. My prophecy made for Ada has been nearly fulfilled—indeed, my success in this forecast has made me not a little conceited, since I commence this one with all confidence in its fulfillment.

Ada Briggs went on to prophesy the idyllic union of Ada James and her suitor, and she closed by signing herself: "Conceitedly yours,

Sibyl." These "prophecies" not only prove that the close friends read one another's diaries but also demonstrate that they were intimately acquainted with the details of one another's lives. Their mutual affection is readily apparent.

Subsequent diary entries reveal that Ada Briggs' prophecy for her cousin did not come true. Ada James' romance with "C.C." was broken off by her family, and she never married. In 1898, shortly after the death of her beloved sister Annie, she wrote:

> Life at present does look sad, but my religion is to *try* to be happy, at least to seem so and try to make others happy. I am happy because I am busy—and that is everything but how deeply I do feel at times when I am not on my guard. I have thought of this poem often lately and find it so hard this "standing alone." I shall soon be twenty-two, I dread next birthday & I am so weary of "standing alone."

Plagued by increasing deafness, Ada James nevertheless graduated from the University of Wisconsin and became active in social reform movements. She helped found the Political Equality Club, an organization for young women, and she became active in the Wisconsin Woman's Suffrage Association and the Wisconsin Women's Progressive Association. She remained close to her cousin Ada Briggs, and the two women visited one another and traveled abroad together during their adult years.

Ada James continued to keep diaries, although there is a gap in her diaries during the 1920s, when she was suffering from cancer. When she resumed her diary on January 1, 1929, she wrote:

> It is many years & much has transpired since I last kept a diary. Most notable change is my own personal viewpoint, a very different woman will write in this book. I wonder whether death will transform us more than life. I quit keeping a daily record book when I knew that I had a cancer and life seemed too hideous to record. That pall hung over me several years following the operation but little by little all but the scar faded from my mind & body until now I am the happiest I have ever been in my life....

Throughout her life, Ada James remained active in social reform movements. Her many years of work on the Richland County

Children's Board led her to advocate birth control and prenatal care, and she took a highly controversial position in favor of mandatory sterilization of the mentally retarded. In 1949 she resigned from the Children's Board, and she died on September 29, 1952, at the age of 76.

Ada L. James' diaries, which span 45 years, offer convincing evidence not only about how the diary fostered friendship between nineteenth-century American women but also about how the diary itself functioned as a friend and confidante for its writer. The diary embodied virtues that made it a valued companion for many women who saw it as trustworthy and empathetic. The commitment of time, energy and trust that many women made to keeping a diary was a commitment to a friend.

Two Civil-War-era diaries, one kept by Caroline Seabury from 1854-63, and the other kept by Emily Quiner from 1861-63, offer further examples of the diary as trusted confidante. In their integration of personal experience with historical events and in their recognition of an audience that included others as well as themselves, both women's diaries defy easy categorization as either "private" or "public" texts.

Caroline Seabury was born in Southbridge, Massachusetts, in 1827. Early in life she lost most of her family members to consumption. As a young woman, she trained to become a teacher; and in October 1854, she traveled to Columbus, Mississippi, to teach French at the Columbus Female Institute, a school for the daughters of wealthy white townspeople. She remained in Mississippi until 1863, and her diary details her nine years in the South before and during the Civil War.

Caroline Seabury's journey to the South provided the impetus for starting a diary, one that would record her experiences as well as those of her younger sister, Martha:

> Christmas 1854. It has been to be a happy day—My dear Martha is here after the long journey arrived safely this morning... The hum-drum life of a teacher gives little variety save what one's own thoughts afford. I think as my journey has been noted down, for the first time in my life, I will keep a sort of journal, perhaps not [to] be seen once in three months, but when I feel like scribbling it may help to while away time, perhaps now & then something may happen which I will like to look over in after years—my sister and I together....

Unfortunately, like other family members, Martha died of consumption a few years later, and Caroline was left on her own in Columbus. Increasingly, her diary became the one friend in whom she could confide her experiences and relate her horror at the instances of slavery she witnessed.

Once the Civil War began, Caroline used her diary to report on battles and to describe the townspeople's adjustment to a wartime economy. She also inscribed her conflicting feelings about the war. On June 1, 1862, she wrote: "When will this agony be over—From the hour where I first saw the Confederate flag flying to this evening there has been a conflict of feeling—personal attachments— struggling against inborn principles—."

Later that same year, Caroline was dismissed from her position at the Columbus Female Institute when its president decided that only Southern teachers could be trusted to teach there. Caroline managed to find work tutoring the daughters of the owner of Waverley Plantation, just outside Columbus. In January 1863, she wrote in her diary that Abraham Lincoln's Emancipation Proclamation "is laughed at here—as the powerless words of an ignorant man."

The summer of 1863 brought the siege of Vicksburg, which culminated in a Union victory and the re-opening of the Mississippi River for travel north. By this time Caroline was desperate to leave Mississippi; in late July, she wrote in her diary that an "unexpected opportunity" had come her way. She undertook an arduous journey through the Mississippi countryside, hidden in a covered wagon, eventually reaching the Mississippi River, where she waved a homemade Union flag to attract the attention of a boat carrying Union soldiers back up the river. Slowly she made her way back to the north, finally returning to her aunt and uncle's home in Brooklyn. There, in their sitting room, Caroline wrote the final entry in her diary:

> In port again—after this tedious journey—in which though a "lone woman"—I had found friends and help every-where—In no other than my native land would this have been possible. Most devoutly I thank God that He has protected me through so many dangers—once more to see "the land of the free"—soon I hope to grasp the hand of my uncle & his family—then my only brother—As I sit—this morning—thinking over all three years since I was last here—I seem to have been living in another world—and slowly traveled back to this—
> For what—

On this poignant and uncertain note, Caroline Seabury's diary concluded. Just when Caroline Seabury was struggling to escape to the North in July 1863, Emily Quiner was traveling south from Madison, Wisconsin, to Memphis, Tennessee, to begin working as a volunteer nurse at a Union Army hospital.

Born in Madison in 1840, Emily trained at the Normal School there and began teaching in the late 1850s. She made the first entry in her diary in April 1861, just after the firing on Fort Sumter by Confederate forces. She continued writing in her diary for two and one-half years. In July 1863 she went to Memphis, Tennessee, volunteering as a Union army nurse following the siege of Vicksburg. Her diary concluded upon her return from the South in September 1863.

On July 8, 1863, Emily confided in her diary about her work as a nurse: "I went at it rather awkwardly, I expect, but I shall soon learn how to work, I hope." Subsequent diary entries recount, sometimes in gruesome detail, the suffering and deaths of individual soldiers—the majority of whom died from infectious diseases rather than from wounds suffered in battle. For instance, on August 10, 1863, Emily wrote:

> In my ward and Ward B all day. There was a boy about 19 in Ward B, who has been under the influence of opium for two days so that he was perfectly stupid and could not be roused. The Dr. told me to give him strong coffee every half hour all day. I did so but it did no good and about 8 o'clock in the evening he died. I felt very badly about it, as I believe he died from an overdose of the drug.

Other diary entries echo these feelings of helplessness and sorrow. On August 25, 1963, an exhausted Emily left Memphis to return to Madison. In her diary she wrote of her sadness as she bade farewell to the men for whom she had cared. On August 28 she arrived back in Madison.

Emily immediately began planning her return to Memphis; however, her father, a historian, disapproved of her plans, and he prohibited her from leaving Madison again. Instead, he ordered her to remain with him and help him write a history of the Civil War. September 27, 1863, marked the date of Emily Quiner's final diary entry, which filled the last four pages of the diary. It was a highly introspective, integrative commentary on her growth in self-awareness over the past two-and-one-half years. She wrote about her father's unwillingness to allow her to return to Memphis and about her misery at having to give up an opportunity to serve her country. The entry concluded:

> It is true, soon I shall bid you adieu, faithful friend, after having gone in your company for nearly two years and a half, laying you among the relics of my *dead past*, no more to look upon your pages, save as reminders of what I have been as chronicled in you, and what I shall be no more forever...
>
> Farewell my Journal, thou hast chronicled many pleasant scenes, thou bearest on the pages the names of many friends to me in the past. Keep them sacredly. I give thee them in trust.

Like the closing entry in Caroline Seabury's diary, the concluding entry in Emily Quiner's diary is poignant. That poignancy is underscored by the fact that no other diary by either woman is extant today. It remains open to conjecture whether Caroline Seabury or Emily Quiner kept other diaries and, if they did, what happened to these texts. Nonetheless, both women's texts demonstrate how well each woman's diary functioned as a "faithful friend" who helped the diarist give voice to her own reality. This reading of Seabury's and Quiner's texts is reinforced by Belenky, Clinchy, Goldberger and Tarule's analysis of the ways in which some women use a diary as a means of nurturing a sense of defiance in external authority and a trust in their subjective truth (67).

Motherhood, daughterhood, sisterhood and *friendship* are simple terms that cannot adequately describe the nature of the complex relationships that they name. It would be incorrect to assert that women's diaries depict such relationships as inherently blissful, uninterrupted or uncomplicated. It would be just as incorrect to assert that women's diaries depict such relationships as fraught with secrecy and disagreement. For many women, past and present, diaries serve an important function: they help to weave the threads of such relationships into the fabric of women's experience as part of the domestic ritual that women continue to create daily.

Ann Romines asserts that many women's thoughts often take the form of "writing domestic ritual" in which "the story of housekeeping, the 'home plot' of domestic ritual, has generated forms and continuities very different from those of the patriarchal American canon" (17). Such forms push "readers to attend to texts that are not inscribed in conventionally literary language" (17). In fact, Domines explains, "Domestic language often seems invisible to those who have not learned it" (17). Romines' detailed study of women, writing and domestic ritual has been very helpful in my analysis of women's diaries, which, I would assert, are a key component in the creation of what Romines calls the "home plot":

> The home plot is my name for a complex of narrative strategies examined in this book. What these strategies have in common is an effort to respond to, replicate, continue, interrogate, and extend the repetitive rhythms of domestic life, which emphasize continuance over triumphant climax and often subordinate the vaunted individual to an ongoing, life-preserving, and, for some women, life-threatening, process. (293)

For this, and for many other reasons, the diary as a form of autobiography is an important medium for the expression of women's relationships. Diaries verify that many kinds of friendships between women do exist, and diaries demonstrate how women's diaries embody the dynamics of such friendships.

Janice Raymond has analyzed female friendships within the larger cultural context in order to understand the ways in which relationships between women are constituted. Raymond uses the phrase, "a genealogy of female friendship," to define "the lineage of women who have been and are primary to each other" and who put one another first (35). In reading and interpreting diary entries by Emily and Sarah Gillespie, Ada James, Ada Briggs, Caroline Seabury and Emily Quiner, I have examined various "genealogies" of female friendship for three reasons: to trace lines of contact between women, to learn how their intimate friendships have been chronicled in their diaries and to examine the ways in which the diary itself has extended and enriched communication and affection between women.

Read in the context of Carol Gilligan's recent work on women's psychological development, women's diaries such as those discussed in this essay illustrate what Janet Surrey defines as "*relationship*: the ongoing, intrinsic inner awareness and responsiveness to the continuous existence of the other or others and the expectation of mutuality in this regard" ("The Self-in-Relation" 61). As Surrey explains, such a definition of relationship "involves the capacity to identify with a unit larger than the single self and a sense of motivation to care for this new unit," yet it "does not imply continuous physical or emotional contact, nor does it imply a contractual, externally defined pattern of relationship" (61). In this model of *relationship*, communication becomes "interaction and dialogue rather than debate" (62).

Women's diaries help to illustrate the importance of *relationship* as interaction and dialogue; they embody text as process rather than product; and they reflect the value of friendships between women and friendships between women and their/our diaries. Just as importantly, women's diaries illustrate what Janet Surrey calls the "power with" or "mutual power" model of empowerment, a model that differs radically from the "power over" or "power for oneself only" model represented by much traditional thinking ("Relationship and Empowerment" 165). "Competition for power," explains Surrey, "pits people against each other in zero-sum power contests," while the alternative model which she describes "assumes that power or the ability to act does not have to be a scarce resource, nor based on zero-sum assumptions—certainly not in interactions between human beings" (165-66).

If, as Surrey asserts (and, as I believe), relational empowerment involves the enlarging of vision and energy and the building of connection through dialogue to create a "framework of emotional connection" (170), then the diary has been and continues to be an effective vehicle for relational empowerment, particularly for women. Women's demonstrated passion for keeping diaries represents the same kind of passion about which Rossetti wrote in "Goblin Market": namely, the fervor with which women protect and sustain one another.

Works Cited

Aptheker, Bettina. *Tapestries of Life: Women's Work, Women's Consciousness, and the Meaning of Daily Experience*. Amherst: U of Massachusetts P, 1989.

Arcana, Judith. *Our Mothers' Daughters*. Berkeley: Shameless Hussy P, 1979.

Baer, Elizabeth, ed. *The Civil War Diary of Lucy Buck*. Columbia: U of South Carolina P, 1993.

Beauchamp, Virginia, ed. "Introduction." *A Private War: Letters and Diaries of Madge Preston, 1862-1867*. New Brunswick: Rutgers UP, 1987.

Begos, Jane DuPree, ed. "Introduction." *A Women's Diary Miscellany*. Weston, CT: Magic Circle P, 1989.

Belenky, Mary Field, Blythe McVicker Clinchy, Nancy Rule Goldberger, Jill Mattuck Tarule. *Women's Ways of Knowing: The Development of Self, Voice, and Mind*. New York: Basic Books, Inc., 1986.

Bunkers, Suzanne L., ed. *"All Will Yet Be Well": The Diary of Sarah Gillespie Huftalen, 1873-1952*. Iowa City: U of Iowa P, 1993.

_____, ed. *The Diary of Caroline Seabury, 1854-1863*. Madison: U of Wisconsin P, 1991.

_____. "Diaries: Public and Private Records of Women's Lives." *Legacy: Journal of Nineteenth-Century American Women Writers* 7.2 (1990).

_____. "'Faithful Friend': Nineteenth-Century Midwestern American Women's Unpublished Diaries." *Women's Studies International Forum* 10.1 (1987).

_____. "Midwestern Diaries and Journals: What Women Were (Not) Saying in the Late 1800s." *Studies in Autobiography*. Ed. James Olney. New York Oxford UP, 1988.

Chodorow, Nancy. *The Reproduction of Mothering: Psychoanalysis and the Sociology of Gender*. Berkeley: U of California P, 1978.

Culley, Margo, ed. "Introduction." *A Day at a Time: The Diary Literature of American Women from 1764 to the Present*. New York: Feminist P, 1985.

Faderman, Lillian. *Surpassing the Love of Men: Romantic Friendship and Love Between Women from the Renaissance to the Present*. New York: William Morrow, 1981.

Franklin, Penelope, ed. "Introduction." *Private Pages: Diaries of American Women 1830s-1970s*. New York: Ballantine, 1986.

Gillespie, Emily Hawley. Unpublished Diary Manuscripts 1858-88. In the Sarah Gillespie Huftalen Collection. Iowa City: State Historical Society of Iowa.

Gillikin, Dure Jo. "A Lost Diary Found: The Art of the Everyday." *Women's Personal Narratives: Essays in Criticism and Pedagogy*. Ed. Leonore Hoffman and Margo Culley. New York: Modern Language Association, 1985.

Gwin, Minrose C., ed. "Introduction." *A Woman's Civil War: A Diary, With Reminiscences of the War from March 1862, by Cornelia McDonald*. Madison: U of Wisconsin P, 1992.

Huff, Cynthia. "From Faceless Chronicler to Self-Creator: The Diary of Louisa Galton, 1830-1896." *Biography* 10.2 (1987).

Huftalen, Sarah Gillespie. Unpublished Diary Manuscripts. 1873-1952. Iowa City: State Historical Society of Iowa.

James, Ada L. Unpublished Diary Manuscripts. 1892-1947. In the Ada L. James Papers. Madison: State Historical Society of Wisconsin.

Jordan, Judith V., Alexandra G. Kaplan, Jean Baker Miller, Irene P. Stiver, and Janet L. Surrey, eds. *Women's Growth in Connection: Writings from the Stone Center.* New York and London: The Guilford P, 1991.

Lensink, Judy Nolte, ed. *"A Secret to be Burried": The Life and Diary of Emily Hawley Gillespie.* Iowa City: U of Iowa P, 1989.

Motz, Marilyn Ferris. *True Sisterhood: Michigan Women and Their Kin, 1820-1920.* Albany: State U of New York P, 1983.

Quiner, Emily C. Unpublished Diary Manuscript. 1861-63. Madison: State Historical Society of Wisconsin.

Raymond, Janice G. *A Passion for Friends: Toward A Philosophy of Female Affection.* Boston: Beacon P, 1986.

Rich, Adrienne. *Of Woman Born: Motherhood as Experience and Institution.* New York: W. W. Norton, 1976.

Romines, Ann. *The Home Plot: Women, Writing, and Domestic Ritual.* Amherst: U of Massachusetts P, 1992.

Rossetti, Christina. *Goblin Market.* 1862. Boston: David R. Godine, 1981.

Ruddick, Sara. *Maternal Thinking: Toward a Politics of Peace.* New York: Ballantine Books, 1989.

Smith-Rosenberg, Carroll. *Disorderly Conduct: Visions of Gender in Victorian America.* New York: Oxford UP, 1985.

Surrey, Janet. "The Self in Relation: A Theory of Women's Development." *Women's Growth in Connection.* Wellesley, MA: Wellesley College Stone Center, 1985.

———. "Relationship and Empowerment." *Women's Growth in Connection.* Wellesley, MA: Wellesley College Stone Center, 1987.

Linking Women Across Generations:
The Journals and Letters of Lessing and Sarton

BARBARA FREY WAXMAN

Until as recently as the 1970s, our youth-centered American culture tended to distance itself from old age and the elderly. Caro Spencer, the 76-year-old narrator of May Sarton's novel *As We Are Now*, writes in one entry of her journal:

> The trouble is that old age is not interesting until one gets there,
> a foreign country to the young and even to the middle-aged. (17)

Caro observes that the young and middle-aged typically socialize with their age cohorts. They are aloof from elders, have not wanted to learn about old age, and have not chosen to prepare for it. The untouched and untouchable status of elders in our society leads many elders to painful isolation and uncertainties about their very existence. As Kathleen Woodward writes in *Aging and Its Discontents: Freud and Other Fictions*, elders are touch-starved, and "one thing is sure: if we are not touched, we might begin to suspect that we are not here" (175). Invisible to the young, elders may begin to see themselves as nonentities. Ashley Montagu argues in his book *Touching* for people's need to touch and be touched, to be acknowledged physically, throughout the life-cycle:

> this is where we fail the aging quite miserably—as we do in so
> much else. Because we are unwilling to face the fact of aging,
> we behave as if it isn't there. It is this massive evasion that is the
> principal reason for our failure to understand the needs of the
> aging. (quoted in Woodward 175)

Barbara Macdonald, writing at age 69 in a 1983 collection of essays on aging called *Look Me in the Eye: Old Women, Aging, and Ageism*, also observes our culture's evasion of the elderly, noting the absence in our culture of any discourse on aging and especially on old women:

> Now nothing told me that old women existed, or that it was possible to be glad to be an old woman. ...[The] silence held powerful and repressive messages. (5)

The silence suggests that old women, even more than old men, are especially excluded from our society. Cynthia Rich, who at 41 co-authored *Look Me in the Eye* with Macdonald and interweaves her chapter-length essays with Macdonald's, characterizes the isolation of old women from society as a serious form of oppression. Citing Simone de Beauvoir's analysis of oppression "'One of the ruses of oppression is to camouflage itself behind a natural situation since, after all, one cannot revolt against nature'"), she sarcastically describes the "natural" isolation of old women from younger:

> How natural that young people, or even the middle aged, should have nothing in common with an old woman. Unthinkable that she should have formed friendships with anyone who was not in her or his 70s or 80s or 90s. It is natural that without family, who must tolerate the stigma, or other old people, who share the stigma, she would have no close ties. (85-86)

However, the oppression and isolation of older women are now being fought in literature. That older women and younger can establish mutually beneficial ties, that older women should demonstrate and celebrate their presence among youth, that younger women—as literary characters and as readers—are traveling to the country of old age, are evident in the recent flourishing of a whole discourse of aging.

This literary discourse has flourished since the 1970s because of the Women's Movement, the graying of the American populace, and women's comparative longevity, creating a readership interested in understanding women's aging. Included in this discourse is a new kind of fiction called the *Reifungsroman* or Novel of Ripening, which I have written about in *From the Hearth to the Open Road: A Feminist Study of Aging in Contemporary Fiction*. In the *Reifungsroman*, an aging heroine grapples with aging's problems while also finding in old age opportunities for true *reifung*, or ripening, of intellect and spirit. In addition to the *Reifungsroman*, the discourse of aging includes belletristic nonfiction: autobiographical essays, journals, and diaries that confront senescence and may help to diminish the isolation of elderly women.

The literary discourse of aging, fictional and nonfiction, self-consciously and purposefully describes elders' thoughts and feelings, physical sensations, philosophical and spiritual questing, and the development of relationships both among elders and between elders and younger people. Journal-keeping elders and elderly narrators of fictive texts present their own private analyses of their lives in journal entries and letters. In addition, some younger narrators, in an effort to understand the psyche of one from the Other Generation, imaginatively project journal entries that might have been written by the character from the Other Generation. This literary discourse of aging offers, in particular, inter-generational rapprochements between women and means by which real women form relationships across generations and strengthen already existing intergenerational friendships. Readers come to appreciate how aging influences the psyche and the conduct of daily life as well as how people can benefit from friendships with elders.

My essay demonstrates how two contemporary American female writers, Doris Lessing and May Sarton, through fictional and authentic journals create a discourse that depicts old age vis-a-vis youth and provide contexts in which older and younger women communicate physically, psychologically, philosophically. As a critic, I also create a discourse whose aim is to build inter-generational bridges by acquainting readers with the texts and by celebrating these works' literary, psychological, and political merits.

Several critics have written about the fictional representatives of this discourse of aging, including Woodward, who in *Aging and Its Discontents* takes a post-Freudian psychoanalytic approach to her analysis of fiction on aging. Mary Sohngen identifies typical themes of many novels on aging in a 1977 essay in *Gerontologist*, also offering an extensive bibliography of novels on the topic. Marlene Springer, in her 1980 *Frontiers* essay on May Sarton, focuses on Sarton's realistic yet positive presentation of the aging experience and on the narrative structural features of Sarton's fiction, as they capture the elder's thought processes and "floating" reveries (48). Anne Wyatt-Brown, in her book on Barbara Pym's fiction, also attends to Pym's treatment of themes of aging. However, not much attention has been given to the self-reflexive journals and letters within these novels of aging or to the nonfiction journals and the letters within the journals that capture the experience of aging and portray bridges between younger and older women. This essay will focus on such texts, in Lessing's fictional journal of Jane Somers,

The Diary of a Good Neighbor, Sarton's fictional journal of Caro Spencer, *As We Are Now*, and Sarton's journal *At Seventy*.

In Lessing's *The Diary of a Good Neighbor*, the first part of *The Diaries of Jane Somers*, the middle-aged protagonist Jane Somers records in first-person diary entries the development of her attachment to a 90-year-old woman named Maudie Fowler. She begins her diary by confessing her previous attitudes toward elders, old age, and death. "Physical awfulness," decay, and death she had feared (7) and the old she had avoided or considered invisible. She had avoided even her own mother when she had been ill with cancer: "I couldn't touch her, not really. Not with kindness" (8). She had eschewed the taint of intimacy with elders who would become dependent on her, fearing that her elderly neighbor Mrs. Penney "would take over my life. I feel smothered and panicky at the idea of being at her beck and call" (11). Old men and women on the streets she had not seen "because I was afraid of being like them" (13). Jane's introspective text immediately forces readers to begin to consider the presence of elders in their own lives and their own ambivalence about aging. When Jane soon meets Maudie in a local pharmacy, the streets seem to come alive with old folks (12). Maudie asks Jane to be her intermediary with the pharmacist, beginning her reliance on Jane, and Jane, observing Maudie's resistance to the drug Valium that has been prescribed, begins her tutelage to learn how to live a more impassioned, less stupefied life.

Readers gradually see Jane overcoming her fearful resistance to intimacy with Maudie as she charts their intensifying feelings for each other in her diary. There is a self-conscious creativity about Jane's act of writing this diary, as if it not only records events and Maudie's presence in her life but also creates and concretizes these things and sharpens her awareness of them:

> I see that as I write this diary, I have in mind that observing eye.
> ...It's a funny thing, this need to write things down, as if they
> have no existence until they are recorded. Presented. When I
> listen to Maudie talk, I have this feeling, quick, catch it, don't let
> it all vanish, record it. As if it is not valid until in print. (64)

In recording this relationship between herself and Maudie, she verifies Maudie's presence in her life and establishes the worth of their relationship in her own mind. Jane writes self-reflectively and is, for example, self-conscious about her diary's structure:

All that I have written up to now was a recapitulation, summing-
up. Now I am going to write day by day, if I can. (30)

Her decision to shift to daily entries reveals her increasing self-
analysis and self-knowledge as well as her growing intimacy with
Maudie. While she does not completely follow through with her
resolve to write entries daily, she writes enough so that "now I look
back through the year and begin to know what was important"
(137).

One of those important aspects of her year is Jane's
vanquishing of her resistance to intimacy with Maudie, most evident
in the entry that Jane titles "Maudie's Day." Here she imagines and
describes a typical day in the life of Maudie, the external challenges
and the interior moil of fears, frustrations, anger, affections. The
narration of the day shifts between a third-person omniscient Jane-
perspective that explains and analyzes Maudie's actions and
thoughts, and a first-person Maudie point of view that speaks aloud
her reactions to events in her body and in her home during the day.
Lessing/Jane with remarkable vividness writes the aged woman's
body in this entry. Jane's imaginative journey into Maudie's world
allows her and the reader to understand the old woman's anger,
shame at betrayal by her unpredictable body, and loss of physical
control: loss of strength and mobility, incontinence, and fear of
illness in her bowels (she later learns she has cancer). Jane captures
Maudie's intermittent confusion or disorientation, her doubting of
her own existence, because of the numbness of her body and
because of the loneliness of her day. Only the sound of her cat
moving about assures Maudie she is alive (113). The sheer physical
difficulties and the psychological hardships which elderly women
face each morning are clearly delineated.

Jane also conveys in this entry the great extent to which (she
thinks) Maudie's needy thoughts must revolve around her
dependency on Janna. Yet she also gives Maudie credit for a heroic
spirit and resourcefulness in coping with daily physical challenges:

A general planning a campaign could not use more cleverness than
Maudie does, as she outwits her weakness and her terrible
tiredness. (115)

For example, she has clever ways of figuring out how to economize
on her movements to feed the cat, build a fire, and walk to the
bathroom, in order to compensate for the failings of her body.

Maudie also escapes her oppressive loneliness by spinning reveries of happy moments from her past and by fantasizing a future in which Janna will come to live with her. These actions and her dozing are punctuated by her yearning for Janna's return, expressed in the increasingly frequent and urgent refrain, "Perhaps Janna will come soon" or "Oh, if Janna would come now" (116, 117). Jane does finally insert herself into Maudie's imagined day, stretching her inventiveness and empathy to consider how Maude perceives her lateness, rushing around, efficient shopping, and crashing energy. She also depicts Maudie's fear of Jane's departure, her fear that Jane will notice something wrong with her bowels when she washes out the commode and her fear of Jane's disapproval of the household mess that Maudie is unable to attend to. Through this written discourse, this imaginary glimpse into Maudie's mind and day, Jane is better able to figure out Maudie's unexpressed needs and to become a better caretaker and a more sympathetic friend.

Jane ends this entry of Maudie's by having a dozing Jane wake up in the middle of the night to hear words from Maudie that confirm their friendship and express Maudie's joy in it:

> I have been thinking that this is the best time of my life...now, I know you will always come and we can be together. (122)

In writing this imaginary conversation, Jane has revealed her growing understanding of Maudie, has accepted intense friendship with her, and has reduced her own anger and resentment at Maudie's dependency on her. Jane may still be on guard against the hungry neediness of other lonely old people, "for into that terrible vacuum you can be sucked before you know it" (146), but she does assent to be depended upon by Maudie. In addition, by allowing herself intimacy with Maudie through the act of writing Maudie's day and by actually accompanying Maudie through her final days, Jane grows emotionally and spiritually. She learns from Maudie to slow down and appreciate small daily pleasures, the "real slow full enjoyment" of an elder's day, from relishing a leaf fallen on a curbside to observing with affection a young mother's interactions with her child in the park (166). In many ways the period of Jane's friendship with Maudie is also "the best time of [Jane's] life."

Sarton's novella is also written as a series of journal entries which enable the protagonist Caro to understand aging and its impact on her life, as well as to analyze her existence in Twin Elms nursing home and her relationships with staff members there. Some of the entries serve as an outlet for the intensity of her emotions and a reassertion of her own identity:

> How *expression* relieves the mind! I feel quite lively and myself again just because I have managed to write two pages of dissent about old age. (75)

Her dissent is against the stereotypical notion that the old enjoy serenity. Moreover, many of the earlier entries express her brimming resentment of the brusque, unsympathetic supervisor of Twin Elms, Harriet Hatfield. This prison warden of a woman starkly contrasts to the woman who enters Caro's life while Harriet is on vacation, Anna Close. Caro writes several journal entries that focus on Anna and enable Caro to sort through the passionate attachment she develops for the kind and affectionate woman, who although a grandmother herself, is younger and more robust than Caro, probably in active late middle-age. In addition to the journal entries, Caro also writes a letter to Anna after Anna leaves Twin Elms, in which Caro declares and explains her love for the younger woman.

Both the "private" journal entries (which we read) and the "published" letter (which Caro intends to mail to Anna) make Caro's relationship with Anna more intimate, intense, and psychically restorative for Caro than the relationship between caregiver and elder often is. As in Lessing's novel, written discourse intensifies intergenerational friendship because it affords opportunities for revealing and understanding elders' psychic lives. Texts that write elders' psyches reveal their humanity and bring opportunities for intergenerational connections. Although Caro fears that an honest written communication, a "true cry from the heart of an old person," alienates the young, "creates too much havoc in a [younger] listener, is too disturbing, because nothing can really be done to help us on the downward path" (73-74), these journals become the basis of friendship that slows the "downward path."

Before Anna enters Caro's life, Caro articulates her longing for female companionship. Besides herself, Twin Elms has only male residents, and neither Harriet nor her daughter Rose, who assists Harriet in her work, can provide Caro with such companionship:

> Sometimes I dream that another woman might be sent...I long for a woman with whom to share quite ordinary things, like how I can get my hair washed. (37)

When Harriet later washes her hair, Caro feels as if she has suffered "an assault on my person" (71). Not surprisingly, her recording of the gentle Anna's appearance in her life is marked in written discourse by the rhetoric of contrast to Harriet. She is described as a miracle, angelic, and the opposite of Harriet's harsh, grudging and judgmental qualities; she is a Beatrix Potter character, blue and white of clothing, pink of face, gentle, graciously caring, wise and efficient (76). The act of writing down their moments of real communication and mutual respect, which are the foundations of a relationship that extends beyond that of caregiver and patient, concretizes the interactions for Caro: Their exchange of looks suggests the look "between two women who understand each other," while her squeezing of Caro's hand "*affirmed* our humanity and regard for each other" (75). Caro writes that Anna's presence is a restorative and a reprieve "from despair and decline" (79), bringing Caro from emotional torpor into a rush of feeling that challenges the myth of old age as "Golden Pond" serenity and calmness. Also challenged is the notion of old people as no longer needing to love and be loved:

> Whatever lives in us, the heart and its capacity...for joy never dies, and must have an object. The sin would be to stop loving. (78)

Because of her blossoming feelings for Anna, which Caro in her writing frequently connects with the budding pink rose that accompanies the first breakfast Anna served Caro, Caro is humanized, energized, and rejuvenated, ready to extract the joy out of daily living again:

> I know that I can still respond to life in a normal human way...The rose has opened during the day. I have lain here for an hour really paying attention to it. (78)

Like Maudie, Caro is now "avid for life" and attentive to its beauties because of her friendship with a woman who cares for her as if she "were worthy for care...not humiliated but treasured" (86). Because of Anna's care, Caro, like Maudie, can experience the exquisiteness of a rose or the "distilled beauty of a Mozart quartet" (90).

The verbal discourse Caro and Anna share is of minimal significance; they communicate during comfortable spells of silence when they are together, and Anna's physical gestures of affection are what Caro chooses to record in her journal:

> So we talk, but it is not the words that matter. When she goes she pats my hand and sometimes kisses me on the cheek. (88)

Almost disbelieving the reality of this heavenly interaction, Caro uses her journal to describe and corroborate it; her notebooks are her "touchstone for sanity" (88). The written discourse is important because it sanctifies and preserves their nonverbal communication. Caro records in her journal the "healing grace of [Anna's] sensitive hands" and her "amazing clear eyes" that note and respond to Caro's every need (93).

Caro also speculates in her notebook on the nature of friendships between women. She wonders what she can offer Anna in exchange for what Anna offers her; in her journal she practices the calculus of real friendships:

> I sometimes ask myself what I do for her...I suppose it is a glimpse of a woman's life not entirely spent in physical struggle to keep going...she gets a romantic delight out of what I am and plies me with questions about Europe. (88)

In a later entry after Anna has left, analyzing Anna's way of looking at her, Caro with wise insight tentatively identifies tenderness as the essence of a woman/woman friendship:

> She used to look at me with such a tender, amused look sometimes—is that what women have most deeply to give to each other? Tenderness? (107)

Although she fears that with Anna's departure (when Harriet returns from her vacation) their "mode of expression will be gone," Caro takes some comfort in the promise that she will be able to *write* to Anna at her farmhouse (92-93). The only problem is Anna's lack of articulateness in writing, which limits the reciprocal aspect of their friendship-through-writing:

> I could see that the idea of putting feeling into written words was disturbing. "I'm not very good at writing letters," she said... "I'll try, dear,...but you mustn't expect too much." (92)

Despite Anna's not being "a word-person," and maybe because of it too, Caro can now contact and express in written discourse the essence of her love. She writes in her notebook:

> I myself am on the brink of understanding things about love I never understood before.... [True love] always comes as revelation, and we approach it always with awe...for the very essence of its power is that it makes all things new. (92-93)

The written discourse of Caro's journal, which also records their conversations, is testimonial to the legitimacy and power of this friendship. The passages on Anna are there for Caro to reread and thereby reaffirm the presence of this miracle of love in her life (97).

The letter as medium for conveying Caro's love to Anna is more inhibiting than the journal. Caro feels she must suppress much of her intensity when writing to Anna to publish her feelings (99). In the letter, she asks permission to visit Anna (the minister's daughter has agreed to bring her there) and tries to explain the miracle of her love for Anna, her gratitude for the gentle touch of her hands, the gesture of the rose, her heavenly voice. She attributes the intensity of this love to her awareness that there is only a short time for it. The letter ends with Caro's gift to Anna of the blouse from Paris that she had admired, "from my old love [bought to please her lover Alex] to you, my miracle of new love," and with her acknowledgment of the limited capacity of words to sustain their relationship: "What we had was a *silent* communion. Words are laden by comparison" (99). While the words are limited, they comfort Caro in her loss of Anna's presence and reaffirm the reality of this love.

There is some question as to whether the letter contributes to the friendship between the two women because it is not mailed after Harriet discovers it and Anna never reads it (113). Moreover, after Harriet discovers both letter and journal, Caro, emotionally violated, stops writing and begins to doubt the existence of Anna and their relationship together. However, the letter gives readers a different voice of Caro, a sincere, if slightly less candid, more restrained, and more "public" side of the character, helping us to appreciate even more the complexity of this elderly woman. We believe in her intelligence and sensitivity, value her passionateness, and understand how friendships with elders can develop.

In their brief verbal discourse at Anna's home, recorded by Caro in her journal afterwards, Caro stumblingly tries to convey what her unmailed letter had said:

> I'm so glad I knew you for a little while. I wish I could tell you what it meant, what I tried to say in the letter... (115)

In this passage, which contrasts conversation with written text, the bittersweet richness and profundity of the written discourse of elder-love is most clear.

Written discourse thus heightens the intensity of the interactions between Caro and Anna, also educating readers about paths of communication between generations and the tenderness that underlies friendships between women of different ages. However, Sarton does also seem to caution us about possible misconstruction of the text of one woman's love for another if it should reach an audience for which it was not intended (such as Harriet). Insensitive readers of Caro's text may misinterpret relationships such as Caro's and Anna's, assigning them to what Harriet calls the sordid realm of lesbian "dirt" (100). The letter drives a deeper wedge between Harriet and Caro, with Caro violated by Harriet's reading, and this "reading-rape" seals her suicidal commitment to destroy Twin Elms. It may well be that there has been an erotic element in the two women's friendship, not uncommon among elderly women, but Sarton, herself a bisexual, rejoices in the rejuvenating quality of this eroticism in elders and condemns Harriet's conclusions by emphasizing her cruel small-mindedness. Sensitive readers will not be threatened by a discourse of friendship between elder and younger that pulls elders in from the margins of society to enjoy a full emotional life, while at the same time escorting younger people briefly into "the foreign country" of old age for contact with a land that they will someday inhabit.

In her nonfiction journals, May Sarton also explores the written discourse of intergenerational friendships between women. The journal entries in *At Seventy* are not, as they are in Caro's notebook, neatly plotted with rising suspense to a climax of epiphanic insight and an earth-shattering decision about how to end her life. However, they do, like the fictional journal, contain real characterizations, vivid settings, and quietly dramatic events that teach readers about intergenerational relationships as Sarton traces the experiences of her 70th year. She is the fulcrum of relationships with women both younger and older than herself, and her journal entries make a point of characterizing both sorts of interactions. The book is structured in chronological journal entries, and there are texts within the text of each entry that flesh out Sarton's friendships: she frequently quotes letters from friends to her and from herself to friends, poems she writes for friends (her Christmas-message poetry booklet, for example), or excerpts from letters, articles, and reviews that comment on Sarton's fiction and poetry. Moreover, she regularly offers portraits of women friends that include the dialogue of recent visits, that bear witness to political struggles and sufferings of these women (such as those of Ursula Nicholls Heathcote 312-13), or that capture their shared memories of past experiences and mutual friends, especially those connected to Sarton's friend and lover Judy, "who gave [her] a home and made [her] know what home can be" for 15 years (213). Finally, some entries become more eulogy than journal in their impassioned tribute to friends such as Judy and Mildred Quigley (212-14; 275-77). The discourse of *At Seventy* is enriched and complicated by this multi-generic intertextuality.

Furthermore, by positioning herself in the middle of friendships with women of 30 or 50, on the one hand and 80 or 90 on the other, Sarton can present women's diverse attitudes toward elders and the aging process, including her young friends' views of her and her reactions to her older women friends. In particular, her discourse enthusiastically celebrates the richness and intensity of very old women's lives such as those of Eva Le Gallienne, Elizabeth Roget, Lotte Jacobi, and Camille Mayran. Sarton relishes her relationships with such elders:

> I take strength and joy in the friendship of someone older than I.
> It is a rest to be with someone who has made her peace with life
> and enjoys everything so much. (76)

Here Sarton speaks of her relationship with 83-year-old Elizabeth Roget, about whom she also says:

> It is a pleasure to be with someone who says that the eighties are
> her happiest years...I feel at home with her partly because she
> was born in Switzerland, so her roots are European [Sarton is
> Belgian by birth], and also because I admire her resilience and
> toughness. She is very realistic and not afraid to be blunt. (74-
> 75)

In such portrayals of women older than herself, as well as in her passages of self-reflection about her 70th year, Sarton attempts to deconstruct myths of aging which have been barriers to intimacy between older and younger women: of aging as deterioration of identity, increasing helplessness, fading joys, and loss of love.

Sarton says she is more comfortable with herself and more relaxed about her life at age 70 than she was earlier:

> I am far better able to cope at seventy than I was at fifty. I think that is partly because I have learned to glide instead of to force myself at moments of tension.... I realize that seventy must seem extremely old to my young friends, but I actually feel much younger than I did when I wrote *The House by the Sea* six years ago.... And that...is because I live more completely in the moment these days, am not as anxious about the future, and am far more detached from the areas of pain, the loss of love, the struggle to get the work completed, the fear of death. (37)

In a journal entry that is a written transcription of an earlier oral text (which occurs frequently in this book), Sarton describes how she had reached out to an audience of college students at a poetry reading by expressing her vision of old age as a time of empowerment; at 70 she is surer of her identity and of what her life means:

> "I am more myself than I have ever been. There is less conflict. I am happier, more balanced, and...more powerful...better able to use my powers." I am surer of what my life is all about. (10)

Sarton at 70 feels less of a need to be who she is not. She celebrates the integrity of the older woman, an unvarnished integrity that rejuvenates her:

> Now I wear the inside person outside and am more comfortable with my self. In some ways I am younger because I can admit vulnerability and more innocent because I do not have to pretend. (61)

At the same time that she extends herself into relationships with younger and older women, she refuses to blur the distinctions between age and youth; proud of how aging has transformed her, she says:

...for someone of forty to say to someone of seventy "We are exactly alike" is ludicrous and an underestimation of what life itself does to force us to maturity. (181)

Such hard-won maturity is precious to Sarton.

In her journal Sarton celebrates this maturity's various incarnations in her friendships with elders. These relationships with elders are inspirational. Sarton marvels at their courage and *joie de vivre*. Like Maudie Fowler, Sarton's elders emphasize the essence of life and put her in touch with it; these elders are "civilizing" influences (66). Friendships with younger women, in contrast, impress Sarton with the younger women's courage and spirit of adventure; for example, she calls Betsy Swart's abandonment of a half-finished thesis when she discovered Sarton's works and began to write her dissertation on Sarton "spontaneous combustion, grand and courageous" (67), and from Karen Saum, who gave up worldly life out of her zeal to do missionary work Sarton extrapolates lessons of "love and dedication...and the fire that makes it possible" (33). Friendships with other younger women also enable Sarton to mentor and nurture, ordinarily satisfying roles for her.

In the closest of all these friendships, regardless of the ages of the friends, one element is common: a history of shared experiences and memories that facilitate an easy, often silent, communication, not unlike that between Caro and Anna. For example, she describes dinner conversation with her 50-year-old friend Janice, an "imaginatively kind" woman (82) whom she admires for her decision to make her life less work-centered and more life- and people-centered. Janice is a friend with whom she feels a peaceful accord and with whom "I can relax and enjoy, enjoy not being May Sarton, the writer, and talk about all the things that really matter, such as our dogs, dreams of the garden this spring, politics, and life in general" (279-80); moreover, in this "rare friendship" with Janice, "we are able to give each other, in a very easy way, all that has been happening to us, inwardly and outwardly" (192). Sarton's entry explores how she and her friends communicate satisfyingly, comfortably, their psychic as well as external lives, preserving the continuity of their shared history in person even after extended separations. Similarly, in a meeting with old friends Cora DuBois and Jeanne Taylor, she describes the tranquillity of their conversation, in which "so much does not need to be said, so much can be taken for granted" (147). Much of the discourse of intergenerational friendships between women is an unspoken discourse. Sarton ends the chronicle of her 70th year with an entry about the quiet discourse between friends as she recounts her visit with Jean Lieberman, a friend from her school days. Here she sums up the essence of good communication between friends:

> I simply felt at home, at ease, with a friend to whom nothing has to be explained, where the past flows into and informs the present. (332)

In such passages about reunions with old friends, Sarton points out the essence of these relationships and emphasizes the importance of in-person sharing of lives. However, she also teaches readers that these long-term relationships have been sustained and nurtured by other forms of communication, especially letters. Sarton's journal reveals how much of the fabric of her social and emotional life is woven by these letters from friends, acquaintances, and readers of her poetry and fiction. Although she sometimes grumbles about the burden of maintaining her extensive correspondence because it keeps her from her other writing projects, Sarton acknowledges that even letters from strangers "have enlarged my heart" (159). Many of these fan-letters "are precious, each in a different way" (242), bringing her such a "renewed sense of how remarkable human beings can be and are that I felt overwhelmed to be the receptacle of so much love and to be allowed into so many lives" (245). Even more precious is Sarton's extended correspondences with friends, such as her 30-year, letter-writing relationship with French writer Camille Mayran.

Sarton and Mayran met at a tea at the Julian Huxleys' in 1938 or 1939, were separated by the war, and Sarton visited her twice, years later. Hence, theirs was a friendship fostered by letters:

> I rejoice in this correspondence of nearly thirty years and like to believe that the friendship it communicates will one day become, for someone who finds it, as fresh and alive as it was for us who met almost entirely by letter and became intimate by letter and grew to understand each other, little by little. (282-83)

Her journal's commentary on these letters underscores the importance of the written word in the gradually developing intimacy between the two women—two women who happen to be professional writers. The journal's commentary also implies that the discourse of friendship through letters is meant to be shared with readers, to teach them how to develop mutual understanding in correspondences and how to use these correspondences in their own relationships.

As the older woman and as a European woman, Mayran in her "written" friendship with Sarton gives the younger woman an important link with her own French roots, a perspective on her own identity, and a wise and appreciative analysis of Sarton's writings:

> For me she has been a shining link with France itself, and with the part of me that was born with the French language.... The marvelous language she wrote in was civilization itself and taught me more by the way she expressed herself in it than I can possibly say. Because she had time, and because she cared, and because she was ultrasensitive to English literature...her letters about my poems and novels came to me like manna from heaven. No one else has read my poems with such attention and such generous appreciation. (283-84)

Sarton's reflection in the journal on this lengthy correspondence enables her to extrapolate the salient features of this intergenerational friendship: its shared European background and tastes; its shared interest in French and English language and literature; the elder's willingness to share her mature wisdom with the younger woman and to praise and nurture the younger's work; the emotional commitment and commitment of time to one another in the act of writing regularly; and the use of letter-writing for complex reflections, for the unraveling, discovery, and creation of emotions and ideas. It is not surprising, then, that Sarton emotionally records in her journal her decision to turn this correspondence over to the archives of the Berg Collection and that she has to mourn this separation from the letters:

> Each time I separate myself from a correspondence, it is like dying a little and also burying the dead. (282)

This entry, which concludes with Sarton's promise to herself to write another letter to Camille beyond the "ending" of the Berg Collection, resists the closure suggested by Sarton's wrapping up of the correspondence for the archives, and is testimonial to the intensity of an intergenerational relationship built upon the written word.

One leaves *At Seventy* feeling more knowledgable about aging and better informed about some ways of building and sustaining satisfying intergenerational friendships. Perhaps even more than the fictional journals discussed in this essay, *At Seventy* is optimistic about ending the isolation of elderly women in our society and about tapping their wealth of spiritual/philosophical maturity by encouraging contact between older and younger women. The healing tenderness of these intergenerational women's friendships is also apparent on every page of Sarton's journal, as well as in the passages of *As We Are Now* that deal with Anna and in Jane Somers's entries about Maudie Fowler. The journals of Sarton and Lessing and the letters embedded in them demonstrate in different ways how the goals of socially reclaiming old women and making intergenerational companionship desirable are furthered in a purposeful written discourse. This discourse of aging simultaneously records and shapes emotions, attitudes, and values that make women (and probably men too) more receptive to intergenerational relationships. This discourse shows, once again, how language creates desire, because we can see how it intensifies existing intergenerational friendships. Lessing and Sarton's texts on aging, with their passionateness, meditativeness and self-reflexiveness, are responsive not only to a literary intertextuality that grows exponentially with the graying of America, but also to the needs of aging readers and of a society in search of a visionary plan for its increasingly elderly populace.

Works Cited

Lessing, Doris. "The Diary of a Good Neighbor." *The Diaries of Jane Somers*. New York: Random House, 1984.

Macdonald, Barbara, with Cynthia Rich. *Look Me in the Eye: Old Women, Aging, and Ageism*. San Francisco: Spinster's Ink, 1983.

Sarton, May. *As We Are Now*. New York: Norton, 1973.

_____. *At Seventy: A Journal*. New York: Norton, 1984.

Sohngen, Mary. "The Experience of Old Age as Depicted in Contemporary Novels." *Gerontologist* 17 (Feb. 1977).

Springer, Marlene. "As We Shall Be: May Sarton and Aging." *Frontiers* 5 (Fall 1980).

Waxman, Barbara Frey. *From the Hearth to the Open Road: A Feminist Study of Aging in Contemporary Literature*. Westport, CT: Greenwood P, 1990.

Woodward, Kathleen. *Aging and Its Discontents: Freud and Other Fictions*. Bloomington, IN: Indiana UP, 1991.

"Women Alone Stir My Imagination": Intertextual Eroticism in the Friendships/Relationships Created by Virginia Woolf

PAMELA J. OLANO

> Much preferring my own sex, as I do, or at any rate, finding the monotony of young men's conversations considerable, and resenting the eternal pressure that they put, if you're a woman, on one string, [I] find the disproportion excessive, and intend to cultivate women's society entirely in the future. Men are all in the light always: with women you swim at once into the silent dusk. (Letters III: 164)

Virginia Woolf expresses these sentiments in a letter dated 5 February 1925. Having just completed *Mrs. Dalloway*, to be published in the late spring, she was resting after a bout with influenza and was unable to attend a party the night before. In her letter, she imagines the scene at the gathering, wondering why there is such a disparity between the men and the women who attend. The young men waltz, while the lovely girls sit together. She finds it curious that Bloomsbury parties are always thus composed—40 young men, all Oxford intellectuals, and a handful of young women, "who are admitted on the condition that they either dress exquisitely, or are some man's mistress, or love each other" (III: 164). Finding "the disproportion excessive," Woolf proclaims that she plans to "cultivate women's society," preferring their company to that of men.

Her letter offers insight into her perception of sexual differences and the centrality that women held in her life. Based "on one string" (sex), the male/female relationship is stressful and monotonous. She elects, instead, female companionship which she finds fuller and more complex, resonant in a way which "one string" cannot be. "Men are all in the light," she declares, believing them to lack depth. Women, in Woolf's estimation, do not possess the same shallowness. She demonstrates the amplitude of female relationships by imagining that in these she swims at once into the silent dusk of vast and uncharted waters.

Virginia Woolf constructed labyrinths of female friendships and relationships throughout the pages of her letters and journals. There she seeks to explore the "silent dusk"—a domain that holds a strong allure. This is especially true during the years 1922-30, a period of personal sexual awakening during which Woolf felt compelled to investigate her emerging desire through the female characters of her fiction and non-fiction. Her works exhibit forays into the realms of friendship and *jouissance*. These intimate webs of connection reveal a matrix of associations between Woolf and the women who would influence her life and drive her fiction. From her early relationships with her mother and sister, through adolescent and young adult friendships with tutor Janet Case and Violet Dickinson, and in adult associations with Vita Sackville-West and Dame Ethel Smythe, Virginia Woolf demonstrates her strongest desire: to communicate with women.

The intricate psychological constructions of Woolf as female friend, lesbian lover, incestuous sister and woman who craved from other women that which only women could provide—the stimulus to create, the security to seek health and, finally, her decision to end a life suddenly bereft of this female infrastructure—are evident in her writing. A study of Woolf's letters and journals helps us to reconstruct the relationship between the writer's life and the female friendships she composes for her fictional characters. Woolf's own words, "Women alone stir my imagination," lead us to an investigation of the associations she shared with women and of how these relationships are played out in an intertextual environment.

For Virginia Woolf, her most exciting and potentially inspiring female relationships moved far beyond the limits of social interactions. Certain of her friendships were indeed erotically motivated. In this essay, I consider the homoeroticism of Woolf's female friendships—both those she experienced in reality and those she immortalized in her fiction. I argue that these homoerotic friendships/relationships are also indicative of Woolf's strong desire to experience her own agency and *jouissance*.

When she published *Mrs. Dalloway* in May 1925, Virginia's friendship with Vita, soon to become her first adult erotic relationship, was just beginning. It was not the earliest, nor would it be the last, of Woolf's homoerotic experiences. Throughout her lifetime, she established many meaningful relationships with women. As Woolf avows in another letter, written in August 1930:

> But I am the most passionate about women. Take away my affections and I should be like sea weed out of water; like the shell of a crab, like a husk. All my entrails, light, marrow, juice, pulp would be gone. I should be blown into the first puddle and drown.... It is true that I only want to show off to women. Women alone stir my imagination. (IV: 202-03)

Many women had stirred her imagination. Involvements with Madge Vaughan and Violet Dickinson preceded the one with Vita Sackville-West, and a later liaison would develop with Dame Ethel Smyth, to whom the 1930 letter is actually written. Yet, despite the evidence of her on-going intimate associations with women, Woolf's homoeroticism and the strength and encouragement she received from these interactions have not been foregrounded.

Of course, certain facts concerning Woolf's sexuality, in keeping with the bohemian picture of a writer, were acknowledged: her liaison with Vita Sackville-West (de-emphasized by male biographers), her close relationships with women (Violet Dickinson, Madge Vaughan, Dame Ethel Smyth) throughout her lifetime, her presumed platonic marriage to Leonard Woolf, the absence of any male romantic figures. However, biographical studies interpreted these "facts" within traditional parameters, portraying her as uninterested in a physical relationship, as a child in search of her mother, as a dysfunctional wife, or as an asexual creature. Quentin Bell, for example, in *Virginia Woolf: A Biography*, describes his aunt as follows:

> I think that the erotic element in her personality was faint and tenuous...she regarded sex, not so much with horror, as with incomprehension; there was, both in her personality and in her art, a disconcertingly aetherial quality and, when the necessities of literature compel her to consider lust, she either turns away or presents us with something as remote from the gropings and grapplings of the bed as is the flame of a candle from its tallow. (2: 6)

Nigel Nicholson, Vita Sackville-West's son, is guilty of the same minimization of the female erotic capacity, as illustrated by his comments on the relationship between Virginia Woolf and his mother. In *Portrait of a Marriage*, he contends that "Vita and Virginia did no damage to each other.... The physical element in their friendship was tentative and not very successful, lasting only a few months, a year perhaps. It is a travesty of their relationship to call it an affair" (207). Such evaluations may have diverted critics from any consideration of sexual desire because there "appeared" to be none.

Assumptions such as these have hindered our study of the importance and vitality of women's intimate relationships. Homoeroticism in Woolf's fiction and non-fiction exists but has been undertheorized and has not taken center-stage in Woolfian criticism. Traditional critics and biographers have historically glossed over evidence of her lesbian orientation. Blanche Wiesen Cook points out that we have now begun the process of "restoring the full range of lesbian options, of woman-loving choices...[of] consider[ing] the full implications of women's friendships and the crucial role played by female networks of love and support" (720). Although aware of the difficulties in ferreting out the details of female erotic relationships, Cook urges that we piece together the threads of this important aspect of women's lives. When, as in the case of Virginia Woolf, these relationships have been depreciated, we are compelled to re-evaluate what has been misinterpreted as a result of the prejudices or the misguided protections of phallocentric scholarship which overlooks inscriptions of homoerotic desire, misreads or completely ignores them. Cook articulates the problem: "In a hostile world in which women are not supposed to survive except in relation with and service to men, entire communities of women were simply erased. History tends to bury what it seeks to reject" (720). This is true on an individual level as well. Family members and friends often disguise or erase evidence of relationships between sisters, mothers, or wives and other women. What is lost is a rich heritage of female experience, friendship and interaction.

The reasons for the invisibility of female homoeroticism in the literary critical tradition are many. Foremost is the gender specificity of representations of desire. The same "disappearing act" which has been performed on woman's desire has also kept homoerotic sexuality from view. Luce Irigaray submits one argument to explain this invisibility. She insists that "the feminine" is only a construct of the patriarchal system: "[T]here are not really two sexes, but only one. A single practice and representation of the sexual" (86). Whatever falls outside the phallic mode is *unrepresented* and therefore has no existence in the dominant discourse.

Teresa de Lauretis amplifies Irigaray's assertion and declares that the configuration of "sexual difference" in our society is, as a result, really sexual *indifference*—"what woman wants" has been derived from phallocentric imperatives and is defined by what man himself desires. De Lauretis alleges that "within the conceptual frame of that sexual indifference, female desire for the self-same, an other female self, cannot be recognized" (156).

The ramifications of sexual indifference for feminine *jouissance* are immense; for homoerotic desire, they are extreme. De Lauretis explains:

> That a woman might desire a woman *like* herself, someone of the *same* sex, that she might also have auto- and homosexual appetites, is simply incomprehensible in the phallic regime of an asserted sexual difference between man and woman which is predicated on the contrary, on a complete indifference for the *other* sex, woman's. (156)

However, this does not mean that homoerotic desire has ceased to exist; it has simply gone "underground." Like woman's desire, it is expressed in an intertextual code. As de Lauretis comments, lesbian writers and artists have sought "to inscribe the erotic in cryptic, allegorical, realistic, camp or other modes of representation, pursuing diverse strategies of writing and of reading the intransitive and yet obdurate relation of reference to meaning, of flesh to language" (159).

Turning again to the denial of woman's desire by our phallocentric culture, it is clear that homosexual imagery and motifs in women's literature have usually been unacknowledged. The homogeneity of the same-sex relationship has made it possible to interpret lesbian interaction as mere friendship, thus denying the erotic implications. For example, in reviewing traditional interpretations of Virginia Woolf's "female friendships," Cook finds that once removed from Quentin Bell's interpretations, Woolf's journal record presents an entirely different view of her intimacy with women. For every interpretation by Bell, there exists a contradictory statement by Woolf, particularly if we acknowledge her homoerotic orientation (726).

This is illustrated by a comparison between Bell's and Virginia Woolf's own view of her association with Vita Sackville-West. Quentin Bell assumes that they could not have [had] very satisfying relations. He concludes: "There may have been—on balance I think that there probably was—some caressing, some bedding together. But whatever may have occurred between them of this nature, I doubt very much whether it was of a kind to excite Virginia or satisfy Vita" (2: 119). Bell promotes a diluted version of the Woolf/Sackville-West relationship. He wonders how deeply in love Virginia could have been, citing her criticisms of Vita's personality and writing. He concludes: "[I]f the test of passion be blindness, then her affections were not very deeply engaged" (2: 119).

Cook challenges Bell's interpretation, declaring: "Now in whose world is the test of love, or passion, 'blindness'? Few women, I think, will recognize as familiar even the idea of such a test" (726). In Cook's opinion, as feminists we "see with different sensibilities, and we begin with different interests and questions. We seek, in fact, a different vocabulary" (728). She proposes to let Virginia Woolf's description of Vita Sackville-West speak for itself. The following is taken from Woolf's diary entry, dated 21 December 1925:

> I like her and being with her and the splendour—she shines in the grocer's shop in Sevenoaks with a candlelit radiance, stalking on legs like beech trees, pink glowing, grape clustered, pearl hung.... What is the effect of all this on me? Very mixed. There is her maturity and full-breastedness; her being so much in full sail on the high tides, where I am coasting down backwaters.... Then there is some voluptuousness about her; the grapes are ripe; and not reflective. (III: 52)

Both the sensuous quality of the sketch and the romantic images signify the intensity of Virginia's interest in Vita. It becomes difficult to imagine that this relationship could be "of no great importance," as Bell insists (2: 119).

The inadequacy of his depiction is also obvious in his observation that Vita loved Virginia "much as a man might have loved her..." (2: 117). Bell's inability to interpret the homoerotic involvement in terms other than those of his own masculine conception of desire is one aspect of a larger problem. Perhaps his opinions simply reflect the patriarchal denial of erotic love between women; or perhaps it is his protection for his aunt that we see operating behind his comments. No matter the cause, Quentin Bell's portrayal of Virginia Woolf's relationship with Vita Sackville-West is biased and inaccurate, giving the impression that their involvement exhibited neither love nor lust.

But, as Cook points out, it contains both. Woolf's sensual description of Vita certainly belies an uninterested, unaffected sensibility. In the diary entry quoted above and in later letters, she writes erotically of her impressions of Vita and their experiences together. To her sister Vanessa, for example, Woolf writes: "Vita is now arriving to spend 2 nights alone with me.... June nights are long and warm; the roses flowering; and the garden full of lust and bees, mingling on the asparagus beds" (III: 275). The enclosed garden—where lust might be experienced upon the "asparagus beds"—again illustrates the all-important spatial conceptualizations of female desire. There can be no doubt that the thought of spending time alone in the presence of her beloved excites Woolf's imagination. She portrays her anticipation in images of physical sensation: the warm nights, the sight and smell of roses, the sound of bees, the feel of feathery asparagus plants on the skin, the lust of lovers. With such vivid records available to Quentin Bell and other biographers, one wonders how Virginia Woolf could possibly have been characterized as "sexless" and "coldly dispassionate."

Not only is the familial denial associated with lesbianism found in both Quentin Bell's and Nigel Nicholson's biographies, it is also present in critical scholarship generated outside the family circle. Sherron E. Knopp challenges the traditional narrow-mindedness surrounding the Woolf/Sackville-West relationship. She comments:

> Yet the extent to which Vita and Virginia did love each other—profoundly and, in every sense of the words, erotically and sexually (the frequency or infrequency with which they went to bed is irrelevant)—is something that continues to be resisted, denied, ignored, qualified out of significance, or simply unrecognized.... There seems to be an unspoken agreement that whatever else one might call Virginia—asexual, bisexual, androgynous—she was not a "sapphist." (25)

Many feminist critics have begun to revise these traditionally homophobic or homo-insensitive assessments of Woolf's relationships. As critic Louise A. DeSalvo writes, "Virginia Woolf and Vita Sackville-West would become as tinder and flint to one another, striking in each other and from one another the sparks of love, sexuality, support, friendship, and literary inspiration" (197). A look at two letters exchanged between these women friends clearly calls into question the interpretations of their biographers. Vita writes:

> My darling, Last night I went to bed very early and read *Mrs. Dalloway*—It was a very curious sensation: I thought you were in the room.... I felt quite light, as though I were falling through my bed, like when one has a fever. Today I am quite solid again, and my boots are muddy. They weight me down. Yet I am not as solid as usual,—not quite such an oaf,—because there is at the back of my mind all the time...a glow, a sort of nebula, which only when I examine it hardens into a shape; as soon as I think of something else it dissolves again, remaining there like the sun through a fog, and I have to reach out to it again, take it in my hands & feel its contours: then it hardens, "Virginia is coming on Saturday." (Berg Collection, as quoted in DeSalvo, "Lighting the Cave" 201-02)

Vita's letter to Virginia shows that there exists an atmosphere of excitement and anticipation around their relationship. Vita's acute perception of Virginia's presence, imagined and awaited, arouses expectations of things to come. Similarly, Virginia's warm sentiments for Vita are expressed in a teasing 1927 letter which begins "Look here Vita—throw over your man, and we'll go to Hampton Court and dine on the river together and walk in the garden in the moonlight and come home late and have a bottle of wine and get tipsy...." Soon her playfulness disappears, and in its stead the promise of more intimate offerings is extended: "[A]nd I'll tell you all the things I have in my head, millions, myriads—They won't stir by day, only by dark on the river. Think of that. Throw over your man, I say, and come" (III: 393). DeSalvo neatly summarizes the Woolf/Sackville-West relationship as follows: "Together they would light the cave of darkness that each held within herself" (197). Their mutual desire, like a glowing nebula of stars in the night sky, is not always visible to the naked eye; but there, "by the dark on the river," Virginia and Vita discover the "shape" of their *jouissance*.

Without a doubt, Woolf neither wrote nor read from a phallocentric point of view, and to impose the rigid grid of traditional interpretation upon her texts is to leave undeveloped the rich homoerotic texture of woman's desire manifested in her female friendships. She introduces the homoerotic element in *Mrs. Dalloway* through the relationship of Clarissa Dalloway and Sally Seton; in *Between the Acts* through Miss LaTrobe, the lesbian artist; and in *A Room of One's Own* through the mysterious relationship of the scientists, Chloe and Olivia. Other suggestions of lesbian sensibility can be identified in *To the Lighthouse* (Lily Briscoe), *Orlando* (the gender metamorphosis of the main character), and "Friendship's Gallery" (a short story written in tribute to Violet Dickinson).

Jane Marcus illustrates how Woolf embeds "seductive sapphistry" in her works. Using material from *The Pargiters*, Marcus examines Woolf's encoded lesbian suggestion. This passage is taken from the conclusion of a speech given in January 1931 before the London National Society for Women's Service. In closing, Woolf constructs a romantic description of a working woman's room:

> There in the privacy of your own room, you can sit and write or paint...what will be the next step? There will have to be one. And I predict that the next step will be a step on the stair. You will hear somebody coming. You will open the door. And then—this at least is my guess—there will take place between you and some one else the most interesting, exciting, and important conversation that has ever been heard. But do not be alarmed; I am not going to talk about that now. (xxxxiv)

Marcus makes the following observations: "What sex is *'somebody'*? What sex is *'someone else'*? Why is this *'alarming'*? This lecture as lupine plot, feminist conspiracy, is another seductive *sapphistry*. It stops just short of sedition" ("Bull" 152).

Marcus continues, pointing out the parallel construction of the "Chloe and Olivia" passage from *A Room of One's Own* to the one quoted above. *The Pargiters* contains "a script with missing lines like the ellipses in 'Chloe liked Olivia. They shared a...'" (152). Marcus posits that "the audience (or the reader) supplies the missing dialogue in 'the *most* interesting, exciting, important conversation that has ever been heard.'" She wonders, "Has Chloe come to visit Olivia after the laboratory has closed?" (152). Furthermore, Marcus contends that Woolf, as woman writer, is attempting to seduce the woman reader. She argues, "Not only narration but even punctuation is enlisted in [Woolf's] seductive plot: 'Chloe liked Olivia. They shared a...' Dot dot dot is a female code for lesbian love" ("Sapphistry" 169).

The laboratory, like the room of one's own, is an enclosure wherein the "discovery" of feminine *jouissance* is possible. In *The Pargiters* and *A Room of One's Own*, Woolf constructs the spaces in which her characters experience their own desires. Moreover, both speeches were given before audiences of women (*A Room of One's*

Own) is based upon two papers read to the Arts Society at Newnham and the Odtaa at Girton in October 1928). We might consider the implications of this fact as well. In the safety of an environment composed entirely of women, Woolf expresses her own desire in the presence of others who do not violate the space. She asks several times in *A Room of One's Own* if the women are certain that no men are hiding nearby. Assured that there are none, Woolf decides to disguise the lesbian text only thinly: "Then I may tell you that...'Chloe liked Olivia...' Do not start. Do not blush. Let us admit in the privacy of our society that these things sometimes happen. Sometimes women do like women" (85-86). She describes the desire of "women [who] like women" metaphorically as "vast chambers" lit in "half lights and profound shadows," and as "serpentine caves where one goes with a candle peering up and down, not knowing where one is stepping" (88). Lesbian desire is subtly inscribed in *half-said* references to the dual representations of the room that houses the women (the laboratory) and the room that the women house (the vagina).

However, Woolf is not always so circumspect in her inscription of homoerotic experience. She uses vivid descriptive metaphors in letters to Vita Sackville-West when alluding to their sexual intimacy. The following example illustrates. Angry with Vita for teasing her with hints at involvements with other partners, Woolf writes: "Yes, you are an agile animal—no doubt about it, but as to your gambols being diverting, always...I'm not so sure. Bad, wicked beast!...You only be a careful dolphin in your gambolling, or you'll find Virginia's soft crevices lined with hooks" (III: 395). This sample and other unmistakable sexual references in her letters indicate that Woolf indeed experiences homoerotic intimacy.

She also inscribes distinctly lesbian experiences beyond the borders of her personal letters. In the short story, "Moments of Being: 'Slater's Pins Have No Points,'" Woolf's language is particularly homoerotic. Written in 1928 during the peak of her relationship with Vita Sackville-West, the narrative takes place in a music room where young Fanny Wilmot is studying with Miss Julia Craye, her piano teacher. On this day, Fanny wears a carnation pinned to her dress. During the lesson, the pin holding the flower becomes detached, and both pin and carnation fall to the ground. Watching Miss Craye retrieve the flower, Fanny observes that "the pressure of [Miss Craye's] fingers seemed to increase all that was most brilliant in the flower; to set it off; to make it more frilled, fresh, immaculate" (Dick 211).

Julia Craye, we learn, has never married, a fact which is the subject of Fanny's thoughts. Believing that marriage endangers one's freedom, Fanny concludes that Miss Craye's decision not to wed is based upon her desire to exercise her habits freely: "They remained safe, and her habits would have suffered if she had married. 'They're ogres [men],' she had said one evening, half laughing.... An ogre would have interfered perhaps with breakfast in bed; with walks at dawn down to the river" (213). The story proceeds with the reminiscences of Miss Craye, who remembers a life filled alternately with passionate excitement (she had visited Waterloo) and utter boredom (Edinburgh was too bleak). Returning from the wanderings of Julia's recollections, we realize that Woolf has tricked us with her manipulation of time. The entire story, as the title suggests, occurs in a moment. Fanny spies the pin from her flower and picks it up from the carpet.

Sitting next to Julia who is "half turned away from the piano, with her hands clasped in her lap holding the carnation upright," Fanny is aware of the "sharp square of the window, uncurtained, purple in the evening, intensely purple after the brilliant electric lights which burnt unshaded in the bare music room" (214). Fanny becomes attuned with that purple shape and all around her becomes "transparent." She is drawn into "the very fountain of [Julia's] being" which spurts up in "pure, silver drops." The young woman is transported "back and back into the past behind her" where she sees Julia "going round and about the corridors of that ancient Cathedral dwelling place...obstinately adhering whatever people might say in choosing her pleasures for herself. She saw Julia—" (214).

Having constructed the environment where one might investigate her own desires, Woolf flashes back to the present, where she inscribes the homoerotic experience:

> [Fanny] saw Julia open her arms; saw her blaze; saw her kindle. Out of the night she burnt like a dead white star. Julia kissed her. Julia possessed her. "Slater's pins have no points," Miss Craye said, laughing queerly and relaxing her arms, as Fanny Wilmot pinned the flower to her breast with trembling fingers. (214)

Thus ends the story of another of Woolf's homoerotic relationships.

Many memorable homoerotic scenes are also presented in Woolf's *To The Lighthouse*, a self-confessed autobiographical novel. Surrogate daughter Lily Briscoe, an undisguised stand-in for Woolf, struggles to understand her relationship with Mrs. Ramsay, the mother-figure in the narrative. Starting "the tune of Mrs. Ramsay in her head," Lily recalls a night when the older woman arrived at her bedroom door, tapped lightly, and entered the moonlit room. Mrs. Ramsay, wrapped in [perhaps only] an old fur coat, enters the room. After telling amusing stories about the male guests, Mrs. Ramsay would insist that she must go, "it was dawn, she could see the sun rising"; then she would "half turn back, more intimately, but still always laughing, insist that she must...they all must marry" because an unmarried woman "has missed the best of life" (76-77).

Mrs. Ramsay's admonition that all women must marry does little to diminish the erotic tension of the scene. In fact, this hetero-centric mandate should not overshadow what is really afoot in the room: flirtations described in strongly sensual terms. Woolf is creating a crackling atmosphere filled with all the elements for sexual interaction between the two women. As the night wears on, Lily explores her own desires: "[S]he would urge her own exemption from universal law; plead for it; she liked to be alone; she liked to be herself; she was not made for that [marriage]" (77-78). Even timid Lily Briscoe dares to express the desires of an agent/self. In articulating her own desires, is Lily simply a child seeking return to the mother or is she an adult woman who is aware that her desire is directed toward the beautiful woman who is wrapped in fur and standing in the moonlight before her? The fluidity between Mrs. Ramsay as mother and as sexual subject opens the possibilities for the daughter.

While the traditionally held view is that Lily Briscoe seeks to become one with the mother-figure and to possess the mother's power, a revised interpretation suggests that Lily Briscoe is erotically aware of the woman who has joined her. Her laughter, while she lays her head on Mrs. Ramsay's lap, is released in waves of recognition—she has caught a glimpse of Mrs. Ramsay, not in the the maternal omnipotent role which the child accords to the mother, but as a female equal (*Lighthouse* 78).

The remainder of the scene suggests that Lily seeks recognition of her own authentic desire (for nurturance and/or erotic union) in the safety of the space of women's friendship. In sensually descriptive terms, Woolf creates a space in which Lily Briscoe might discover what she desires:

> ...she imagined how in the chambers of the mind and heart of
> the woman who was, physically, touching her, were stood, like

the treasures in the tombs of kings, tablets bearing sacred inscriptions, which if one could spell them out, would teach one everything, but they would never be offered openly, never made public. What art was there, known to love or cunning, by which one pressed through into those secret chambers? What device for becoming, like waters poured into one jar, inextricably the same, one with the object one adored? Could the body achieve, or the mind, subtly mingling in the intricate passages of the brain? or the heart? Could loving, as people called it, make her and Mrs. Ramsay one? for it was not knowledge but unity that she desired, not inscriptions on tablets, nothing that could be written in any language known to men, but intimacy itself, which is knowledge, she had thought, leaning her head on Mrs. Ramsay's knee. (78-79)

Woolf inscribes what woman desires as something which cannot be written in "any language known to men."

Moving on to another of Woolf's well-known narratives, let us investigate how homoeroticism is inscribed in *Mrs. Dalloway*. Clarissa Dalloway is compelled to examine homoerotic feelings in her relationship with Sally Seton. We discover that her thoughts (echoing those of the author?) are precipitated by failure to engage successfully in sex with her husband: "[S]he had failed him.... She could see what she lacked. It was not beauty; it was not mind. It was something central which permeated; something warm which broke up surfaces and rippled the cold contact of man and woman, or of women together. For *that* she could dimly perceive" (46). Clarissa describes what she yearns for—her own desire:

[Y]et she could not resist sometimes yielding to the charm of a woman...she did undoubtedly then feel what men felt. Only for a moment; but it was enough. It was a sudden revelation, a tinge like a blush which one tried to check and then, as it spread, one yielded to its expansion, and rushed to the farthest verge and there quivered and felt the world come closer, swollen with some astonishing significance, some pressure of rapture, which split its thin skin and gushed and poured with extraordinary alleviation!... Then, for that moment, she had seen an illumination; a match burning in a crocus; an inner meaning almost expressed. But the close withdrew; the hard softened. It was over—the moment. (47)

It would be inaccurate to read this passage in phallic terms. Woolf is reciting feminine *jouissance*, not the subject/object dynamic of phallocentric desire. Clarissa feels "what men feel"—not the need to objectify women, but the *agency of desire*. The rest of the section, when read erotically, denotes the physiological sensations of *female*, not male, orgasm. The blush, the expansion, the quiver of the swollen clitoris precedes the orgasmic rush—the pressure of rapture, the gush, the pouring. Woolf's knowledge of female anatomy and sexual response, most likely gained in intimate physical relationships with other women, is evident in her description. Since her heterosexual experiences were less than fulfilling, we must credit her lesbian sexual involvements as the source of her awareness of orgasmic sensations.

Many examples to support the assumption that Woolf shared physical intimacy with another woman can be found in her letters. For instance, writing to Violet Dickinson in 1906, Woolf announces:

> If you could put your hand in that nest of fur where my heart beats you would feel the thump of the steadiest organ in London—all beating for my Violet. Sometimes, when I am ordering dinner, or emptying—a flower vase—a great tide runs from my toe to my crown, which is the thought of you.... Now then will you believe that I am devoted to every hair, and every ridge and hollow, and every spot upon your body? (I: 245)

The sensual references should be understood as exactly what they are—a 24-year-old woman's sensual description of her female anatomy and her knowledge of its sexual capacity. In another letter to Dickinson, Woolf writes that "it is astonishing what depths—hot volcano depths—your finger has stirred...." (I:85). Woolf's propensity to pay tribute to the women in her life through her fiction is, in fact, illustrated in *Mrs. Dalloway*. Sally Seton resembles Virginia's "first love," Madge Vaughan, and hints of Violet Dickinson are also in her character (Hawkes 51).

Echoing the sensibilities presented in Woolf's 1906 letter, Clarissa Dalloway experiences a similar "rush" when she recalls the excitement of Sally Seton's visits. The spatial imagery we have come to expect fills her memories of the past. She wonders, "Had not that, after all, been love?" (48). The two women spend hours in a bedroom at the top of the house, undisturbed by the world. Clarissa's memories are distinctly erotic:

Sally's power was amazing, her gift, her personality. There was her way with flowers, for example. At Bourton they always had stiff little vases all the way down the table. Sally went out, picked hollyhocks, dahlias—all sorts of flowers that had never been seen together—cut their heads off, and made them swim on the top of water in bowls. The effect was extraordinary—coming into dinner in the sunset.... Then she [Sally] forgot her sponge, and ran along the passage naked.... "Suppose any of the gentlemen had seen?" Indeed she did shock people. (50)

This scene is brimming with sexual innuendo. Woolf's metaphoric example of woman's power disrupts the phallic economy. Sally exercises her own desire, thus shattering the singular mode of representation. The "stiff little vases" that line the table represent the phallus; the bowls of water and the flowers, woman's genitals. Dissatisfied with the arrangement, Sally gathers "dahlias and hollyhocks" and floats them "on the top of water in bowls." The contrast between the phallic-like vases and the womb-like bowls is apparent.

Although Woolf couches her description in floral images, she soon divulges her meaning. To close the scene, she portrays the naked Sally running down the passageway and adds the voice of disapproval, "Suppose the gentlemen had seen?" Is it the flowers swimming in the water of the bowls that would shock the men, or is it the naked Sally (with sponge for bathing in a larger bowl) that would have this effect? Woolf, doubtless, would have us understand that they are one and the same. Desire, expressed in unexpected floral arrangements or in the female formulation, is shocking to phallocentric society.

In a 1927 letter to her sister, Vanessa, Woolf compares the garden of heterosexuality with her own homoerotic environs. She writes to Vanessa: "You will never succumb to the charms of any of your sex—what an arid garden the world must be for you! What avenues of stone pavements and iron railings!" (III: 381). Of her own garden, however, she speaks in the following manner:

The gardens...lay before me in the spring twilight, wild and open, and in the long grass, sprinkled and carelessly flung, were daffodils and bluebells.... Somebody was in the hammock, somebody, but in this light they were phantoms only, half guessed, half seen, raced across the grass—would no one stop her...All was dim, yet intense too, as if the scarf which the dusk had flung over the garden were torn asunder.... (Room 17)

A cursory comparison of the imagery reflects the hard, dry, "man-made" aspects of the heterosexual habitat, while the garden occupied by women is fecund both with flora and with possibilities. Echoing Jane Marcus' queries, we wonder who the *"somebody"* is in the hammock, the phantom only "half-guessed, half seen," racing across the grass. We know the "somebody" is a *woman*, who has been enfolded by the dusk. The erotic atmosphere of Woolf's garden is conspicuously present.

The same atmosphere pervades the relationship of Sally Seton and Clarissa Dalloway. In fact, Woolf uses flowers to signal that an erotic experience between women is immanent. She writes:

> Then came the most exquisite moment of [Clarissa's] whole life
> [as she passed] a stone urn with flowers in it. Sally stopped;
> picked a flower; kissed her on the lips. The whole world might
> have turned upside down!...And she felt that she had been given
> a present, wrapped up, and told just to keep it, not to look at
> it—a diamond, something infinitely precious, wrapped, which,
> as they walked (up and down, up and down), she uncovered, or
> the radiance burnt through, the revelation, the religious feeling!
> (52-53)

The diamond—lying deep inside the earth, slowly taking shape, waiting to be discovered—is a metaphor for female desire and is also representative of female anatomy. Clarissa's own body already houses the diamond which Sally has "given" to her. The clitoris lies buried in the folds of the labia. Its hardness when stimulated is symbolized by the diamond, as is the multifaceted dimension of woman's eroticism. "Infinitely precious," radiant, revelatory: the gift heralds the recognition of desire, an overwhelming moment when the "world might have turned upside down." In that moment, Clarissa experiences her own feminine *jouissance*. She accepts the gift, keeps it, does not look at it; but the radiance of that "diamond shape" burns through, is revealed.

Woolf blends together the images of a flower, the kiss on the lips, and the wrapped shape. The allusions to lesbian love-making are buried in the metaphors. Sally, whose "beautiful voice...made everything she said sound like a caress" (52), whose presence makes Clarissa feel that "if it were now to die 'twere now to be most happy" (51), is the reciprocal agent (the female lover) in this dual recognition of desire.

Jane Marcus emphasizes this point, stressing that "female heterosexuality is most often represented in Woolf's fiction as victimization or colonization" ("Liberty" 77). Homosexuality carries no such representations; it is magical, exquisite, a kind of ecstasy. Marcus speculates on the effect of these dissimilar treatments by Woolf:

> If the historian had only Woolf's novels from which to deduce the position of women in England, she would be forced to conclude that marriage was a primitive institution in decline; that many women perceived male sexuality as rape; that lesbianism and homosexuality were widespread; that spinsterhood, aunthood, sisterhood, and female friendship were women's most important roles; that motherhood and wifehood were Victorian relics. ("Liberty" 77)

Woolf's strategies for developing alternative images of woman's desire are found throughout her fiction, non-fiction, letters and diaries. Her techniques for the inscription of the homoerotic open new horizons and exciting vistas for women's friendships. However, we also note that Sally Seton gives Clarissa Dalloway a wrapped present, a diamond hard and *impervious to assault,* perhaps for good reason. Lesbian desire has not only been denied visibility in the phallocentric world, it has also been attacked. We need only to place Woolf's works in the historical context of their times to understand her discretion.

Jane Marcus provides substantial evidence of Woolf's awareness of the homophobic climate. Citing an early fragment of *A Room of One's Own*, Marcus observes that after the words "Chloe liked Olivia. They shared a...," Woolf writes:

> The words covered the bottom of the page: the pages had stuck. While fumbling to open them there flashed into my mind the inevitable policeman...the order to attend the Court; the dreary waiting; the Magistrate coming in with a little bow...for the Prosecution; for the Defense—the verdict; this book is obscene + flames sing, perhaps on Tower Hill, as they compound (?) that mass of paper. Here the paper came apart. Heaven be praised! It was only a laboratory. Chloe-Olivia. They were engaged in mincing liver, apparently a cure for pernicious anaemia. (Monk's House Papers, as quoted in Marcus, "Sapphistry" 186)

Woolf's references are to the obscenity trial of Radclyffe Hall's lesbian novel, *The Well of Loneliness* (1928). Banned by English courts, the book significantly affected women's freedoms to explore homoerotic relationships in the pages of their books or in the lines of their poetry. Woolf planned to testify at the trial but was never called to do so. We can only conjecture as to why she decided to eliminate the above passage from her final draft of *A Room of One's Own*. "The paper of her own pages is singed by the flames that burned the banned book," Marcus theorizes ("Sapphistry" 186). Nonetheless, Virginia Woolf continues to inscribe homoerotic desire in her works, bringing "buried things to light and [making] one wonder what need there had been to bury them" (*Room* 96).

Once we are able to follow Woolf on her journey into the silent dusk of feminine *jouissance*, we too wonder "what need" there is to bury woman's desire or to minimize the importance of women's friendships. Significantly, through her texts Woolf has given her readers a "laboratory" in which to make exciting discoveries. We join in "stirring the imagination"—with Virginia and Vita, Chloe and Olivia, Julia and Fanny, Sally and Clarissa and countless others whose quiet footsteps fall on the stairs, whose whispered voices are heard, whose shadowy outlines can be seen in the garden on a moonlit night—until by sheer force of *will*, desire is created in the company of women.

Works Cited

Bell, Quentin. *Virginia Woolf: A Biography*. New York: Harcourt, 1972.

Cook, Blanche Wiesen. "'Women Alone Stir My Imagination': Lesbianism and the Cultural Tradition." *Signs: Journal of Women in Culture and Society* 4 (1979).

De Lauretis, Teresa. "Sexual Indifference and Lesbian Representation." *Theater Journal* (May 1988).

DeSalvo, Louise A. "Lighting the Cave: The Relationship Between Vita Sackville-West and Virginia Woolf." *Signs: Journal of Women in Culture and Society* 8 (1982).

DeSalvo, Louise, and Mitchell A. Leaska, eds. *The Letters of Vita Sackville-West to Virginia Woolf*. New York: William Morrow, 1984.

Dick, Susan, ed. *The Complete Shorter Fiction of Virginia Woolf*. New York: Harcourt, 1985.

Hawkes, Ellen. "Woolf's 'Magical Garden of Women.'" *New Feminist Essays on Virginia Woolf*. Ed. Jane Marcus. Lincoln: U of Nebraska P, 1981.

Irigaray, Luce. *This Sex Which Is Not One*. Trans. Catherine Porter. Ithaca: Cornell UP, 1985.

Knopp, Sherron. "'If I Saw You, Would You Kiss Me?': Sapphism and the Subversiveness of Virginia Woolf's *Orlando*." *PMLA* 103 (1988).

Marcus, Jane. "Liberty, Sorority, Misogyny." *Virginia Woolf and the Languages of Patriarchy*. Bloomington: Indiana UP, 1987.

_____. "Sapphistry: Narration as Lesbian Seduction in *A Room of One's Own*." *Virginia Woolf and the Languages of Patriarchy*. Bloomington: Indiana UP, 1987.

_____. "Taking the Bull by the Udders: Sexual Difference in Virginia Woolf—A Conspiracy Theory." *Virginia Woolf and the Languages of Patriarchy*. Bloomington: Indiana UP, 1987.

Nicholson, Nigel. *Portrait of a Marriage*. New York: Anthenaeum, 1973.

Woolf, Virginia. *The Diary of Virginia Woolf*. Volumes I-V. Ed. Anne Olivier Bell. London: The Hogarth P Limited, 1980.

_____. *The Letters of Virginia Woolf*. Volumes I-VI. Eds. Nigel Nicholson and Joanne Trautmann. New York: Harcourt, 1977.

_____. *Mrs. Dalloway*. New York: Harcourt, 1925.

_____. *The Pargiters*. Ed. Mitchell A. Leaska. New York: The New York Public Library, 1977.

_____. *A Room of One's Own*. New York: Harcourt, 1929.

_____. *To The Lighthouse*. New York: Harcourt, 1927.

"The Medicine She Trusted To": Women, Friendship and Communication in *The Voyage Out* and *Night and Day*

ELIZABETH COOLEY

> "Chloe liked Olivia" I read, and then it struck me how immense a change was there. Chloe liked Olivia perhaps for the first time in literature. Cleopatra did not like Octavia.... But how interesting it would have been if the relationship between the two women had been more complicated. All these relationships between women, I thought, rapidly recalling the splendid gallery of fictitious women, are too simple. So much has been left out, unattempted. (*A Room of One's Own* 82)

Despite her narrator's shock at reading these words written by the fictitious novelist, Mary Carmichael, by 1929, the year *A Room of One's Own* was published, Woolf herself could very well imagine that Chloe liked Olivia. With Clarissa Dalloway and Sally Seton, Mrs. Ramsay and Lily Briscoe, Orlando and the eighteenth-century London prostitutes, Woolf had successfully depicted female friendship, both conventional and otherwise, in *Mrs. Dalloway*, *To the Lighthouse* and *Orlando*. She would go on to explore female relationships, though arguably in a less positive light, in her final three novels as well. In her two earliest novels, *The Voyage Out* and *Night and Day*, we also can detect the theme of female friendship, but we must search for it more actively and recognize its prototypical, embryonic quality in light of her later novels.

Friendship between women is an important but generally overlooked aspect in *The Voyage Out* and *Night and Day*. Often characterized as apprentice works that reflect Woolf's Victorian heritage rather than reveal her modernist innovations, these novels are generally viewed as romances whose conflicts and resolutions rely on young love and, in the case of *Night and Day*, on what Jean Kennard in her book *Victims of Convention* calls the "two suitor plot." Similarly, both novels appear to follow the pattern of nineteenth-century women's novels that Rachel Blau DuPlessis examines in *Writing Beyond the Ending* and elsewhere. DuPlessis notes the inherent contradiction between love (heterosexual romance) and quest or Bildung (maturation and self-realization) in nineteenth-century novels with female protagonists. She observes that this contradiction is generally resolved through "an ending in which one part of that contradiction, usually quest or Bildung, is set aside or repressed, whether by marriage or death" (Feminist 323).

Although DuPlessis and others note that "Woolf conducted a serious and continual scrutiny of these issues throughout her career" (324), certainly Woolf's earliest novels appear to fit this death-or-marriage pattern. In *The Voyage Out* Rachel Vinrace's quest is aborted by death. In *Night and Day*, dismissed by many critics as a failed "social comedy," Katharine Hilbery's marriage is generally interpreted as her acceptance of convention and of second class citizenship in a patriarchal society. However, if we look beneath the dominant plot of each novel, beneath boy-meets-girl and its death-or-marriage conclusion, we realize these novels are more than failed Bildungsromans or mediocre Victorian romances. Each novel's muted plot presents the protagonist's maturation and growing self-awareness. Within each muted plot we also find a relationship just as significant, in fact prerequisite, to the love relationship.[1] In each case the protagonist experiences her first adult friendship with another woman, Rachel with her aunt, Helen Ambrose and Katharine with her would-be rival, Mary Dachet. Katharine also renews or re-visions her relationship with her mother and this, too, is essential to her growth. Significantly, Helen and Mary are unconventional, both in their directness and in their language use; both embody a certain freedom with words that the protagonists admire but never try to emulate. By examining each novel in turn, we can explore how female friendship and, more specifically, female conversation teach each protagonist essential lessons about communication and human relations, lessons necessary to her psychological and emotional growth as well as to the more traditional heterosexual relationship she finds after she experiences friendship with another woman.

While most critics of *The Voyage Out* focus on the relationship between Rachel Vinrace and Terence Hewet, Rachel's earlier friendship with her Aunt Helen is crucial to her maturation and to her future relationship with Hewet. Although 24 years old, Rachel is very much the "unlicked girl" that Helen perceives her to be at the beginning of the novel, and this is reflected in her linguistic attitude and idiosyncrasies (23). Her slight stammer, her preference for music over speech and her reticence reflect a tendency to avoid communication. Raised by her taciturn father and two maiden aunts, Rachel has had little experience with friendship or communication. Although her aunts wish Rachel would "come to" them, when Rachel questions her Aunt Eleanor about her fondness for her Aunt Lucy, Eleanor replies, "'My dear child, what questions you do ask!'" (36). Thus Rachel is convinced that "Her efforts to come to an understanding [of human relationships] had only hurt her aunt's feelings," and "that it is better not to try.... It was far better to play the piano and forget all the rest." Before her friendship with Helen, Rachel sees people as "symbols" in a world where "nobody ever said a thing they meant" (37). Despite her early assumptions about what can and cannot be discussed, she has a natural desire to express herself and to communicate with others. This is a healthy desire; as Woolf wrote, paraphrasing Montaigne, and echoed later in *Mrs. Dalloway*, "communication is health, communication is truth, communication is happiness" (Montaigne 23-24).

Rachel initially attempts to fulfill this desire for talk through conversation with the voluble Dalloways whom she mischooses for companionship over her abrupt and sometimes intimidating Aunt Helen. Walking about the deck with Mrs. Dalloway, "She was overcome by an intense desire to tell [her] things she had never told anyone—things she had not realized herself until this moment" (60). While trying to discuss politics with Richard Dalloway, she experiences a "thrusting desire to be understood" (67). The Dalloways' apparent interest in her and their willingness to talk to her on an intimate level flatter Rachel and provide a welcome relief from her Aunt Helen's apparent rudeness. Helen's silences and her tendency to come "unexpectedly to the point" intimidate Rachel, and their early attempts at communication fail. Furthermore, by violating what H.P. Grice calls the Cooperative Principle,[2] she makes Clarissa Dalloway as well as Rachel "decidedly uncomfortable" (45). Her outright contradictions and her questions seem "to Clarissa in extraordinarily bad taste" (48). Naturally Rachel finds Clarissa, who conveys "an extraordinary degree of sympathy and desire to befriend" (58) and Richard, who always seems to mean what he says, more appealing than the "perverse" Helen. Rachel is particularly attracted to the fact that the Dalloways spend much time talking about talk and personal communication. Mr. Dalloway, with his noble sounding phrases, especially appeals to Rachel's desire for intimate communication: "'Here I sit,'" he says, "'there you sit; both, I doubt not, chock-full of the most interesting experiences, ideas, emotions; yet how communicate?'" (68). His declaration that "'This reticence—this isolation —[is] what's the matter with modern life!'" comes only seconds before he kisses Rachel (75).

A more worldly woman might not be surprised by this stratagem, but Rachel is baffled. The apparent juxtaposition of a high-minded desire for communication with an underhanded desire for illicit intimacy alerts Rachel to the true nature of the ephemeral and self-serving relationships offered by the Dalloways. The revelation about the Dalloways does not come in an epiphanic flash, however. It is only through talking to Helen that Rachel can integrate the experience and use it positively in her process of maturation.

Despite Helen's earlier conclusion that Rachel is "an unlicked girl, no doubt prolific of confidences" that Helen doesn't much want to share (23), she decides that she would like "to know what the girl was like" (79). At this point in the novel she becomes Rachel's self-appointed tutor. In some ways Helen seems an unlikely teacher for a young girl. Her silences, her bluntness and her disregard for the Cooperative Principle are suitable enough for her role as the wife of a scholar who lacks any semblance of social grace, but not necessarily for her role as instructor for a young lady. Ultimately, however, this bluntness forces Rachel to dispense with the vacant small talk that Helen, and Woolf herself, saw as a hindrance to real communication.

In *Moments of Being*, Woolf recalls the Victorian manner that she and Vanessa were forced to put on during tea at 22 Hyde Park Gate:

> We learnt it partly from remembering mother's manner; Stella's manner, and it was partly imposed upon us by the visitor who came in.... We should have first to make conversation. It was not argument, it was not gossip. It was a concoction; light ceremonious and of course unbroken. Silence was a breach of convention. (149)

Throughout the novel Helen breaches convention both through her silence and through her candor, yet her disregard for convention allows her much freedom. By dispensing with the light concoction of conversation she is not encumbered by superficial talk. And yet Helen is quite capable of following convention when necessary. In her conversation with Rachel about the Dalloways, she "indulged in commonplaces to begin with" easing Rachel into the topic (79). With the help of Rachel's own desire to confess, she comes straight to the point. Helen realizes from the beginning that Rachel must verbally express herself and her experiences in order to understand either. "Talk was the medicine she trusted to, talk about everything, talk that was free, unguarded..." (124). As Rachel talks, the incident with Dalloway becomes clearer in her own mind. Helen's words also help clarify things. They "hewed down great blocks which had stood there always, and the light which came in was cold" (81-82). The sudden awareness of sex and the realization that men could be "brutes" shocks Rachel, yet Helen "could think of no way of easing the difficulty except by going on talking" (82). By verbalizing the incident, Rachel better understands it and keeps it in perspective.

During the conversation, Rachel draws several other conclusions as well. She realizes that "most people had hitherto been symbols; but that when they talked to one they ceased to be symbols" (83). For Rachel, reality slowly becomes more than "what one saw and felt but did not talk about" (37), and she decides she likes talking with people and "could listen to them for ever" (84). As they talk the two women realize that they like each other; "That fact, together with other facts, had been made clear by that twenty minutes' talk, although how they had come to these conclusions they could not have said" (84). Paradoxically, the ability to define and appropriate reality through conversation is a process which itself cannot be defined or explained. In fact it can hardly be written about. As Woolf speculates, again referring to her maverick novelist:

> I wanted to see how Mary Carmichael set to work to catch those unrecorded gestures, those unsaid or half-said words, which form themselves, no more palpably than the shadows of moths on the ceiling, when women are alone, unlit by the capricious and coloured light of the other sex. (*Room* 84)

This conversation with Helen is Rachel's first real lesson. She begins to see what honest discourse can accomplish, and she also has intimations that some feelings and phenomena cannot be expressed verbally.

To Rachel, "the end of the voyage meant a complete change of perspective" (88). Ironically, with the end of her sea voyage, and seachange, her friendship with Helen recedes and the novel surrenders to the dominant romance plot. Although Rachel could never have reached the understanding about herself and about communication necessary to a successful heterosexual relationship had it not been for lessons learned from Helen, the recession, even repression, of their friendship undercuts it and disappoints the reader. Submitting to a pattern that Annis Pratt describes in *Archetypal Patterns in Women's Fiction*, Woolf allows Rachel and Helen to share "the brief energy...that characterizes only a transitional period in [women's] mutual quest for male appropriation" (97) before calling in the appropriate male. Helen herself is primarily responsible for this change in her relationship with her niece. In a letter home she writes, "I now pray for a young man to come to my help; someone, I mean, who would talk to her openly, and prove how absurd most of her ideas about life are" (97).

Once again marveling over Mary Carmichael's novel, the narrator of *A Room of One's Own* exclaims that after Mary had broken the sentence, "she had gone further and broken the sequence—the expected order.... the effect was somehow baffling; one could not see a wave heaping itself, a crisis coming round the next corner" (91). In *The Voyage Out* Woolf breaks the sequence but then sets things "right" again. And yet in setting things right, in allowing the novel to fall back into the well-regulated death-or-marriage pattern DuPlessis outlines for us, she must make things go wrong for Rachel Vinrace. Once the sequence is re-established, Rachel must die, a victim of convention. Even so, through this early depiction of female friendship Woolf prepares for the more lasting friendships and more permanent breaks in the sequence in her later novels.

Like Rachel's friendship with her aunt, Katharine Hilbery's tentative friendship with Mary Dachet and her renewed relationship with her mother are essential to her growth from a young woman who "did not like phrases" (41) or personal relationships to one who understands the necessity of communication for mutual understanding. Described by Shirley Garner as "the most deeply felt" relationship in the novel (322), Katharine and Mary's friendship depends on honest, if somewhat disjointed and chaotic, verbal communication. Similarly Katharine's mother, initially "the last person she wished to resemble" (41), becomes a source of comfort and wisdom once Katharine decodes the meaning behind the apparent nonsense of her words.

Just as *Night and Day* might be seen as a social comedy in the traditional sense, it is also a novel structured around what Jean Kennard calls "the convention of two suitors" (11), a convention which represents half of DuPlessis's death-or-marriage conclusion to the conventional woman's Bildungsroman. Dominant in Victorian novels with female protagonists, the two-suitor plot involves the protagonist coming of age by distinguishing Mr. Right from Mr. Wrong. In the course of the novel the protagonist's emotional and psychological growth are "defined through comparison with two male characters": in *Night and Day*, William Rodney and Ralph Denham. Katharine Hilbery must break her engagement with the foppish, verbose and egotistic Rodney before she can mature and, apparently, find fulfillment in the sensitive, poetic (and perhaps equally egotistic) Denham. Jean Kennard correctly describes this structural convention as sexist because the heroine "appears to have subordinated her own personality to that of the hero" (14). Marriage to Mr. Right is hardly the greatest reward we would hope for our protagonist's hard-earned maturity. Thus, Kennard notes, at the end of the two-suitor novel we are asked to "respond to two mutually exclusive conclusions: the maturation of the heroine and the completion of the romantic comedy plot" (15). *Night and Day* certainly seems to ask us to respond in this manner, and yet there is a definite story of individual growth hidden beneath the dominant two-suitor, comic-romance plot. As with *The Voyage Out*, we find this growth by focusing not on the heterosexual relationship but on female friendship in the novel and, more particularly, on scenes involving female conversation.

Like Virginia Woolf, Katharine Hilbery was born into what Woolf describes as "a very communicative, literate, letter writing, visiting late Nineteenth Century world" (Moments 65). Also like Woolf she stands in the shadow of her literary forefathers, realizing that "the history [and literature] of England is the history [and literature] of the male line, not of the female" (Women 141). Katharine is silenced by the symbolic order into which she is born. She feels alienated from a society that apparently takes for granted that words can not only express reality, but do so "beautifully," "fitly" and "energetically" (38). Unable to express herself fluently she moves outside of the dominant mode of expression and, like Rachel with her music, chooses an alternative symbolic order for personal expression: "mathematics were directly opposed to literature.... She preferred the exactitude, the star-like impersonality of figures to the confusion, agitation, and vagueness of the finest prose" (40). Like Rachel, Katharine initially denies the need for articulation and so denies language's ability to reveal aspects of the self and reality. She ignores what Adrienne Rich describes as the "transforming power" of language. Her most necessary symbolic system, her language, is inadequate, and "as long as our language is inadequate, our vision remains formless, our thinking and feeling are still running in the old cycles" (Rich, *On Lies* 247-48). It is only after her conversation with Mary that she is able to break out of her cycles of thought, especially about Rodney, Denham and love, and use language adequately.

Although Katharine's acceptance of language's "transforming power" first reveals itself in the scene where she finally communicates with Rodney and refuses to marry him, it is in the previous scene with Mary that Katharine experiences the power of honest discourse. It is significant that although both of Katharine's suitors are self-proclaimed poets, neither introduces to her the knowledge about language necessary to her maturation and growth; Mary does that. While the relationship between Katharine and Mary remains secondary in a traditional reading of the novel as social comedy, it comes to the fore when we look into the palimpsest[3] of *Night and Day* and allow the two-suitor plot to recede.

Like Helen Ambrose, Mary is unconventional and uses language in a direct, probing and sometimes disconcerting manner. A suffragist who lives and writes in rooms of her own, she is more independent than Katharine, yet she is also oppressed by the male tenders of language, most particularly by Ralph Denham who interrupts her work to tell her "that she couldn't write English" (281). While Denham's criticism accounts for "those frequent blots and insertions" in her work, Mary pushes ahead "with such words as come her way." Mary's treatise, "Some Aspects of the Democratic State," is full of "generalizations" suggesting that her use of a traditionally masculine form, the political essay, results in alienation from language and, more fundamentally, from herself. Even so, the fact that she tries to write down her thoughts at all reflects some freedom. More importantly, her ability to break through the silence imposed by female rivalry (she is at first jealous of Katharine), social inequality and personal intimidation reveals her to be the most sensitive communicator in the novel.

The conversation between Katharine and Mary begins awkwardly; Katharine is self-absorbed and Mary is determined to make her realize the need for "the impersonal life" (286). However, as Mary recognizes "the simplicity and good faith that lay behind

Katharine's words" the conflict between the two diminishes (287). Despite Mary's declaration that "she wanted to talk to her so much," Katharine attempts to leave, feeling "better fitted to deal with figures than with the feelings of men and women" (288-89). Then Mary speaks and puts "flight and further silence beyond [Katharine's] power." Mary's words, at this point, are much less important than the fact that she makes verbal contact with Katharine. This verbal contact is accompanied by a slight physical contact: Mary takes up the fur trim of Katharine's skirt. This gesture creates a bond of intimacy not found in Katharine's relationship with Rodney or, until much later, with Denham. Mary's words are simple and disorganized by conventional standards: "'I like this fur...I like your clothes. And you mustn't think that I'm going to marry Ralph,' she continued in the same tone, 'because he doesn't care for me at all, he cares for some one else'" (289-90). Katharine's response is equally disconnected, "'It's a shabby dress,'" as is Mary's next line, "'You don't mind my telling you that?'" (290).

Here we find Woolf attempting two things that she later praises her fictitious novelist, Mary Carmichael, for doing successfully. First she breaks the sequence; Mary, the foil to the romantic heroine, overcomes her jealousy and tries to form a friendship with her. Then Woolf catches "those unrecorded gestures, those unsaid or half-said words, which form themselves...when women are alone..." (*Room* 84). Once underway, the conversation becomes more personal and even less conventional as Mary declares Denham's love and her jealously for Katharine in the same breath. For Mary, making this confession serves two purposes. First, it allows her to clarify the very feelings she confesses as she "[tries] to explain...her motives for making the statement" (291). Second, she invites Katharine to help her overcome these feelings of envy. "'I don't want to be jealous of you,'" she admits, "'If I tell you, then we can talk; and when I'm jealous I can tell you'" (292).

Although Mary finds it difficult to talk, she also recognizes the danger of cycles of thought, of "going about with something in [her] mind all [her] life that never changes" (292). Mary recognizes the power of language to transform her jealousy of Katharine into understanding. By forcing herself to speak the truth, to make language adequate to the situation, Mary breaks the old cycles of female rivalry and isolation. Furthermore, she achieves a kind of catharsis and simultaneously gives Katharine new knowledge about human relationships and communication. Katharine leaves Mary's rooms for Rodney's with single-minded intent: "I've only got to speak now. I've only got to speak" (294). Once Katharine realizes the value of communication, she is ready to express honestly and to understand her feelings about Denham and Rodney.

Like her conversation with Mary, Katharine's conversation with her mother near the end of the novel is essential to her growth. Until this scene, Katharine represents a classic example of "matraphobia" which, as Adrienne Rich defines it, is "the fear not of one's mother or of motherhood but of *becoming one's mother*." For Katharine, it is "easier by far to hate and reject a mother outright than to see beyond her to the forces acting upon her" (Rich, *Of Woman* 235). Mrs. Hilbery initially provokes in her daughter a silent anger and is the "last person she wished to resemble" (41); however, by the end of the novel she becomes a kind of fairy godmother who rescues her daughter from "the detestable authority" of her unsympathetic father and sets things right with Denham. Mrs. Hilbery returns to London from visiting Shakespeare's grave like some benevolent supernatural being, "a moving mass of green which seemed to enter the room independently of any human agency" (507). As usual, she talks confusedly, but this time Katharine listens and understands how to decode her message. For perhaps the first time in her adult life, Katharine recognizes the value of her mother's words. In an act that parallels Mary touching the fur of her own dress, Katharine begins, "like a child to finger a tassel hanging from her mother's cloak" (508). Again this slight physical contact helps to initiate confession and communication between the women. As in the scene with Mary, the conversation is highly disorganized and digressive by conventional standards. Mrs. Hilbery recalls her courtship with Katharine's father, asks about Denham's home life, and speculates "about the meeting between Keats and Coleridge in a lane" (510). Rather than stifle Katharine, this apparent indirection and confusion "draw from [her] further descriptions and indiscretions" that would have been impossible in more orderly discourse.

Instead of the matraphobia she experienced in the first half of the novel, she finds "an extraordinary pleasure in being thus free to talk to some one who was equally wise and equally benignant, the mother of her earliest childhood." In Katharine's eyes Mrs. Hilbery becomes mythic, the Great Mother, "a figure of indefinite size whose head went up into the sky, whose hand was in [Katharine's] for guidance" (514). This newfound respect for and relationship with her mother, like her friendship with Mary, and like Rachel's relationship with Helen, teaches her the necessity for honest expression and the importance of matriarchal, not patriarchal guidance. As in *The Voyage Out* this lesson is important to her growing self-awareness in the muted plot.

However, matriarchal guidance soon gives way to a love relationship and the ruptured sequence is restored. Mrs. Hilbery, like Helen Ambrose, is primarily responsible for Katharine's heterosexual relationship with Mr. Right. After having provided emotional comfort and support, she too prays for a young man, so to speak, and visits Ralph Denham "in the capacity of ambassador" (517). She then brings Ralph to the Hilbery home, which precipitates his engagement to Katharine. Once again Woolf surrenders to the expected sequence and female friendship shines with only a "brief energy." Our protagonist, like protagonists of other female Bildungsromans who "share the formative voyage with friends, sisters or mothers" (Abel, Hirsch, Langland 12), enjoys and learns from the company of women, but only during a transitional stage that ends with the advent of heterosexual love.

In later novels such as *Mrs. Dalloway* and *To the Lighthouse*, women's friendships become more complex and more integral to both theme and plot. While Woolf's first two novels are undeniably apprentice works in some ways, they are more than failed Bildungsromans or mediocre romances. In fact they might be seen as precursors to these later works where the relationships between women, Clarissa Dalloway and Sally Seton or Lily Briscoe and Mrs. Ramsay, are at least equal in importance to the heterosexual relationships. In *The Voyage Out* and *Night and Day* woman-talk and women's friendship are good medicine, a cure for reticence and a tonic for the growing protagonist. Furthermore, they were just the thing modern fiction needed to remedy the facile renderings, the simplification of characters, in that "splendid gallery of fictitious women" to which Woolf added her own unparalleled portraits.

Notes

[1] The terms "muted" and "dominant," loosely adapted from the work of cultural anthropologists Shirley and Edwin Ardner, have been used by various feminist critics to describe what Elaine Showalter calls "the double voiced discourse" of "two alternative oscillating texts" that we must keep "simultaneously in view" as we read ("Feminist Criticism in the Wilderness" 266).

[2]In general, the Cooperative Principle involves mutual agreement between the communicating parties to follow conventions of quantity, quality, relation and manner in conversation. For a more in-depth discussion of this principle, see Grice's "Logic and Conversation" in *Syntax and Semantics: Speech Acts*. Eds. P. Cole and J. Morgan.

[3]In *The Madwoman in the Attic* Gilbert and Gubar define palimpsestic works as "works whose surface designs conceal or obscure deep, less accessible (and less socially acceptable) levels of meaning" (73).

Works Cited

Abel, Elizabeth, Marianne Hirsch, and Elizabeth Langland, eds. *The Voyage In: Fictions of Female Development*. Hanover, NH: UP of New England, 1983.

DuPlessis, Rachel Blau. *Writing Beyond the Ending: Narrative Strategies of Twentieth Century Women Writers*. Bloomington: Indiana UP, 1985.

_____. "Feminist Narrative in Virginia Woolf." *Novel* 21 (1988).

Garner, Shirley Nelson. "'Women Together' in Virginia Woolf's *Night and Day*." In *The (M)other Tongue: Essays in Feminist Psychoanalytic Interpretation*. Eds. Shirley Garner, Claire Kahane and Madelon Sprengnether. Ithaca: Cornell UP, 1985.

Gilbert, Sandra M., and Susan Gubar. *The Madwoman in the Attic: The Woman Writer and the Nineteenth-Century Literary Imagination*. New Haven: Yale UP, 1979.

Kennard, Jean E. *Victims of Convention*. Hamden, CT: Archon Books, 1978.

Pratt, Annis. *Archetypal Patterns in Women's Fiction*. Bloomington: Indiana UP, 1981.

Rich, Adrienne. *On Lies, Secrets, and Silence*. New York: Norton, 1979.

_____. *Of Woman Born: Motherhood as Experience and Institution*. New York: Norton, 1986.

Showalter, Elaine. "Feminist Criticism in the Wilderness." *The New Feminist Criticism: Essays on Women, Literature and Theory*. Ed. Elaine Showalter. New York: Pantheon Books, 1985.

Woolf, Virginia. *Night and Day*. London: Duckworth, 1919.

_____. *The Voyage Out*. New York: George Doran Co., 1920.

_____. *A Room of One's Own*. New York: Harcourt, 1929.

_____. "Montaigne." *The Collected Essays*. Vol. III. Ed. Leonard Woolf. New York: Harcourt, 1967.

_____. "Woman and Fiction." *The Collected Essays*. Vol. II. Ed. Leonard Woolf. New York: Harcourt, 1967.

_____. *Moments of Being: Unpublished Autobiographical Writings*. 2nd ed. Ed. Jeanne Schulkind. New York: Harcourt, 1976.

"Islands" of Peace:
Female Friendships
in Victorian Literature

LAURIE BUCHANAN

Female friendships have been seen as arising from a young woman's need to re-establish the mother-daughter bond and complete the process of merging with and separating from her mother, the process which should encourage pride in herself as a woman and the development of an autonomous self. As Nancy Chodorow explains in her study *The Reproduction of Mothering*, because the daughter's acceptance of herself as a woman and her ability to develop a separate identity from that of her mother depend on her early relationship with her mother—the primary caretaker and also the same-sex role model—the mother must have provided her daughter in infancy and childhood with a confident and secure symbiotic relationship. The difficulty in this theory is that the merging must be simultaneously accompanied by the mother's encouragement of her daughter's autonomy. But because mothers and daughters are the same sex, many mothers identify too closely with their daughters throughout their daughters' lives, seeing them as narcissistic extensions of themselves, and thus keeping their daughters tied to them by rewarding sameness with love and difference with disapproval. The ambiguous message the daughter receives from her mother is that nurturance and autonomy are at the expense of each other. This cripples the daughter's attempts to separate and leaves her feeling bound to her mother, unable to establish clear relational boundaries and ambivalent about her gender.

It is to female friendships that woman may turn in order to replace the mother-daughter relationship. Friendship offers her the intimacy, support and nurturance she needs without the identity issues that confuse the relationship. As Elizabeth Abel says in "(E)Merging Identities: The Dynamics of Female Friendships in Contemporary Fiction by Women," "[W]omen friends, as well as children, play a crucial role in relaxing ego boundaries and restoring psychic wholeness" (418) in some fiction by women. It is the interdependence on which women's friendships are based, which the mother-daughter relationship cannot sustain, that allows for separation and autonomy.

This need for nurturance and validation defines women's friendships in the Victorian novel. Indeed, women often found their only means of comfort and support in other women. Referring to Elizabeth Barrett Browning's *Aurora Leigh*, Tess Cosslett says, "The friendships often spring from an intense 'mother-want' on both sides—not just because actual mothers are absent, but because they are inefficient, or because other women have acted as betrayers and oppressors" (12). And indeed, the model for these friendships is often the maternal one, in which "friends act as mother-substitutes for each other" (Cosslett 12).

Female friendships in the Victorian novel by women, however, are rarely developed thoroughly, as being interesting in themselves for what they say about women and women's lives. Instead, they are often subordinated to the traditional marriage plot. Charlotte Bronte's *Shirley*, for example, a novel in which women's friendships are central, is often seen as a critical failure because the exploration of women's friendships "disrupts the conventional [plot] structure," says Cosslett:

> The structure of the novel is noted for its unconventional postponement and inactivity in the love-plots.... The absence of men allows Bronte to explore both the suffering, empty life of Caroline as a single woman, and the enjoyment and fullness of Shirley's independent life.... But this "true narrative" has structural problems: the whole point about Caroline's life from now on is going to be that *nothing happens* to her: 'passion, and stimulus, and melodrama' are missing. (113)

Thus, *Shirley*, which should stand as a model for depicting women's lives and their friendships with women as vital and important in themselves, is a critical failure because of this very aim: Bronte cannot sustain literary interest in her characters' lives without the intrigues of the marriage plot.

Other women writers avoided this criticism by outwardly accepting literary custom and developing their heroines' friendships as peripheral to the action. As Cosslett notes, in the Victorian novel, "[t]he world of women's friendships seems to be perceived as something *static*, outside the action that makes the story" (11). In these novels by women, plots are devised to suppress women's interest in women and instead adhere to the traditional structure, where the characters and heroine are rendered to fulfill a male ideal, and where marriage is a woman's goal and her reward for molding herself to this ideal. In fear of "supposing herself a monster when she did not fit the acceptable narrative of a female life," says Carolyn G. Heilbrun in her text *Writing a Woman's Life*, women were writing for and as men (45). Under these conditions, the problem for women of trying to write a text that arises from and provides female perspectives and values, Heilbrun suggests, is "not so much women's lack of language as their failure to speak profoundly to one another" (43). Thus, because women novelists generally felt it necessary to conform to traditional plot structures and character development, their writing, rather than telling true stories of female experience, often reveals instead the oppression and ambiguity of women's lives and identity as they must necessarily be interpreted to fit a male world. Nancy K. Miller writes that "the plots of women's literature are not about 'life'...They are about the plots of literature itself, about the constraints...of rendering a female life in fiction" (qtd. in Heilbrun 44-45).

Heilbrun suggests that by the end of the nineteenth century, women were beginning to feel "trapped in a script they did not write but were slowly beginning to analyze, [and they began to] look about them for a way out, a way on to a different life" (42). But perhaps it was in the Victorian novel, as early as Jane Austen's fiction, that women, recognizing the constraints imposed upon them as they tried to write their own texts, began to create "a way out, a way on to a different life" for themselves. And perhaps this new text is delineated in their portrayal of women's friendships.

Because women are taught to be mothers, their lives largely revolve around relationships, nurturing and self-sacrifice. Carol Gilligan, in *In a Different Voice*, says that women's lives are defined by the closeness of their relationships: "Intimacy goes along with identity, as the female comes to know herself as she is known, through her relationship with others" (12). In the Victorian novel, perhaps *because* women's friendships are drawn "outside the action that makes the story" (Cosslett 11), women writers felt more free to develop women's relationships and experience. These literary friendships are drawn to delineate the care, trust and support that define the female experience. What women readers found in the depiction of these friendships was at once a consolation for the difficulties of being a woman, a maternal model of (a female text for) re-establishing mother-daughter bonds, and a reinforcing, and therefore a validation of, their feminine identity. Thus, women's friendships, while developed peripherally to the plot, are central to the heroines' (and therefore all women's) psychological development, for they provide assurance about female issues and experience and develop and sustain communication between women that allows them to gain self-confidence and feel loved and nurtured. In this way, the friendships Victorian women portray in their novels seem to me to be the embodiment of what Heilbrun seeks: a way for "women [to] turn to one another for their stories" (44).

Thus, women's friendships as delineated in novels by women both reflect and validate female experience; but just as importantly, they provide a text for women's lives, a text that allows women to communicate their experience to each other. Furthermore, it is within that text, that center of communication, that female friendship "stands out as uniquely precious, an 'island' of peace and understanding...in some world beyond normal social relations" (Cosslett 11).

The mother-daughter relationship creates the essence of female identity. As has been explained, because the mother sees the daughter as a narcissistic extension of herself—the daughter, in fact, if she is behaviorally and emotionally like her mother, reinforces and validates her mother—the mother's relationship with her daughter is at best ambivalent, and this pattern of confusion which was established in childhood is replayed in adolescence.

It is at this point, in adolescence, that women's friendships work to replace the daughter's tie to her mother. Sensing the need to define herself, yet unable to do so both because of her fear of her mother's rejection of her and because she has no models of female independence, the daughter finds friends who do what her mother has been unable to do: help her develop pride in herself as a woman and support her as she attempts to define herself autonomously. She develops a relationship with a "best friend," another girl or woman with whom she can identify as a female but who does not have the biological ties that fuse them into one person and deny her individuation. Chodorow says of adolescent female friendships, "This friend in part counteracts the feelings of self-diffusion which result from the intensely experienced [tie to the mother]. Her friendship permits her to continue to experience merging while at the same time denying feelings of merging with her mother" (137-38).

These issues can be seen in nineteenth-century novels by women, who, while developing characters who deal with common Victorian themes of moral growth and self-knowledge, are also delineating specifically female psychological conflicts through their heroines' personal growth and relationships. These adolescent issues tend to be portrayed through opposing personality traits of their heroines; and the pairings can be seen to unconsciously suggest a psychological manifestation of merging and separation issues. For example, Jane Austen's practical Elinor Dashwood contrasts with her overly emotional sister, Marianne. Indeed, the theme of *Sense and Sensibility* is most often seen to be the need to balance reason and emotion, as the novel is developed around each sister's extreme practicality or sensitivity and her growth as she comes to self-understanding and her responsibility to society for right action. As the rational sister, however, Elinor's independence is really her rejection of the "femininity" her mother and sister represent, for Marianne's extreme sensitivity is the part of her that is most emotional and dependent—or "womanly" in the Victorian script for acceptable female behavior—the most merged with her similarly endowed mother.

The difficulty for women that Austen explores in her depiction of the sisters is twofold and reflects women's divided self: the woman who has not successfully merged with and separated from her mother and is therefore dependent on her mother for her very identity; and the opposing fear of independence as encompassing a state of rejection and alienation. Thus, Marianne, as an example of a woman whose mother has encouraged too close merging, is defined as being "strikingly" like her mother in her inability to "govern her feelings" (5). Mrs. Dashwood, in fact, whose "feelings were strong" (4) "valued and cherished [Marianne's]...excess... sensibility" (5). And further, "[Mother and daughter] encouraged each other now in the violence of their affliction" (5). This commiseration, while initially appearing as a warm and close tie that protects Marianne, is really her mother's way of validating herself through her daughter. It has tragic consequences, for it keeps her daughter tied to her to affirm herself by approving and reinforcing the very aspects that keep Marianne dependent and lacking in self-awareness and ability to make rational decisions that would allow her to grow independently and act reasonably in the world.

Thus, when Willoughby leaves, Marianne falls ill: "The violent oppression of spirits continued the whole evening. She was without any power, because she was without any desire of command over herself" (71). Like her mother, "common sense, common care, common prudence, were all sunk in...romantic delicacy" (73), and she thus "would have thought herself very inexcusable had she been able to sleep at all the first night after parting from Willoughby" (71). Eva Margolies says that women who have maintained a too exclusive bond with their mothers often retain a childlike dependence on others and a constant need for attention and for having their needs met by others. "Ironically," says Margolies,

> it is often a friendly, positive relationship with a traditional mother [that makes women dependent on others for their identity]. Too friendly, in fact, which is why these women often don't develop much of a desire for independence. While a close relationship with [her mother] might feel emotionally nourishing, as a rule, the better relationship with a [traditional mother], the less separated the girl. (74)

Marianne's extreme emotions, while on the surface a warning from Austen of incorrect behavior, become, from a female psychological perspective, a manifestation of her too complete merging with her mother, which results in her inability to know her own feelings and guide them rationally.

Marianne's relationships are always formed from shallow traits of dependence and need; that is why her relationship with Elinor initially does not contain the honesty and support needed to build an intimate and nurturing relationship. Knowing her tie with her mother to be based on protection and merged feelings rather than on guidance and support, Marianne sees Elinor, who consistently takes on the more sensible role of a wise, rationally-guiding mother, not as a replacement for her mother but as the opposing and distant authority figure, the self-denying independent woman who has no feminine characteristics or needs, while Elinor sees Marianne as an overly emotional, unself-guided and dependent child with few admirable characteristics on which to model herself. Thus, though they love and wish to protect each other, they are not "friends" as yet because, without role models or texts, they both feel the need to guard themselves from the unwanted extreme of opposite the other represents.

Yet Elinor, as the independent daughter, the more rational of the two, though possessing the self-control and intelligence to conduct her affairs with little emotional interference, is overwhelmingly alone. It is true that Austen develops the other characters as flawed and really more of an "aggravation" to Elinor than a comfort or support. And surely, with her more mature self-awareness, Elinor has few peers with whom to share intimate feelings. Yet there is a sense of desolation with which Elinor handles her emotional trials, so that with all her praise of Elinor, Austen cannot avoid the silence which enclouds Elinor's emotional existence:

> From [her mother's and Marianne's] counsel, or their conversation she knew she could receive no assistance, their tenderness and sorrow must add to her distress, while her self-command would neither receive encouragement from their example nor from their praise. She was stronger alone. (121)

"Stronger alone," Elinor yet seems to be outside of the action, silently enduring her own emotional trials and watching others while having little nurturing support of her own. Indeed, without the support of other women, Elinor appears to lack a sense of or confidence in her own feminine self. "Femininity," says Gilligan, "is defined through attachment...[and] female gender identity is threatened by separation" (8). Elinor's is a world of the mind, intelligent, practical and sensitive, but cut off from a woman's life of intimacy, nurturance and support, from the connectedness with other women that reaffirms their feminine selves.

Thus, in contrast to Marianne, while Elinor might represent the moral maturity that is Austen's ideal, she also manifests the subconscious threat to women of too severe separation from her mother and thus from her feminine self. To Marianne, Elinor's rationality appears as her being superior; it distances her from Marianne and her mother. In this way, Elinor appears to reject the world of women and the intimacy, support and nurturance that defines female identity. Thus, though it is Elinor's independence and rationality of mind that she feels protect her from the chaotic, irrational world of her mother and sister, these qualities in fact define her as unfeminine. Because of this, Elinor's text does not provide a model for women, for she is isolated, where Marianne at least has spontaneity and the enjoyment of people around her.

Furthermore, Elinor's lack of friendships, while denying her validation as a woman, also inhibits her ability to know herself. For, as Elizabeth Abel explains, "Through the intimacy which is knowledge, friendship becomes a vehicle for self-definition for women, clarifying identity through relation to an other who embodies and reflects an essential aspect of the self" (416). Elinor, while not losing her independent spirit, must also learn to soften her emotions, to communicate honestly and openly with other women. Until her confrontation with Marianne, she rejects the feminine within herself because she knows it only as it is manifested in Marianne and in her mother, as weakness of character, or as she sees it in Lucy Steele, who epitomizes the "person who joined insincerity with ignorance" (110), the shallow woman Elinor most disdains. For her part, Marianne refuses to see herself as independent because she understands it only to mean the isolation and solemn reserve she sees in Elinor.

The sisters' confrontation, then, has to do with what it is to be female. When Marianne accuses Elinor of having no feelings, she has in fact questioned Elinor's femininity. Elinor, "in some confusion" at her sister's strong reproach, is shocked that she appears to others as cold and aloof and uncaring, and she begins to recognize her own and her sister's need for "greater openness" (146, 147), for connectedness, the relational aspects that define a woman's life. Admitting the pain of holding in her strong emotions, she is at the same time recognizing both that she has strong feelings and that she has alienated herself. It is in defense of her feminine self, then, that Elinor feels compelled to reveal to Marianne the details of what she has gone through over Lucy's revelation and her promise to Lucy of secrecy:

> "If you can think me capable of ever feeling—surely you may suppose I have suffered *now*. The composure of mind with which I have brought myself at present to consider the matter, the consolation that I have been willing to admit, have been the effect of constant and painful exertion;—they did not spring up of themselves;—they did not occur to relieve my spirits at first— No, Marianne.—*Then*, if I had not been bound to silence, perhaps nothing could have kept me entirely—not even what I owed my dearest friends—from openly shewing that I was *very* unhappy—" Marianne was quite subdued. (229-30)

In expressing the suffering her isolation causes her, Elinor is asking for the intimacy that will help her merge with Marianne, which will in turn cause her to recognize and accept her feminine self as strong rather than vulnerable. Opening up to her sister, Elinor establishes the bonds of female friendship, the connectedness that reveals her feminine self. Though Marianne hardly becomes a role model for Elinor, communicating with her has revealed a shared need for understanding, and it has provided Elinor with the support of the friendship itself that she needs to define and validate her own femininity. No longer fearing that she is too like her mother, Elinor does not need to reject femininity and to portray herself through "negative identification (I am what [my mother] is not)" (Chodorow 137); no longer disliking the woman in herself, she is able to establish relationships and fulfill her need to connectedness.

The result of this confrontation is that her relationship with Marianne changes from that of Elinor-as-mother-to-Marianne to one in which more sharing and communication occur. It is also seen in her willingness to accept other women in her life. Sharing the commonly female task of nursing her sister with Mrs. Jennings (whom she previously disliked), Elinor now appreciates Mrs. Jennings' "kindness of heart which made Elinor really love her" (269).

For Marianne, Elinor's independent practicality becomes less threatening and female-denying after Elinor's confession. She sees that a woman can be intelligent and rational and still need friendship and connectedness. Marianne, in fact, begins to understand that Elinor is a woman of great feeling but that she controls her emotions out of a sense of responsibility to and love and concern for others. Thus, Elinor becomes a model for Marianne. She says to Elinor of her past blindness,

> Your example was before me: but to what avail? Was I more considerate of you and your comfort? Did I imitate your forbearance, or lessen your restraints, by taking any part in those offices of general complaisance or gratitude which you had hitherto been left to discharge alone?...
>
> You, my mother, and Margaret, must henceforth be all the world to me; you will share my affections entirely between you. (304)

This might be seen as Marianne transferring her dependence from men to women. But, in fact, she is proving her newly *separated* self. Her friendship with these women, because it is based on mutual support rather than weakness and fear, suggests that Marianne is actively pursuing growth as an independent woman.

Merging is completed through each woman appearing as a model for and reflection of the other; separation is achieved once that support system is established. With these issues resolved, each woman has formed her own identity and begins autonomous growth. Their friendship has brought them closer together while simultaneously allowing them to become independent individuals and bringing new understanding to themselves, each other and the world. Thus, Austen's delineation of the sisters' growth through their relationship in itself provides a text for women's lives.

In Elizabeth Gaskell's *Ruth*, the contrasts set up between the passive and obedient Ruth and the unruly and "passionate" Jemima can also be seen as a manifestation of the merging and separation process that occurs between friends because of the inability of the mother to help her daughter develop autonomously. In this novel, though Ruth is the central figure, she functions as the vehicle for Gaskell's social message about Victorian sexual double standards that victimize women. Seduced and with a fatherless child, Ruth is yet pure and innocent from the beginning, and she matures only in terms of embodying more fully the Christian ethic of human caring. It is Jemima, a relatively minor character in terms of Gaskell's theme of the "fallen angel," who embodies the text for female self-revelation and growth in the novel.

Jemima is one of those "passionate" Victorian women who needs to be silenced. Willful, knowing her own mind and feeling that "there was something degrading in trying to alter herself to gain the love of any human creature" (217), Jemima represents the liberated woman trying to reconcile her place in the repressive patriarchy. As an adolescent, she is trying to define herself as a woman who is feminine and loving yet independent and respected. But she has no role models who can both provide a text for her and give her approval as she struggles with her freedom and her identity. Her mother, "sweet and gentle-looking, but as if she was thoroughly broken into submission" (152), is Jemima's only female role model; like Mrs. Dashwood for Elinor, she projects the dismal text for Jemima's life in her own submissive actions. Merging with her mother for Jemima would mean becoming like her mother, adopting her "weak and anxious mind" (229), rather than developing pride in herself as a woman.

The appearance of Ruth in Jemima's adolescent life provides her with a different feminine model from her mother, with a friend who can reflect and help define and reinforce the feminine in Jemima. To Jemima, Ruth is what a woman should be. She embodies the dignity of person and pride in her femininity that Mrs. Bradshaw lacks, indeed denies.

Furthermore, Ruth is a single mother (not by choice, of course, since remaining unmarried is her lifetime punishment for being seduced), who overcomes her shame by acting with love, dignity and integrity. Asserting a sense of pride that will not allow her to be manipulated, even by the powerful Mr. Bradshaw (he has offered his patronage, but Ruth refuses his gifts), Ruth is someone Jemima admires and is thus someone on whom she can model herself. Her friendship provides Jemima with the companionship, honesty and support Jemima needs to form her own identity. In this way, Ruth takes over Mrs. Bradshaw's place by providing Jemima with a woman with whom she can merge and thus find positive definition as a woman. Indeed, Ruth replaces Jemima's parents in terms of needing to win Ruth's approval: "She valued Ruth's good opinion so highly, that she dreaded lest her friend should perceive her faults" (231).

So it is when Mrs. Bradshaw reveals to Jemima that Ruth is acting for Mr. Bradshaw in helping to subdue her so that Bradshaw can marry Jemima to his associate, Mr. Farquhar (a relationship that, unbeknownst to her blind father and mother, Jemima and Farquhar have already established), that Jemima feels anger at Ruth because of Ruth's betrayal of the devotion and support they have established. This betrayal feels particularly cutting to Jemima for two reasons. One is because it was told to her by her mother. Thus, she feels that even her mother, who, if she lacks the strength to guide her, will not be even a silent support system as she goes through this particularly female struggle. What underlies the dynamics here is the problem that it is not just the patriarchal system that devalues women but women who devalue women. In her article, "The Conflict between Nurturance and Autonomy in Mother-Daughter Relationships and within Feminism," Jane Flax explains that because of unresolved issues within mother-daughter relationships, women's relationships "are often filled with conflict" (182). Because the roots of the conflict are not understood, they are not worked through, and women's friendships are abandoned in disappointment. Thus, Gaskell emphasizes the ambivalence between mothers and daughters by appointing Jemima's mother as the one to bring the news about Ruth's "deception." Furthermore, by drawing the situation as if Mrs. Bradshaw is subconsciously trying to break up the friendship between her daughter and Ruth, Gaskell suggests that Jemima is being stuck in a helpless triangle in which women work against each other and thus guarantee the failure of their relationships with women.

Jemima also feels betrayed because Ruth now appears not as the independent, self-esteeming woman she had represented herself to be to Jemima but, instead, as one who compromises her own principles and gives into a man's demands. (Jemima, of course, does not know Ruth has refused to obey Mr. Bradshaw: "If she had seen anything wrong in Jemima, Ruth loved her so much that she would have told her of it in private" [225].) Furthermore, because she has been a model for Jemima, Ruth's betrayal portends the end of Jemima's hopes of integrating her own feminine self-love and her need for independent growth, the end of her search for a sense of her self as autonomous. As Mrs. Bradshaw has suggested, Ruth appears now to have proven: a woman cannot embody both femininity and independence. The message from these female friends is that in the end, women are forced to submit; they are powerless against the patriarchy.

Feeling betrayed by her mother and her friend, Jemima loses not only her support system but also in Ruth a model and text for developing feminine self-esteem. Thus, Jemima is left angry and isolated, and with no hope of building a full life for herself. The issue here is anger, and surely Jemima has no female models to show her how to deal with that emotion. Indeed, anger is not allowed in women. Margolies explains that, unlike men, whose lives and identities are based on competition, who are encouraged to acknowledge and relieve anger through physical activity, women are taught that anger is unacceptable, that kindness and tolerance should replace anger in them. However, Margolies says,

> What we call tolerance for rules is really a coverup for [women's] inability to express anger, [their] struggle with assertiveness, [their] fear of being rejected. [Thus, w]ith no channels for feelings of aggression to be released directly, [women's] hostile, competitive impulses are forced underground, seeping out in malevolent ways. (30)

And Jemima, not thinking of expressing true anger, turns it inward and becomes sullen and depressed.

But Jemima's anger does "seep out in malevolent ways." She finds an object for her anger, and this object is in fact the one "acceptable" channel for women's anger: competition with another woman for approval and for a man. In adolescence, Margolies says, as women's social spheres become more confined, "the arena in which girls are allowed to compete narrows, getting the boy increasingly becomes the name of the contest, and love the battlefield" (53). Indeed, Gaskell devises the plot of *Ruth* to shift the attentions of Farquhar (who, in fact, had admired Jemima's independence and disagreed with Bradshaw's insistence on Jemima's obedience and submission) from the "rebellious" Jemima to the quieter, more obedient Ruth.

But seen in terms of the psychology of women's friendships, Jemima's anger, now directed at Ruth, reflects her confusion about her identity and place in the world. Part of the force of women's anger, as Margolies explains, is that "when a girl expresses aggression towards another girl, she is also expressing aggression symbolically toward her mother and by definition toward herself" (30-31). This unconscious anger toward her mother is a response to messages her mother has given her about being a woman, messages that convey the mother's own feelings about her life, which she may see as stifling and hopeless, and which she fears for her daughter. As explained by Flax:

> Because women tend to identify more strongly with their girl children, more internal conflict is likely to be stimulated by their role as mother.... [T]he mother, knowing the difficulties of being female in a man's world, might also wish that for their daughter's own sake, she could have been born male. (174-75)

Gaskell brings up this aspect of feelings of self-worth as communicated from mothers to daughters in Mrs. Bradshaw's attitude towards her son as opposed to her feelings toward her daughter. Mrs. Bradshaw's preference for boys appears to be one of her weaknesses as a mother. Gaskell says, "Her son was her especial darling, because he very seldom brought her into any scrape with his father.... Mrs. Bradshaw, somehow, contrived to be honestly blind to a good deal that was not praiseworthy in Master Richard" (230). The self-deception here is also made clear in Gaskell's description of the limited way she views her daughter: "Her perception was only of external beauty, and she was not always alive to that, or she might have seen how a warm, affectionate, ardent nature, free from all envy or taking care of self, gave an unspeakable charm to her plain, bright-faced daughter, Jemima..." (187). Furthermore, both parents are obviously blind to their son's true character. He ultimately disappoints them by forging Mr. Benson's signature to get his money.

Thus, what Jemima's anger ultimately reflects is her learned dislike of being a woman and her loss of support and role models, not the loss of her romantic interest. Angry at the betrayal and at her lack of power and a sense of self, angry at the patriarchy that forces (and the women who enforce) her dependence and powerlessness, but with no means by which to express and resolve these feelings, Jemima rejects Ruth and turns her anger inward, blaming herself for the loss of Farquhar: "Yes! by every means in her power had Jemima alienated her lover, her beloved" (239). When Jemima discovers the truth about Ruth's past, she is provided with information that would allow her an "acceptable" outlet for her anger. Gaskell sets up the perfect situation for female competition, challenging another's goodness and purity to ensure or prove one's own. And indeed, Jemima feels "the power which the knowledge of this secret gave her over Ruth" (322).

In Ruth's death from typhus, which she contracts from her seducer, Bellingham, after nursing him through an epidemic, Gaskell has had to sacrifice Ruth to patriarchal rules. Her study of female friendships and what they ultimately mean in terms of personal growth for women must rest on Jemima and how she decides to utilize this power. Pauline Nestor characterizes Gaskell's work as

> depicting women united by circumstances and by choice and celebrates their talent for mutual support. [She delineates] the fundamental bonds between women...in terms of shared maternal feelings and a common lot as victims of the social and sexual passivity to which women are inevitably subjected. (142)

Indeed, it is significant in looking at *Ruth* as challenging a traditional depiction of women's friendships that Jemima, rather than ultimately allowing her anger to "seep out in malevolent ways," sees her love for Ruth and the community they shared as more important to her than her need to compete with Ruth. Her discovery, in fact, only oppresses her:

> [S]he would watch and wait. Come what might Ruth was in her power. And, strange to say, this last certainty gave Jemima a kind of protecting, almost pitying, feeling for Ruth. Her horror at the wrong was not diminished; but the more she thought of the

struggles that the wrongdoer must have made to extricate herself, the more she felt how cruel it would be to baffle all by revealing what had been.... For the present she would neither meddle nor mar in Ruth's course of life. (324)

Jemima's determining whether or not to reveal Ruth's past poses a moral dilemma in which her decision not to interfere in Ruth's life shows that she is more concerned with the caring and responsibility of her relationship with Ruth instead of with the power she holds over Ruth, and this can be seen in Jemima's ultimate knowledge that her only happiness and fulfillment have been in developing her friendship with Ruth. It is upon this recognition and her sense of connectedness with Ruth that she bases her decision to keep Ruth's past to herself.

Furthermore, part of Jemima's decision not to reveal Ruth's past arises from her recognition that Ruth exemplifies what could happen to all women. In Ruth are manifested the possibilities all women face at the insistence of society that they remain innocent and pure. "[I now see]," says Jemima, "how I might just have been like Ruth, or rather worse than she ever was because I am more headstrong and passionate by nature" (361). Thus, the knowledge which she could have used to destroy Ruth, Jemima instead uses to empathize with her. This recognition could be seen as another reminder that she is, as a woman in a patriarchy, a victim, always vulnerable and powerless. It can be seen as Jemima's initiation into Victorian womanhood, an initiation in which, as Gaskell states, Jemima has "purified [herself of] pride" (366-67). This is an adult world where imaginative and passionate women are silenced and humbled, where, as Sandra M. Gilbert and Susan Gubar say of Austen's heroines, "[Women] must acquiesce in their status as objects after an adolescence in which they experience themselves as free agents" (161).

However, Gaskell's choice is for Jemima to use her knowledge to strengthen rather than break her ties to Ruth and thus to show how their friendship empowers Jemima. When Mr. Bradshaw finds out about Ruth and admonishes and blames her—"the more depraved, the more disgusting you" (344)—Jemima refuses her father's orders to leave the room "in an opposition that was strange even to herself, but which was prompted by the sullen passion which seethed below the stagnant surface of her life and which sought a vent in defiance. She maintained her ground, facing round upon her father..." (333). The anger that has seethed in her, together with the strength of Jemima's love for Ruth, encourages her and she finally can stand up against her father.

But this solidarity only infuriates Mr. Bradshaw; Jemima's sympathy for Ruth "called out all Mr. Bradshaw's ire afresh; he absolutely took her by the shoulders and turned her by force out of the room" (337). Thus, Jemima's support of Ruth is seen by Mr. Bradshaw as another example of her defiance; and it furthermore weakens him, he feels, because their friendship has given Jemima the courage and assertiveness to disobey him. If their relationship strengthens Jemima, it is thus a threat to his authority and power. Bradshaw attempts to weaken the women by banishing Ruth from his home and forbidding Jemima to see her. Flax says that when women cannot communicate with each other, they are denied empowerment both in the social network of the home and in their full development as persons: "The lack of intimate female relationships further weakens a woman's position. It reconfirms her devaluation of the female world, denies her a chance to mitigate the mother-daughter conflicts, and forces her to turn more exclusively to men" (182). By denying women's friendships, Mr. Bradshaw feels he lessens female strength and ensures his own. But Bradshaw's fierce control of the women in reality shows his fear of female power, and in this he represents "a patriarchal ideology that devalues women by men's jealousy and discomfort at strong female bonds" (Flax 182). By standing up against her father, then, in favor of her friendship with Ruth, Jemima chooses the liberation of female friendship over submission to the patriarchy, and it is the friendship itself which has given her the will and support to make and assert that choice.

As a Victorian woman, Gaskell was compelled to adhere to the traditional plot by providing Jemima with marriage as her only option emotionally as well as socially and economically. But as Gaskell's concern is female growth and self-knowledge, she presents Jemima's marriage as proof of her maturation in terms of completing the merging and separating process through her friendship with Ruth, for Farquhar, while ambiguously drawn, is ultimately supportive of Jemima. Had he known, for example, of Mr. Bradshaw's attempts to "manage" Jemima and therefore to mold her into the male ideal of the submissive angel, he "indeed would have been as much annoyed at them as Jemima" (238). Just as important is his support of Jemima's friendship with Ruth, even after knowledge of her past is made known and Mr. Bradshaw prohibits their relationship. Thus, Farquhar appears to be the best husband Gaskell can create for Jemima, for he values Jemima for herself.

Appreciating this fact, Jemima marries him not to gain an identity but *because she already has one.*

Finally, the fact that her husband chooses not to dominate her and maintains his affection and admiration for her because of her independent spirit is proof that marriage for Jemima is, within its own confines, freedom from the patriarchy. "'Tell me,'" says Farquhar only half teasingly to Jemima, "'how much of your goodness to me...has been owing to the desire of having more freedom as a wife than as a daughter'" (371), and Gaskell assures the reader that Jemima maintains her spirit and achieves independence within her marriage and that her husband accepts rather than tries to subdue and mold her:

> She imposed very strict regulations on Mr. Farquhar's behavior; and quarrelled and differed from him more than ever, but with a secret joyful understanding with him in her heart, even while they disagreed with one another—for similarity of opinion is not always—I think not often—needed for fulness and perfection of love. (373)

While Jemima's involvement with Ruth and her acknowledgement of Ruth's difficulties and victimization have tempered her passion and appeared to silence her, what has occurred psychologically is Jemima's merging with another woman and emerging as a woman who, though forced to accept her secondary place in society, has nevertheless come to esteem herself, to understand responsibility in the world, and thus to find strength and validation in being a woman. Her friendship and bonding with Ruth have, in exchange for her relationship to her parents, provided her with a model her submissive mother could not, and in this way she has provided Jemima with a text for a woman's life through which she can attain autonomy at least in her perception of herself and within her close relationships.

Gaskell's attestation to the strength and longevity of female friendships is that Jemima does maintain contact with Ruth despite her father's commands to relinquish their friendship. Indeed, her friendship with Ruth continues to replace her relationship with her mother, with each woman encouraging the other's happiness through self-knowledge and fulfillment. In this way of thinking, the independent women are neither silenced, nor do they appear, as Gilbert and Gubar suggest, to "become [their] self-denying double" (161-62). Surely, it cannot be denied that one lesson the women learn in adolescence is their powerlessness in the patriarchy, but in all Victorian novels by women, the growth they achieve has allowed them autonomy at least within their own marriage and, most of all, a sense of themselves as whole people. Indeed, the growth to wholeness is what makes a heroine of a woman.

Furthermore, marriage in the Victorian novel can be seen not as a reward for submitting to male rules but instead as proof of successful merging and separating, where the heroine, with her femininity validated and her self defined, will not in fact lose her identity in marriage. Indeed, Victorian woman writers have developed their heroines so that they can achieve autonomy, albeit within a patriarchal structure, because ultimately, while overtly adhering to male values and ideals in their acceptance of the marriage plot, in their personal growth, the heroines embody power and freedom: whether to marry is not a choice, but whom to marry is. And one way this power is gained is through the growth sustained in female friendships. Indeed, "it [is] in [their] relationships with other women that the real need for validation and approval, that the real power rest[s]" (Margolis 6).

Because women's themes are so consistently (if only subconsciously) developed in women's novels, it is clear that women sought to establish a network and a text, and that this text was in fact the working out of these developmental difficulties, as well as an attempt to create models of female growth. Being drawn outside the marriage plot, they are uninhibited by male rules. Thus women's friendships become a text for feminine lives. For, as Gilbert and Gubar say of Austen's novels:

> Just as [her heroines] manage to survive only by seeming to submit, she succeeds in maintaining her double consciousness in fiction that proclaims its docility and restraint even as it uncovers the delights of assertion and rebellion. Indeed the comedy of Austen's novels explores the tensions between the freedom of her art and the dependency of her characters: while they stutter and sputter and lapse into silence and even hasten to perfect felicity, she attains a woman's language that is magnificently duplicitous. (168-69)

These are the stories, as told outside the traditional plot, that, as Heilbrun says, become "the collective articulation of one's experience of sexuality and gender...[stories that] begin to tell the truth" (45) about women's lives. This "truth," then, is communicated in the novel in the delineation of women's friendships, friendships which create in themselves a female language within its own female text.

It is through their women characters that women prove their need for the approval and support their friendships provide. Marriage, while being the goal in the traditional plot, is not the message these women communicate to each other. Instead, it is the continuing comfort and affection that women give to each other. Thus, entwined within the endings of each novel, in which the heroine has met the necessity of marriage, the authors project their continuing need for female friendships. Perhaps this is the reason why Bronte's Caroline Helstone says, "...I am supported and soothed when you—that is *you only*—are near, Shirley" (264); why in *Sense and Sensibility* Marianne is most upset at Elinor's thinking poorly of her: "Had I died. How should I have lived in *your* remembrance" (303); and why Jemima says to her fiancé, now with a compassionate tone infused with her independent spirit, "You won't forbid my going to see Ruth will you? because if you do, I give you notice I shall disobey you" (371). Indeed women's texts communicate this support and approval. They prove that it is women's friendships, those "'islands' of peace and understanding" (Cosslett 11), that sustain and empower women and validate their experience in the patriarchy.

Works Cited

Abel, Elizabeth. "(E)Merging Identities: The Dynamics of Female Friendships in Contemporary Fiction by Women." *Signs* 6.3 (Spring 1981).

Austen, Jane. *Sense and Sensibility*. Oxford: Oxford UP, 1989.

Bronte, Charlotte. *Shirley*. Oxford: Oxford UP, 1986.

Chodorow, Nancy. *The Reproduction of Mothering*. Berkeley: U of California P, 1978.

Cosslett, Tess. *Woman to Woman: Female Friendships in Victorian Fiction*. Atlantic Heights: Humanities P, 1988.

Flax, Jane. "The Conflict between Nurturance and Autonomy in Mother-Daughter Relationships and Within Feminism." *Feminist Studies* 4.2 (1978).

Gaskell, Elizabeth. *Ruth*. London: Everyman's, 1982.

Gilbert, Sandra M., and Susan Gubar. *The Madwoman in the Attic: The Woman Writer and the Nineteenth-Century Literary Imagination*. New Haven and London: Yale UP, 1979.

Gilligan, Carol. *In a Different Voice.* Cambridge: Harvard UP, 1982.

Heilbrun, Carolyn G. *Writing a Woman's Life.* New York: Ballantine, 1988.

Margolis, Eva. *The Best of Friends, The Worst of Enemies: Women's Hidden Power over Women.* New York: Pocket, 1985.

Nestor, Pauline. *Female Friendships and Communities.* Oxford: Clarendon P, 1985.

"I can step out of myself a little": Feminine Virtue and Female Friendship in Hannah Foster's *The Coquette*

JOHN PAUL TASSONI

Eliza Wharton, hero of Hannah Foster's *Coquette*, at one point describes herself as a "pensioner of friendship" (36). In this instance, the phrase refers to her dependence upon the Richmans, who house Wharton following the death of her betrothed. But Eliza is a "pensioner" in an emotional sense as well. Expressly, she "wish[es] for no other connection than that of friendship" (6), and when companions criticize her "coquettish" activities (27), she struggles to retain what they view as the essential and socially acceptable lines of her identity. "You can see," she writes to her friend Lucy Sumner, "that I can step out of myself a little. Afford an assisting hand, and perhaps I may again be fit for society" (100). Just as our own identities, Bakhtin tells us, depend upon "the point of view of the community to which we belong" (*Marxism* 86), the self to which Eliza refers is a social entity. However, Wharton's continued identification with her socially constructed identity must depend upon Lucy Sumner's "assisting hand[s]," for competing conceptions of self bring Eliza's relationship with her community into crisis.

Yet Wharton overlooks the extent to which *society's* "assisting hands" make her unfit for her community. In her quest for acceptance, she fails to see her friends' situation within a dominant ideology compelling their judgments of normality and deviancy. Universalizing the virtuous self that their culture prescribes for them, women in *The Coquette* trivialize those traits of identity Eliza experiences "out of" their community.[1] This paper examines the discourse of virtue implemented in women's language in late eighteenth-century, middle-class America and Eliza Wharton's struggles with this discourse to preserve both her friendships and her sense of self(s). After discussing the overlapping concerns of feminine virtue and female friendships in America's new republic, I show how rhetoric about virtue hinders affectionate exchange between women in *The Coquette*. My essay exhibits, then, the manner in which virtue acted as an oppressive discourse in women's friendships at a time in middle-class America when personal freedom and communal relations were among the population's chief ambitions.

Previous studies on the values of friendship and virtue in the lives of late eighteenth-century middle-class American women ignore the manner in which these discourses mutually affected female communion. In other words, examinations of female friendships in this period rarely refer to virtue as an operative set of values in women's common experience. And, with the possible exception of recent work on female abolitionists (see Yellin), commentaries on virtue and on the "Cult of True Womanhood" it derived tend to overlook its effects on women's friendships. Below, I summarize conceptions of virtue and companionship in the new republic, and I show the ways that notions of feminine virtue and female friendship reflect economic, nationalistic and essentialistic concerns. Ideas of virtue produced conditions that tied women economically to the domestic sphere, connected their morality to the fate of the nation, and linked them intrinsically with feeling and self-sacrifice. These factors, at the same time, helped construct the social institutions that linked women geographically and emotionally, that formed for them an environment inhabited almost entirely by children and other women (Smith-Rosenberg 36). Together, these conditions affect the rhetorical strategies with which female friends in *The Coquette* read and relate to one another.

Although middle-class Americans in the post-revolutionary years saw an increased attention towards personal liberty and a related disenchantment with patriarchal tyranny, the new nation perceived as well a necessity for communal relations and social stability. Anarchy was to be averted only through the good will of the populace. As Gordon S. Wood writes, "This willingness of the individual to sacrifice his [sic] private interests for the good of the community...the eighteenth century termed 'public virtue.' A republic was such a delicate polity precisely because it demanded an extraordinary moral character in the people" (68). With the advent of industrialization, however, virtue from the capitalist standpoint became associated with deprivation and frugality. Discovering themselves more individualistic than they had heretofore imagined, urban American males found the spoils of commerce more agreeable than the altruistic demands of republicanism (Agresto 495).

The interrelated discourses of virtue and feeling, as much as they promised egalitarian relations and an elevated role for women in the new republic, paradoxically limited their roles in the public sphere by demanding their subjugation to the desires of market society. To maintain harmony within both the domestic and the public spheres, virtuous wives would bend to the wills of their husbands (Lewis 712); the economics of virtue, meanwhile, left them little choice. The consequences of women's viciousness, both in marriage or in the events preceding marriage, might very well be poverty and social exile: few opportunities for employment existed for middle-class women and, generally, social opinion was hostile to middle-class women who worked (see Lerner 84 and passim).[2]

With the economic well-being of women like Eliza Wharton and, indeed, the fate of the new nation itself, so dependent upon their allegiance to a socially inscribed identity, it follows that rhetoric about virtue would strongly influence communication among female friends, especially when one might express inclinations to "step out of" the self prescribed for her. However, the interplay of virtue and feelings among women in the new republic has yet to be satisfactorily explored. Perhaps typical of approaches to feminine virtue, Barbara Welter's "The Cult of True Womanhood: 1820-1860" examines the fruition of a virtuous discourse that intensified in the years following the American Revolution, but neglects the particular forms and effects of the discourse in female friendships. Welter's piece confines itself to the influence that virtue had on the interactions of men and women, thereby overlooking significant positions that female friends might have taken in the distribution of or resistance to patriarchal power. Just what were the effects of republican ideology on communications between women? And conversely, what effects did these friendships have on conceptions of virtue?

At least on the surface, the precepts of virtue, with their emphases on community, intersect with those of friendship: both of them entail concern for others, and both posit feeling as a primary consideration. As the codes of feminine virtue would suggest, feeling predominated in discourses comprising female friendships in the late eighteenth-century. In her article on women's friendships, "The Female World of Love and Ritual: Relations Between Women in Nineteenth-Century America," Carroll Smith-Rosenberg theorizes that the "rigid gender-role differentiation within the family and within society as a whole" spurred "a specifically female world...built around a generic and unself-conscious pattern of

"I can step out of myself a little"

Not ones to allow selfish ambitions to crumble their repu
middle-class Americans sought to ensure the survival of
country's moral integrity through feminine virtue. Although
classical sense "virtue" had been associated with rat
faculties (Bloch 41), by the eighteenth century writer:
Shaftesbury, Hume and Hutcheson had aligned virtue wi
emotions. "This realignment," writes Ruth H. B
"coincided…with a revision of binary gender distinc
rationality, long associated with men, was linked to intere
emotions, long associated with women, to morality"
Because republican writers had visualized their citizens un
affection, by a selfless concern for fellow Americans, and b
women were believed to be intrinsically the more emoti
the sexes, women were the "logical" choice to insure virt
in the home and in the nation at large.

In the years following the American Revolution, w
allegiance to virtue became linked with the success of the r
As Mary Beth Norton puts it, "At times it even seemed a:
republican theorists believed that the fate of the republi
squarely, perhaps even solely, upon the shoulders of its
folk" (242). Following the same line of thought, men
virtuous only if the morals of the women whom they cou
married, the women who raised them, were infallible. "
were vice-ridden," continues Norton

> so, too, would men be; but if women adhered to high star
> of behavior, they would cause men to adopt similar standa
> Because the nation would not survive unless its citizen:
> virtuous, and man's virtue was traditionally linked to wom
> then followed that feminine influence would play a speci
> in the United States. (242-43)

Woman's emotions, long considered a legacy of Eve':
passion, now became the source of moral obligation.

Women's association with virtue, however, c(
detrimental to their participation in the liberty ch
revolutionary thinking. In the home, feminine virtue
values—purity, self-sacrifice, piety and domesticity—se
generate egalitarian relations with men (Welter 152 and
Lewis). "The doctrine [of virtue]," Nancy F. Cott explain:
women's initiative because of its central distinction betw(
self-abnegation and manly self-assertion. More potentl)
women in specifically sexual rather than human terms" (

single-sex or homosocial networks" (35). Examining female relationships from the late 1700s, Smith-Rosenberg describes relationships between women of this era as "a world of emotional richness and complexity" (35), a world where "Women, who had little status or power in the larger world of male concerns, possessed status and power in the lives and world of other women" (40).

But the prevalence of discourse about virtue, which helped produce the "rigid gender-role differentiation" in this era, remains unidentified in Smith-Rosenberg's study, and as a result, it eschews cultural and ideological imperatives that may have existed in women's communications. Emerging associations between virtue and feeling, nevertheless, markedly influenced the ways in which women communicated with each other. Cott's *The Bonds of Womanhood: "Woman's Sphere" in New England, 1780-1835* does explicate the manner in which ideological conceptualizations of gender influenced the discourse of women's communities. For Cott, traditional associations of women with "heartfelt" emotions and men with rationality promoted the intense intimacies of women's friendships: "Although it was intended to stress the complementary nature of the two sexes while keeping women subordinate, the identification of women with the heart also implied that they would find truly reciprocal interpersonal relationships only with other women." With "'heartfelt' caring [identified as their] characteristic virtue" (168), the era's women exercised freely in their interrelationships an affectional vocabulary so intense that, as even Smith-Rosenberg observes, modern readers of their correspondence would have difficulty distinguishing platonic from erotic intent (34).

Conceptions of virtue provided an environment conducive to intimate female friendships; however, other precepts of its discourse generated conditions detrimental to women's communion. Rhetoric about virtue provided women with a claim to an essential emotionalism, it allotted them a significant role in the success of the new republic, and it offered them financial security in marriage. At the same time, the discourse devalued woman's rationality, made her sexual autonomy a threat to the nation, and threatened her with financial deprivation should she resist the social codes. Such essentialistic, nationalistic, and economic conceptualizations of virtue affect communication between women in *The Coquette.* Despite the characteristic devotion these women display towards one another, societal pressures leave little room for a dialogic understanding of Eliza as individual; rather, the discourse of virtue transforms the dialogics of friendship into a platform for monologic pronouncements.

By privileging the potentials of emotional discourse between the virtuous women of America's middle class, Cott and Smith-Rosenberg ignore the ways that social conditions and cultural beliefs can determine the very grammar of affectionate exchange, the ways that ideology can restrict and define the expression of certain feelings in certain situations. Examining the rhetoric of virtue in the context of late eighteenth-century American female friendships, sections below show how cultural beliefs and societal pressures situate the discourse of virtue in a relationship antagonistic to dialogical exchange—the means through which social and personal transformations can be negotiated. My essay, then, takes a course opposite that of Cott's and Smith-Rosenberg's as I examine ways that rhetoric about virtue limits affectionate dialogue between women in Hannah Foster's *Coquette*.

Eliza Wharton's first writings evidence her resistance to prevailing social codes. The book opens with three consecutive letters from Wharton to Lucy Freeman, who later becomes Mrs. Lucy Sumner. The initial letter describes the hero's "pleasure...on leaving [her] paternal roof." This pleasure coincides with the death of Mr. Haly, whom her parents had intended Eliza to marry. Expressly, Eliza's "heart [was not] much engaged in the alliance" (5), and in future letters she discovers herself "cheerful, volatile, and unreflecting" as Haly escapes her memory (7).

When the issue is her marriageability—we soon learn—pleasure, cheerfulness, volatility and unreflectiveness represent values that situate Eliza in opposition to her friends' interpretive community. For much of the novel, Eliza's dilemma will be to define herself in terms of her values, which readers in the novel interpret as marks of deviance, as signs of "coquettish airs" (27), "fanciful folly" (107) and "licentiousness" (83). Because eighteenth-century notions of virtue had made such deviancies national threats, Eliza's evasion of these charges attains for her a desperate importance

Eliza's second letter finds her already in a battle over signification. Apparently responding to Lucy's charges of coquettishness, Foster's hero suggests that her actions "deserve a softer appellation" (7). Resisting the designations of her friends' moral code, Eliza argues against any easy, right-or-wrong interpretation of her life. She defends herself against a rhetoric that, as Bakhtin would say, "is populated—overpopulated—with the intentions of others," and her retorts to friends' criticisms reflect the "difficult and complicated process" of "forcing [language] to submit to [her] own intentions and accents" (*Dialogic* 294). In other words, the discourse of virtue becomes a battleground, one where Eliza must vacillate monologic pronouncements to ensure both a space for her individual wants and a place for herself within her friends' community. By putting into question judgments of her coquettishness, Eliza suggests the arbitrariness of such evaluations and gives notice to her "own intentions and accents" within the virtuous society.

Perhaps sensing the "silence" that would accompany her total capitulation to Lucy's repertoire (8), Eliza in her third letter pens what amounts to a valorization of her own codes and a critique of customs that would suppress them. Narrating the events of a dinner party, Eliza expresses consternation over having her enjoyment curtailed by references to the dearly departed Haly:

> The absurdity of a custom, authorising people at a first interview to revive the idea of griefs, which time has lulled, perhaps obliterated, is intolerable. To have our enjoyments arrested by the empty compliments of unthinking persons, for no other reason, than a compliance with fashion is to be treated in a manner, which the laws of humanity forbid. (9)

At this juncture Eliza's "laws of humanity" allow her an alternative set of values with which to critique the "emptiness" of the prevailing social fiction. In effect, she denaturalizes a social ritual—dictating one articulate condolences to a "grieving" person—by positing a new essence, which privileges pleasure.

In these initial letters we find Foster's protagonist at her greatest degree of confidence. However, it is Eliza's confidence in essences, in "human nature," that later incurs the "disorder" of her mind (89). Rather than view a plurality of discourses, Eliza's friends seem illiterate to alternative codes, or at least suspicious of codes that disturb the essentialized gender typing upon which rested the nation's delicate polity. For Eliza, the scarcity of readers for her social text eventually serves as proof of its deviancy, and she experiences the spaces between systems not as the heterogeneity of culture but as her own invisibility.

In all fairness, Eliza's friends are concerned for her well-being, at least her financial well-being. They worry about Wharton's reputation in society at large, a concern in part provoked by her financial status. Eliza does not have an inheritance of her own, and her friends' advice that she seek a husband rather than a job reflects the limited venues available to women of Eliza's social class (Davidson 144). Although her friends rely predominantly on a discourse of virtue to criticize Eliza's behavior, their anxiety about Eliza's reputation reflects as well a concern for her financial health: they know that their friend's marriageability and, with that, her economic security will depend largely on her reputation as a virtuous woman. In this respect, rhetoric about virtue bonded women against the salacious advances of men like Sanford, *Coquette*'s resident rake. A mutual regard of virtue translated into a mutual defense against male autonomy; such a regard protected not only women's reputations, but also their chances for economic security.

In the case of *Coquette*, however, considerations of virtue overwhelm the affectional discourse that writers like Smith-Rosenberg and Cott see characterizing women's friendships in the new republic. Despite the characters' intense concerns for one another, the regard of Wharton's friends for her economic status and her virginity displaces their affectional vocabulary. Among these friends, Lucy Freeman feels her role towards Eliza should be to "act the part of a skillful surgeon, and probe the wound, which [she] undertake[s] to heal" (107). Indeed, Lucy employs a discourse of virtue to "probe" Eliza's wounds, but nowhere does she display a vocabulary that can negotiate their healing. The complexity of social discourses impelling Lucy's evaluation of her friend's virtue does not permit her a rhetoric conducive to an understanding of Wharton's own "heart felt" feelings.

Representing Wharton's main correspondent throughout the novel, Lucy feels obligated to warn Eliza against "coquettish" activities, a warning that discloses the ideological framework within which the community reads Eliza's actions.[3] "I know your ambition is...to bear off the palm amidst the votaries of pleasure," writes Lucy Freeman:

> But these are fading honor...incapable of gratifying those immortal principles of reason and religion, which have been implanted in your mind by nature; assiduously cultivated by the best of parents, and exerted, I trust, by yourself. Let me advise you then...to lay aside those coquettish airs which you sometimes put on.... (27)

Reflecting her culture's absolutist regard of feminine virtue, Lucy essentializes "principles of reason and religion," while describing coquettishness as a trait extrinsic to Eliza's basic characteristics. In Lucy's eyes, coquettishness is ideological (religion and reason are not), and Eliza's arguments against the appellation are viewed as but "a play about words" (31). Eliza's "essential piety," however, depends more upon interpellation than any natural impulse.

Interestingly, Lucy's favorable reading of Boyer, a clergyman infatuated with her friend, marks for her Eliza's unfitness for the essence that codes of virtue prescribe. The "self" that Eliza eventually "step[s] out of" finds its universalization here in Lucy's criticisms. Lucy's "monitorial lessons" represent her attempts to reclaim for Eliza the bounds of an identity that society insists is hers (7); in her lesson plan, however, Lucy makes no allowance for emotional interference. As we learn later, Lucy is as much a reader of romances as she is a reader of the social fiction, but as such, she reveals an insensitivity to actions that traverse outside the normative social text. "Your truly romantic letter came safe to hand," Lucy writes in the latter stages of Eliza's disintegration: "Indeed, my dear, it would make a very pretty figure in a novel. A bleeding heart, slighted love, and all the *et ceteras* of romance, enter into the composition!" (107). Anxious about Eliza's future, Lucy has difficulty sympathizing with her friend's deviations from the dominant text, deviations that apparently come to light with Wharton's attraction to Major Sanford.

Eliza's relationship with her interpretive community slowly disintegrates over their disparate readings of Major Sanford. Lucy's interpretations in this regard are perhaps most urgent, but her insistence on the integrity of her social fiction continually omits Eliza's difference to it. "Can you," Lucy writes,

> who have always been used to serenity and order in a family, to rational, refined and improving conversation, relinquish them, and launch into the whirlpool of frivolity, where the correct taste and the delicate sensibility which you possess must constantly be wounded by the frothy and illiberal sallies of licentious wit? (58)

Against the moral decrepitude of Sanford, Lucy reads only those qualities of Eliza which align themselves with the code of virtue. Omitted are Eliza's inclinations to coquetry, those traits Lucy finds readily apparent against the impeccable virtue of Boyer's character. Lucy reveals in her readings of Eliza's courtships the dichotomous nature of the community's repertoire. Based on a set of binary oppositions that are mutually exclusive, Lucy's repertoire categorizes objects according to established notions of vice and virtue. Depending on the situation, Lucy will privilege either one of these two extremes. When she reads Eliza beside Boyer, Lucy admonishes her friend's deviancy. When she reads Eliza beside Sanford, Lucy perceives only Sanford's deviance and urges Eliza's allegiance to the codes of virtue. For her own part, Eliza feels it a pity "that the graces [of Sanford] and the virtues [of Boyer] are not oftener united" (22); but Lucy Freeman's reading strategies preclude a discourse outside the mutually exclusive categorizations of vice and virtue. So long as Eliza is read according to these categorizations, her expression of differences and her communion with friends remain problematic.

Eliza exercises rhetoric about virtue to negotiate a place for herself within her friends' interpretive community. For example, in the same letter in which she praises Sanford as "an excellent dancer...well calculated for a companion in the hours of mirth and gaiety" (71), Eliza also catalogues the virtuous accomplishments of Lucy and Mrs. Richman. To the latter, a new mother, Eliza writes:

> Hail happy babe! Ushered into the world by the best of mothers; entitled by birth-right to virtue and honor; defended by parental love, from the weakness of infancy and childhood, by guardian wisdom from the perils of youth, and by affluent independence from the griping hand of poverty, in more advance life!

And about the recently wedded Lucy she writes:

> Her dress was such as wealth and elegance required. Her deportment was every thing that modesty and propriety could suggest.... Every eye beamed with pleasure on the occasion, and every tongue echoed the wishes of benevolence. Mine was only silent.

Eliza's reference to her silence in this quotation signals her crisis with her community. Overwrought with "the idea of separation" (70), Eliza confronts in a single letter her closest friends' embeddedness in the social fiction.

As both Lucy and Mrs. Richman evolve further in the dominant text, Eliza's isolation becomes more and more evident. Where Eliza's "coquettishness" represents to the fictional community her waywardness in relation to their text, one could just as well understand Lucy's and Mrs. Richman's unyielding allegiance to their scripted roles as treks that distance *them* from Eliza. Given this, Eliza's recital of virtuous codes suggests her own fear of social invisibility: we can read her discourse as a recital geared to ensure her place amongst friends. Although Wharton is without "affluent Independence" or "wealth and elegance" (see Hamilton 143), the recital of virtue's codes fends off the invisibility that alliance to her own inclinations incurs; i.e., she procures her presence by espousing a text that her friends recognize and accept without censure.

Curiously, as Eliza stands on the brink of social exile her appeals to her friends' sense of virtue seem the most voluminous:

> But the cause [of my fall] may be found in that unrestrained levity of disposition, that fondness for dissipation and coquetry which alienated the affections of Mr. Boyer from me. This event fatally depressed, and enfeebled my mind. I embraced with avidity the consoling power of friendship, ensnaringly offered by my seducer. (145)

Recited to her friend Julia Granby, these words once again indicate Eliza's attention to her interpretive community, the extent to which she is conscious of her friends' ever-watchful eyes and the codes with which they read their world. However, Eliza in the same passage expresses as well the insufficiency of their codes. "My circumstances called for attention;" she tells Julia, "and I had no one to participate my cares, to witness my distress, and to alleviate my sorrows, but [Sanford]" (145). In other words, although Eliza continues to acknowledge the consequences of her actions in terms of the discourse of virtue, she remains as equally aware of the omissions such a discourse makes in regard to her "distress," "cares" and "sorrow."

Ultimately judged unfit by her suitors and alienated by her friends, Eliza suffers the invisibility that the social text procures for her. Following Boyer's rejection of her and a subsequent affair with Sanford, Eliza falls, as Cathy N. Davidson describes it, "into physical infirmity, mental instability, and narrative invisibility" and "increasingly, others must recount the story that was once her own" (146). Her shrinking voice and health become testimony to the aggressive readings of her culture, the strength with which its repertoire omits Eliza as individual. If, as Bakhtin writes, we give ourselves "verbal shape from another's point of view," then we can view the inability of Eliza's community to "share" with her the "territory" of language as the cause of her exile, her banishment from the text (*Marxism* 86). Symbolically, she becomes an invisible woman: "See you not, Julia, my decaying frame, my faded cheek, and tottering limbs?" she asks the last of her (sympathetic) peers, "Soon shall I be insensible to censure and reproach!" (142). Given her eventual disappearance from her text, we can see that the discourse of virtue has not, as Kristie Hamilton says, "entrap[ped] Eliza in the role of the coquette" so much as it has failed to represent Eliza as Eliza (140). Discourse of virtue registers the word "coquette" where a person ought to be.

Once Eliza becomes pregnant with Sanford's child, she can no longer rely on rhetoric to negotiate her place in virtuous society: her illegitimate pregnancy discloses her abandonment of the self that culture prescribes for her, the only self with whom Eliza's friends are capable of communicating. Friends attribute Wharton's demise to the "*lust* and *brutality*" of Sanford (163), but they could as well blame the social conditions and cultural beliefs which limit their roles as women: socially constructed notions of femininity fail to ensure an environment facilitative to Wharton's needs. Eliza uses her final days to reflect upon "the absence of friends" and to write messages "calculated to sooth and comfort the minds of mourning connections" (162-63); but perhaps the inscription most telling of her friendships is that upon her tombstone, which informs readers that Wharton "SUSTAINED THE LAST PAINFUL SCENE, FAR FROM EVERY FRIEND," and marks that "THE TEARS OF STRANGERS WATERED HER GRAVE" (169).

In the introductory chapter to her *Communities of Women*, Nina Auerbach recreates the story of the Graie, mythical sisters who "have a single eye between them, which is passed unfailingly from sister to sister" (3). For Auerbach, "the only eye possessed by the Graie is that of sisterhood" (4). Metaphorically, the eye is the code which knits their community together (8-9). It represents their shared vision, their shared beliefs, and their mutual dependence. In Foster's *Coquette*, characters like Lucy Sumner, Mrs. Richman, and Julia Granby become a type of Graie of their own, passing unfailingly to one another the discourse through which they read their world. Only where Auerbach's Graie "are emblems of female self-sufficiency which create their own corporate reality" (5), a complexity of social concerns transforms Foster's community into a monstrous singularity. The singularity of their vision comes to represent an oppressive discourse, functioning panoptically to ensure the discipline of subjects in a patriarchal society (see Foucault 195-228).

By reading the rhetoric of Wharton's friends in their socio-historic context, however, we can better understand the conditions which compel their readings. Friendships do not exist in a vacuum but, rather, subsist within the complexity of discourses that constitute people as subjects. The discourse of virtue through which women in *The Coquette* read Eliza Wharton comprises cultural concerns which determined perceptions of woman in the new republic. Identifying the patriarchal dimensions of their discourse, this essay shows the ways that a shared vision can become at once cooptive in nature and alienating in effect; it shows the ways that rhetoric can restrict the "free-play" of selves to which women like Eliza Wharton aspire.

Notes

I would like to thank Jennifer Gehrman, Gail Tayko, Sandy Vrana and Michael Vella for reading and commenting on this paper throughout its composition.

[1] Among the few articles devoted to Foster's epistolary novel, only two have remarked on Wharton's relationship with her female friends. Cathy N. Davidson finds women in *The Coquette* constitutive of a "dialogical" community in which vital feminine issues are discussed (144). Kristie Hamilton, on the other hand, discerns these women's voices as manifestations of the "societal codes...that serve to make of Eliza Wharton a 'coquette' and a victim" (141). With Hamilton, I agree that Eliza's friends succeed more in marginalizing than they do in comforting Foster's protagonist; nevertheless, Hamilton's focus undervalues the devotion with which Eliza considers her friendships. Hamilton sees the major conflict in *Coquette* as that between Eliza's materialist desires and her friends' concerns about virtue; I read the central conflict as that between ideas of virtue and feelings of friendship.

[2] Writers like Nina Baym, Zita Dresner and Nancy Cott have pointed out that views of women as the sources of virtue in society "implied a necessary extension of women's influence into the public sphere with a view to reforming its...market-based structure through the operation of woman's moral sensibility" (Dresner 28), thereby indicating ways in which

women were empowered by their role in the new republic. My point here is that financial insecurity produced by this gender typing could in some cases make challenges to patriarchal structures all the more precarious.

[3]For reasons of space, I confine my analysis to a discussion of Lucy's rhetoric, which I believe is representative of that employed by other women in the text in regard of Eliza. In a longer version of this paper, I discuss the ways that both Mrs. Richman and Julia Granby, as well as Boyer and Sanford, use the codes of virtue in a manner destructive to Eliza.

Works Cited

Agresto, John T. "Liberty, Virtue, and Republicanism: 1776-1787." *The Review of Politics* 39.4 (1977).

Auerbach, Nina. *Communities of Women.* Cambridge: Harvard UP, 1978.

Bakhtin, M.M. *The Dialogic Imagination.* Ed. Michael Holquist. Trs. Caryl Emerson and Michael Holquist. Austin: U of Texas P, 1981.

[Bakhtin]/V.N. Volosinov. *Marxism and the Philosophy of Language.* Trs. Ladislav Matejka and I.R. Titunik. Cambridge: Harvard UP, 1973.

Baym, Nina. *Woman's Fiction: A Guide to Novels by and about Women in America, 1820-1870.* Ithaca: Cornell UP, 1978.

Bloch, Ruth H. "The Gendered Meanings of Virtue in Revolutionary America." *Signs: Journal of Women in Culture and Society* 13.1 (1987).

Cott, Nancy F. *The Bonds of Womanhood: "Women's Sphere" in New England, 1780-1835.* New Haven: Yale UP, 1977.

Davidson, Cathy N. *Revolution and the Word: The Rise of the Novel in America.* New York: Oxford UP, 1986.

Dresner, Zita Z. "Sentiment and Humor: A Double-Pronged Attack on Women's Place in Nineteenth-Century America." *Studies in American Humor* 4 (1985).

Foster, Hannah Webster. *The Coquette.* 1797. Ed. Cathy N. Davidson. New York: Oxford UP, 1986.

Foucault, Michel. *Discipline and Punish: The Birth of the Prison.* Tr. Alan Sheridan. New York: Vintage [Random], 1979.

Hamilton, Kristie. "An Assault on the Will: Republican Virtue and the City in Hannah Webster Foster's *The Coquette*." *Early American Literature* 24 (1989).

Lerner, Gerda. "The Lady and the Mill Girl: Changes in the Status of Women in the Age of Jackson." *Our American Sisters: Women in American Life and Thought.* Eds. Jean E. Friedman and William G. Shade. Boston: Allyn and Bacon, 1973.

Lewis, Jan. "The Republican Wife: Virtue and Seduction in the Early Republic." *William and Mary Quarterly* 44 (1987).

Norton, Mary Beth. *Liberty's Daughters: The Revolutionary Experience of American Women, 1750-1800*. Boston: Little, Brown, 1980.

Smith-Rosenberg, Carroll. "The Female World of Love and Ritual: Relations Between Women in Nineteenth-Century America." *The Signs Reader: Women, Gender, and Scholarship*. Eds. Elizabeth Abel and Emily K. Abel. Chicago: U of Chicago P, 1983.

Welter, Barbara. "The Cult of True Womanhood: 1820-1860." *American Quarterly* 18 (1966).

Wood, Gordon S. *The Creation of the American Republic, 1776-1787*. Chapel Hill: U of North Carolina P, 1969.

Yellin, Jean Fagan. *Women and Sisters: The Anti-Slavery Feminists in American Culture*. New Haven: Yale UP, 1990.

The Bluestocking Circle:
The Negotiation of "Reasonable" Women

SUSAN M. YADLON

In eighteenth-century England, the cult of domesticity functioned as a cultural mechanism that defined femininity. This ideology, as Nancy Armstrong and Mary Poovey explain, reified the concept of an ideal woman and positioned her firmly in the domestic (as opposed to public) sphere. She was constituted by values considered natural and intrinsic to her—modesty, chastity, passivity and frugalness. In essence, she was a vessel of morality. Since these characteristics could only be demonstrated indirectly or negatively (chastity is shown by not acknowledging sexuality; modesty by not speaking), it offered dominant discourses added control in reconfiguring constructed notions of femininity. Such control created a paradigm for women's behavior that functioned as a support for the existent power/privilege system, as well as limited women's ability to act in ways that contested that system. Simultaneously, restricted access to the public sphere limited female contribution to the formation of these codes. The force of this ideology can be seen in how these notions of femininity soon began to function as the "ideal" for all women regardless of class, region, or religion.

However, as Felicity Nussbaum notes in *The Autobiographical Subject,* ideology itself is never monolithic and is always composed of multiple and conflicting discourses. She advocates "a model of ideology which acknowledges contradiction within it in order to allow subjects to misrecognize themselves in prevailing ideologies and to intervene in producing new knowledge" (36). This understanding would allow literature, or any written discourse, to "subtly voice several contradictory codes at one time" (35). Examination of eighteenth-century writings confirms this claim as the written word comes to function not only as a tool of ideological dissemination but also as a site of intervention into domestic ideology's construction of femininity. By investigating the written texts (personal correspondences as well as published works) and the lives of a group of women known as the Bluestockings, one can see how the conflicts inherent in the ideology of domesticity simultaneously reified women's behavior and offered a space from which to intervene in that paradigm.

During the eighteenth century, the written word became a powerful mechanism for defining, refining and disseminating these codes of femininity. This century witnessed an expansion of the popular press, providing greater accessibility to written texts than ever before. Additionally, more people, especially women, became literate. Through a genre of literature called conduct books, whose function served to educate women on how to be the "ideal," this ideology of domesticity became widely dispersed among the literate public. Interestingly, conduct books were often authored by women, creating what Michel Foucault has labeled a "reverse discourse." A reverse discourse occurs when a group "[begins] to speak in its own behalf, to demand that its legitimacy...be acknowledged, often in the same vocabulary, using the same categories by which it was... disqualified" (101). Although a reverse discourse is limiting in that it continues to invoke the traditional categories of classification, speaking in one's own behalf also creates the possibility of voicing the misrecognition Nussbaum speaks of, and provides a platform from which to then intervene in dominant ideology.

One site of intervention occurs within the debate over women's education. The ideology of domesticity required that women be educated, but education was limited to the cultivation of women's "inherent qualities," the very same qualities needed to perform the duties of wife and mother. For example, although women were thought to be naturally modest and frugal, ideology stressed the necessity of teaching them to regulate their natures so they would not be swayed into desire for ostentatious behavior and attracted to material goods. Conduct books ensured this cultivation, and women's education, although primarily focused on domesticity, became a cultural given. However, this acceptance of women's education also created a space from which to argue for access to other kinds of knowledge. Supported by Enlightenment notions of human reason and rationality, many women began to request that education exceed the sphere of the domestic. Mary Wollstonecraft and her polemic *A Vindication of the Rights of Woman* is probably the most widely known example of this.

However, women far more politically conservative than Wollstonecraft also entered the debate on women's education. From 1750 until about 1790, a group of women who would come to be known as the Bluestockings publicly lobbied for an expansion of the female system of education. Though individually these women vocalized a wide range of opinions as to the extent of such change, they were united by a common "desire to reform manners and education in order to reach a higher level of morality and intellectual life" (Williamson 93). Nearly all of the Bluestockings wrote and published in some form, and they are remembered for the intellectual gatherings they sponsored reminiscent of the French salons. As the statement from Williamson suggests, however, the Bluestockings argued for reform, not revolution. To a great extent, their lives complied with dominant codes of femininity, and it is from within that position that they argued for a reform of education and a rethinking of certain tenets of domesticity.

By looking at the works they published, personal correspondences and descriptions of the salons they hosted, one can see the emergence of a Bluestocking discourse that simultaneously perpetuates and resists dominant ideology. Foucault, in *The History of Sexuality,* examines discourse and its possible deployments in ways useful for understanding this contradiction in the Bluestocking's intervention:

> We must make allowance for the complex and unstable process whereby discourse can be both an instrument and an effect of power, but also a hindrance, a stumbling-block, a point of resistance and a starting point for an opposing strategy. Discourse transmits and produces power; it reinforces it, but also undermines and exposes it, renders it fragile and makes it possible to thwart it. (101)

With this understanding, it becomes possible to view discourse as operating in conflicting ways simultaneously. The Bluestocking discourse illustrates this and, in many ways, their power emanated from their ability to negotiate these contradictions. In other words, their support and perpetuation of particular tenets of dominant discourse brought them a certain level of societal sanction, or at least tolerance. Such positioning gave them an opportunity to acknowledge publicly the misrepresentation of themselves in the ideology of domesticity, and through that, critique it, while avoiding the marginalization that many previous critics had been subjected to. It is precisely this ability to somewhat neutralize marginalization that allows them effectively to intervene into dominant codes and carve out a sanctioned space for women to publish.

The ideology of domesticity structured the lives of the Bluestockings in various and crucial ways. The most obvious instance can be seen in their relationships to the institution of heterosexual marriage. Elizabeth Robinson (later Montagu), Hester Thrale and Lady Mary Harley all married men in accordance with the wishes of their family. Their husbands were older and, for the most part, emotionally unconnected to their wives. However, they were economically and socially appropriate matches. These women's journals, letters and diaries testify to minimal affection for their mates, but they remained loyal wives and mothers regardless. Elizabeth Carter, who remained single, had the hesitant blessings of her father in that decision. Additionally, she remained with him, caring for him and her brothers until he died and her brothers married. Catherine Talbot also did not marry, a decision paralleling the wishes of her family. Such compliance had material effects on these women's lives.

For example, marriage often put strict limitations on women's mobility and connections to society. A husband traditionally had the right to approve or deny a wife's relationships with those outside the family as well as her ability to travel. Additionally, popular belief held that a woman's only friendship should be her spouse. Samuel Johnson, the highly respected philosopher of the age, proclaimed "that a married woman can have no friendship but with her husband" (qtd. in Myers 118). With marriages arranged by a woman's family, often for economic and political reasons, women had little opportunity to exercise control over their relationships. In a letter to Elizabeth Carter, Talbot speaks of the difficulties of this imposed lifestyle:

> One of my most favorite, most amiable friends has been married for several years, and I experience that the difference of circumstances make an alteration in the ease and frequency of our seeing one another, which robs me of the gayest, happiest moments I ever enjoyed. But our affection for one another continues the same...we sometimes lament the distance that it puts between us, but are upon the whole mighty reasonable people, and very well satisfied that every thing should be as it is. (qtd. in Ferguson 334)

The image of "reasonable people" provides an interesting way to explore the strategy of the Bluestockings' resistance. They lived during the eighteenth century, the Age of Reason, a time when many utilized the concept of human reason as a platform from which to argue for certain equalities for women. Yet, Talbot invokes "reason" in a way that does not resist the power relation between men and women, but rather perpetuates it by naming it as the natural state of things. Talbot's statement laments this natural state of things rather than contesting it.

Even prior to marriage, friendships were difficult to start and even harder to maintain. The cult of domesticity severely limited women's access to the public sphere, so most middle and upper class women (as the Bluestockings were) lived in relative isolation. For example, it was common for families to live in a country home geographically isolated from other families and polite society. Company often visited, but parents controlled their children's access to individuals outside of the family. For daughters, all education was done in the home, enhancing isolation. This lifestyle allotted women little control over life decisions and social activity. Elizabeth Robinson (recognized as the "Queen of the Bluestockings") once remarked, "I am left wholly to myself & my books & both I own too little to possess me entirely..." (qtd. in Myers 38).

With these physical limitations, it is obvious to see how difficult friendships were to cultivate. This lifestyle kept women isolated and separated and very much under the control of parents and, later, husbands. However, it is precisely the overcoming of these obstacles that eventually allows for a series of personal friendships among women to coalesce loosely under the name of Bluestockings. The formation of the Bluestocking circle began as an attempt to compensate for such isolating conditions, not a unified decision to resist or support dominant codes. Most of the Bluestockings met at social events or at spas patronized by the upper classes. Commonly, friendships began either at social gatherings on family estates or at one of the spas frequented by upper-class society, like Turnbridge. Montagu met Lady Margaret Harley (later Bentick) at the latter's estate at Wimpole Hall around 1730; Carter and Talbot met through a mutual friend in London in 1741. In 1749, Carter became acquainted with Hester Mulso Chapone, and years later she would strike up an avid friendship with Elizabeth Montagu after being introduced at Turnbridge spa in 1758. Earlier, Montagu had become acquainted with Frances Boscawen and Elizabeth Vesey at Turnbridge (Myers 21, 68, 76, 189, 178). These women all shared a love of knowledge and literature as well as lifestyles that left them isolated from a supportive intellectual community.

Friendships were founded on common intellectual interests and a need for some sort of intellectual community, which was denied to women. Because of the isolating conditions women lived under, many of these individual friendships had epistolary origins. In their letters to each other, they explored and encouraged one another's intellectual pursuits, sharing names of books and interpretations of philosophic works. Additionally, they shared common concerns about marriage, children, disease and so on. These individual friendships provided great support to these women, and the Bluestockings found ways to continue them in spite of the restraints that dominant ideology placed upon them.

Elizabeth Montagu illustrates one method of resistance to the lack of control over her decisions. Married to a man years her senior, who spent a great deal of time away from the home or alone in his study, she rebelled against the limitations placed on her ability to visit friends. When Mr. Montagu refused to allow his wife to visit Mrs. Boscawen, she requested that he write a letter to the Boscawens explaining why she can't come. He agreed to allow her to visit for three days. She ultimately refused his limited compromise, and commented by letter to her sister:

> I...was determined either to have my pleasure or give a signal mark of my obedience to his noble exertion of prerogative. ...What do the generality of men mean by a love of liberty but the liberty to...exert their power over others...I am not sure that Cato did not kick his wife. What inconvenience cd be to his honour that I shd be in Hillstreet, in the County of Middlesex rather than at Hatchlands in ye County of Surrey, he being all the while in Coun. Berks. and the pretence of my keeping order in the family is trifling, as I shall leave all the Servants here but my own Maid & footmen. (qtd. in Myers 139)

Notice what Montagu does here. She does not tirade against the system that places women subordinate to their husbands. She makes little connection between herself and the lives of other women (except for Cato's wife).

Rather, she deconstructs the power relation inherent in one element of her relationship with her husband, exposing its impracticality, and renaming it as an effect of power. It becomes crucial for her to mark it in this way. More importantly, however, Montagu has keen insight into the power of bringing personal discourse into the public. Only when she requests that her husband make public his decision by "franking a cover" is he willing to compromise. The Bluestockings later employ this tactic when they publicly mark their need for an intellectual life through both their intellectual gatherings and the publications of their works. It is the making public that violates the taboos of domesticity. But this bringing into the public is also what allows for structural changes to be made in the dominant ideology, and for changes that eventually affect women beyond their circle.

Hester Chapone takes a more philosophical approach than Montagu in her justification of female friendship. She reconfigures the relationship between marriage and friendship, inverting Samuel Johnson's decree that a wife's only friend be her spouse by claiming that marriage will make her a more valuable friend.

> I hope you join with me in the most perfect dissent from an opinion of your favorite Johnson...I flatter myself my heart will be improved in every virtuous affection by an union with a worthy man, and that my dear Miss Carter, and all my friends, will find it more worthy of their attachment, and better qualified for the best uses of friendship, than it ever was before. (qtd. in Myers 118)

This passage from a letter to Elizabeth Carter shows how the written word, originally in the form of personal letters, begins to act as intervention to the ideology of domesticity by suggesting alternative ways of operating within that system.

These personal correspondences testify to the origins of a Bluestocking discourse. These women, long positioned as objects of public discourse about their lives, begin to voice opinions about the conditions under which they live. These epistolary friendships, formed in response to the power of dominant ideology, additionally become an act of intervention in it. This commitment to friendship exemplifies the subtle, yet powerful method of resistance characteristic of the women of the Bluestocking circle. It is their compliance that makes their "perfect dissent" possible. They do not threaten the institution of heterosexual marriage itself, but rather intervene in certain marital practices.

Many of the published texts of the Bluestockings illustrate this complex negotiation of dominant ideology. Hester Chapone provides an interesting case in point. Both her life and her writings contest several of the values of domesticity. Yet, in crucial ways she remains positioned within that ideology. In 1773, Chapone authored a conduct book, *Letters on the Improvement of the Mind*.

In it, she reiterates many of the dominant codes of femininity. For example, Chapone reifies the public/private split that relegates women solely to the latter domain. She claims that "The principle virtues or vices of a women [sic] must be of a private and domestic kind" (95). She also parrots the hegemonic representation of women's bodies as frail and tending toward illness:

> Women in general are very liable to ill health, which must necessarily make them in some measure troublesome and disagreeable to those which they live with. They should therefore take the more pains to lighten the burden as much as possible, by patience and good humor; and be careful not to let their infirmities break in on the health, freedom, or enjoyment of others. (76)

Not only does she perpetuate the notion of women's physical frailty, but she encourages women to place others before them. The message instructs women to suffer in silence rather than to disturb those around them, thus keeping women's bodies imprisoned in the private. Further, it positions women as captives to their biology, an inescapable occurrence of an undeniable essence.

Chapone also perpetuates the class hierarchies inherent in the cult of domesticity. In *The Proper Lady and the Woman Writer*, Mary Poovey investigates how class is deployed in this ideology. The eighteenth century saw the rise of the middle class, and the more successful in this group developed consumer spending patterns "that rivaled that of their social betters" (11). This increase in consumption standards as well as a rise in taxes for landowners put financial pressures on the upper classes. That pressure was often relieved through economically strategic marriages. Wealthy middle-class merchants who were financially liquid married daughters to the landed aristocracy who were cash poor, but had land and respectable family names. This encouraged competition and animosity between women, for middle-class daughters could improve themselves and their family through marital affiliation, yet these associations threatened the marriage potential of aristocratic women as well as the solidarity of their class. Chapone's advice in her conduct book cements this antagonism. She advises women:

> be intimate with those of your rank; but to be with those superior to you is in every way desirable and advantageous.... Above all things, avoid intimacy with those of low birth and

education! nor think it a mark of humility to delight in such society, for it much oftener proceeds from the meanest kind of pride, that of being the head of the company, and seeing your companions subservient to you. (77)

What Chapone sets up here is social mobility for middle-class women through relationships with the upper classes. However, it furthers the antagonism of upper-class women towards middle-class women. Quite simply, to associate with them would be to have "the meanest kind of pride." Additionally, it continues to disparage and separate out working-class women. To interact with working-class women (unless one is one) would evidence a fault in one's character, and because poor women had few economic assets to encourage the crossing of class lines, working-class women became further isolated. Chapone's text reaffirms such animosity.

Despite certain compliance with the ideology of domesticity, Chapone also questions several of its crucial tenets in her *Letters on the Improvement of the Mind*. The title itself asserts the existence of an active and valuable female intellectual capacity that deserves the opportunity for utilization and advancement. Additionally, within this text, she seeks to redirect the motivation for and authority over female behavior. Claiming that reason is limited and "liable to error," she argues that loyalty to God should be the motivation for women's behavior (17). Chapone deploys reason here in a particularly interesting manner. Many had used the notion to argue for equality between the sexes. Chapone, however, discredits reason, and through that displaces man's authority over women. Chapone's brilliance is to call upon the only figure commonly accepted as being more powerful than man—God. Even though God is referred to as a father figure, which has the effect of collapsing husband/father with deity, it is still a crucial relocation of authority beyond the male scope.

Along with this leveling, Chapone argues for a companionate system of marriage, not one completely ruled by the male figure: "As I trust you will deserve the confidence of your husband; so I hope you will be allowed free consultation with him on your mutual interest" (76). This system of marriage would not be threatened by the existence of outside friendships, as long as the marriage remains the highest form of it (86). Since the policy of allowing women no friendships outside of marriage often served to further isolate women and limit the possibility of communal resistance, the space she attempts to open up can potentially have a powerful effect on intervention into dominant ideology.

Additionally, Chapone complicates the very notion of marriage itself. Though the cult of domesticity defined the ideal state of women as married, Chapone's emphasis on God allows her to acknowledge that marriage is sometimes oppressive for women: "The calamities of an unhappy marriage are so much greater than can befall a single person, that the unmarried women may find abundant argument to be contented with her condition...whether married or single, if your first care is to please God, you will undoubtedly be a blessed creature" (59-60). Because the relationship with God supersedes relations with men, women can have value through the former and not the latter. It still defines worth through a connection to a male figure, but does offer alternative lifestyles for women.

However, Chapone and many of the Bluestockings were only able to voice such opinions because they were considered exceptions to the rule and given unusual access to education. For example, Chapone's father allowed her the same education that her brothers had, and both were supportive of her intellectual endeavors. Through this uncommon occurrence, she was positioned in ways that allowed her to venture beyond the domestic sphere. For example, Chapone engaged in an epistolary debate with Samuel Richardson (with Richardson's encouragement also) critiquing his novel, *Clarissa*. Here, she advocates for a social constructionist notion of women's characteristics: "Custom indeed allows not the daughters of people of fashion to leave their father's family to seek their own subsistence, and there is no way for them to gain a creditable livelihood, as gentlemen may." However, anxious about her conversation with Richardson and aware of the codes she has violated, she later apologizes for her boldness: "Forbid it justice! that the sex, and the cause of learning, should thus suffer for the faults of one ignorant girl! For if I have erred, you should impute it rather to my ignorance than knowledge" (qtd. in Myers 145).

Chapone's retraction illustrates the negotiation she makes in order to speak. Her ability to voice her opinion publicly relies on an implicit contract of restrained critique. It is her perception as one who accepts the ideology of domesticity that has given her this platform from which to speak. If she upsets that balance and is seen as one who rejects domesticity, she risks marginalization. Once marginalized, she loses her audience, in this case, the very author of a work that had widespread effect on eighteenth-century notions of femininity.

Many of the Bluestockings also lived under exceptional circumstances that gave them access to classical education and/or allowed them limited power over their life choices. Elizabeth Carter, for example, was raised by a father who provided her with education similar to that of her brothers, and she took full advantage of that opportunity. She was permitted to study the classical languages—Greek, Latin and Hebrew, as well as French, German, Italian and Spanish. It was an intellectually supportive environment:

> We have a great variety of topics in which every body bears a part, till we get insensibly upon books; and whenever we go beyond Latin and French, my sister and the rest walk off, and leave my father and me to finish the discourse, and the tea-kettle by ourselves, which we should infallibly do, if it held as much as Solomon's molten sea. (Pennington 106)

Her father respected and encouraged her intellectual capacity, going as far as securing a position for her as writer at the popular "Gentleman's Magazine." There she came in contact with Samuel Johnson. The two developed a great affinity and respect for each other. Johnson later participated in the Bluestockings' intellectual gatherings, and he formed crucial friendships with Hester Thrale and Elizabeth Montagu as well. It is impossible to underestimate the impact of having a man of Johnson's stature supporting the intellectual endeavors of these women. His encouragement, as well as that of other prominent men (Lord Lyttleton, for example), provided a basis of societal support for the Bluestockings that helped them publicly come to voice.

Carter's father also allowed Elizabeth unprecedented control over her life decisions. He states,

> I must do you the justice to say, that I think you are an exception. I am extremely unwilling to cross your inclination in any thing, because your behavior to me is more than unexceptional. I leave you, therefore, to act agreeably to your own judgment. My exceeding fondness of you must necessarily make me anxious and fearful; but it does not prevent me from being convinced that I may safely leave a great deal to your own judgment. (Pennington 26)

As her father states, this authority over her own life was uncommon at this time. It was power granted to her, earned if you will, by her exceptional behavior towards him. She repaid that favor by supporting him until his death and by negotiating a balance between her intellectual projects and her domestic duties. It is vital not to underestimate how crucially Carter's negotiation impacted her ability to write and be accepted as a female author. Samuel Johnson commented that "his old friend, Mrs. Carter...could make a pudding, as well as translate Epictetus from the Greek, and work a handkerchief as well as compose a poem" (qtd. in Myers 158). It is precisely Carter's ability to live the role of domesticity that allows her to venture beyond it.

For Elizabeth Montagu, her marriage, although limiting in some ways, gave her crucial economic support and sufficient time to engage in intellectual pursuits. Her only child died quite early on in the marriage. Although her husband spent enormous amounts of time away from her or their home and she often complained of isolation, she eventually began to utilize that time. Sylvia Myers states:

> But she had Virgil and Milton for companions...She was determined to be a dutiful wife, however, and to begin with made the effort to be flexible...One such way to make her periods of enforced solitude profitable was serious study. Elizabeth Montagu, like Catherine Talbot and Elizabeth Carter, enjoyed the letters of Madam de Sevigne, who had found in country life a space for reading and reflection. Mrs. Montagu began to order her life on this contrast—the city for sociability and friendships, the country for reading, study, and letter-writing. (187)

Montagu became a widow in 1775, allowing her more freedom of movement. Additionally, she inherited her husband's money, an unusual occurrence in the eighteenth century. As Susan Staves explains, "the law gave a husband rights over his wife's property in exchange for the legal obligation to support her which he assumed at marriage" (7). After the husband's death, the widow would be provided with a jointure, a stipend for widows, but the property would pass to a male heir. Yet, Mr. Montagu's will ensured that Elizabeth would inherit nearly his entire fortune. After his death she had an annual income of £7,000, using this money to construct a large house in Portman Square where she hosted Bluestocking gatherings of considerable size (Myers 250). Additionally, Montagu was able to support Carter by giving her a £100 a year stipend.

Widowhood had previously granted more freedom to several of the women associated with the Bluestockings. In 1761, Hester Chapone Mulso, Lady Mary Bentick and Frances Boscawen all lost their husbands. Although the death of a husband sometimes brought financial difficulties, it eradicated the authority that controlled their freedom of movement. Since women were not required to remarry, widowed Bluestockings could now exercise more control over their physical movement and participation in friendships. Interestingly, the Bluestockings who had remained single also experienced a shifting of their status at this time. As they grew older, questions of whether they would marry faded, and their spinsterhood became accepted. Traditionally, single women received the appellation of Mrs. during middle age, the age when childbearing was no longer possible. These women shifted from the title of Miss, which still located authority in the father to Mrs., which locates power in a husband figure that didn't exist. Linguistically, these women reached parity, a parity that reflected their removal from the marriage market. Materially, it granted more freedom of activity. Sylvia Myers finds this chain of events crucial to the formation of the Bluestockings: "The significant factor which brought them together seems to have been that they had some control over how they used their time, and where they lived and visited. A woman who married and could not live in London or could not afford to visit in the season seems to have been unable to maintain a 'bluestocking circle' friendship" (120).

In and of themselves, the Bluestockings' access to education and economic conditions which granted relative financial independence might have had little power to impact in any substantial way the ideology of domesticity. However, in combination, these conditions led to the formation of a loose community with its own discourse, which made possible resistance to the cult of domesticity.

This formation of this community significantly influenced each woman's ability to enter into public discourse. Nearly all their writing and publication originated through the encouragement of friends. The Bluestockings lived in a time when women did not have a public voice, and they were greatly affected by the code that told women to remain silent. Hesitancy to publish is common among these women. Carter writes to her publisher, "I should choose my name might be concealed, unless you should have any inclination to shew it to Miss Mulso (Hester Chapone), to whose knowledge of the author I have no objection" (Pennington 115). Additionally, she began the work as a favor to Catherine Talbot. Catherine and her mother were in mourning after the death of Archbishop Secker, and asked Carter to translate Epictetus so they could make a project of the reading and thereby pass the time. Montagu published her critique of Shakespeare anonymously, but only after much prodding from Carter. Montagu encouraged Chapone's writing so much that Hester dedicated her work to her, claiming, "perhaps it was the partiality of friendship that led you to encourage me publish" (Chapone dedication). Montagu also edited the book. These women clearly recognized the transgression of codes implicit in publication. Elizabeth Montagu remarked, "a Woman that possess them [talents] must be always courting the World, and asking pardon, as it were, for uncommon excellence" (qtd. in Myers 183). It was only through the formation of community through friendships founded on shared intellectual interests that they were able to overcome hesitancies and break the silencing of the cult of domesticity.

However, the bonds of their supportive community do not necessitate nor ensure any unity regarding the work produced. These women had varying opinions on education, reform, and the role of women in society, and their works echo this range. Chapone wrote a conduct book, Talbot a religious tract. Both echo the dominant codes of femininity in many ways. Hannah More's publications stress religious values over all else. Elizabeth Carter is mostly regarded as the intellectual (and interestingly enough, the feminist) of the group. Her major written work was her translation of Epictetus. And Elizabeth Montagu published a critical essay on Shakespeare.

For Montagu and Carter, writing allowed them a voice from which to critique and interpret classic and canonical texts. Few women had done either before this time, and their entrance into this role directly contested notions of women's intellectual capacity. Translation provided Carter a way to intervene in women's representation in the classic texts. For example, Carter had earlier disagreed with Archbishop Secker (a step-father figure to Talbot) over a Biblical translation. In the translation of the First Epistle to the Corinthians, the translator had given the same verb gender specific meanings. In English it then read, "Let her not leave him. Let him not put her away" (Pennington 125). Carter's recognition of the potentially sexist method of interpretation exemplifies the equally potential possibilities for resistance inherent in her stepping into the role of translator.

Laetitia Barbauld was undoubtedly one of the more conservative members of the Bluestockings. When Montagu offered to fund a private institution for women's education with Barbauld as the principal, Barbauld balked at the idea. She stated, "A kind of Academy of ladies, where they are taught...the various branches of science, appears to me better calculated to form such characters as the *Precieuse* or *Femmes Savantes* than good wives or agreeable companions" (qtd. in Williamson 91). This considerable philosophic variety contributed to the positive reception of the Bluestockings as a group. The range from conservative to mildly conservative helped ensure their acceptance in society. The connection between women like Barbauld and Carter helped to lessen the potential for Carter's being read as a threat to male intellectual society. The contrast served to neutralize views that could be perceived as radical.

This contrast helps to explain the importance of women like Mary Wollstonecraft for the positive reception of the Bluestockings. To a woman, the Blues strongly disagreed with Wollstonecraft's radical notions. Hannah More called her "one who wanders far from the limits prescribed to her sex" (qtd. in Meakin 322). Even Elizabeth Carter, by far the most likely of the Bluestockings to be labeled feminist, thought Wollstonecraft too radical (Pennington 303). Here again, Michel Foucault's work on discourse can help explain this rejection. He suggests that "we must question them [discourses] on the two levels of their tactical productivity (what reciprocal effects of power and knowledge they ensure) and their strategical integration (what conjunction and what force relationship make their utilization necessary in a given episode of the various confrontations that occur)" (102). From this understanding, one can see how the Bluestockings' rejection of Wollstonecraft served two purposes: first, it protected the power they had gained from class privilege; secondly, it ensured their admittance into the male intellectual world.

As noted previously, the ideology of domesticity cemented antagonisms between middle-class women and their aristocratic counterparts. The majority of the women who participated in the Bluestocking circle were from the landed upper class. Even the few who belonged to the middle class (namely Carter and Talbot) had been accepted into this circle and cared for in material ways. Wollstonecraft, on the other hand, clearly associated herself with middle-class interests. In her introduction to *Vindication of the*

Rights of Woman, she states, "I pay particular attention to those in the middle class, because they appear to be in the most natural state" (81). Wollstonecraft represents the upper class as "[w]eak, artificial beings...undermin[ing] the very foundation of virtue, and spread[ing] corruption through the whole mass of society!" (81).

Additionally, to accept the radical implications of Wollstonecraft's reforms could potentially weaken the positions many of the Bluestockings had come to hold. Several Bluestockings had gained significant financial and cultural power through economically/societally advantageous marriages. As a result of this, the Bluestockings argued not against the institution itself, but against certain practices that limited their freedom of movement or decision-making. Wollstonecraft, on the other hand, had far more radical notions about heterosexual marriage. Jane Rendall, in *The Origins of Modern Feminism*, argues that Wollstonecraft thought that "'matrimonial despotism'

> ...was to the key to women's oppression in all spheres of life" (64). Wollstonecraft believed that marriage kept women dependent on men, and advocated changes in the civil laws which would put women on an equal footing with their husbands. Only then would women "not be faced with the choice of marriage, or the most menial of employment, or prostitution." (63)

Due to class positioning, the likelihood that any of the Bluestockings would face "the most menial of employment" was minimal. By the time Wollstonecraft wrote, the Court of Chancery had instituted the "law of equity" which ensured financial protection for widows. It allowed women to retain the assets they brought into a marriage, thus establishing financial stability for women of privileged classes. Considering such financial security, it becomes easy to see the vested interests they had in maintaining the current standards.

Secondly, any alliance with Wollstonecraft's more radical notions could threaten to disrupt the intellectual positioning they had gained. For the Bluestockings to ally themselves with Wollstonecraft, who attacked the virtue and rights of the privileged class, would be intellectual suicide. Certainly, they would risk the loss of societal sanction which they relied heavily upon. If they sided with the marginalized, they, too, ran the risk of marginalization. That possibility, as well as Wollstonecraft's potential threat to their economic standing, ensured Wollstonecraft's rejection by the Bluestocking circle, who continued to seek reform, and not radical transformation.

The rejection of Wollstonecraft helped the Bluestockings gain position in eighteenth-century intellectual society. Supported by influential friends and strengthened by communal encouragement, they became a force to be reckoned with. An experience of Samuel Johnson illustrates this. After a disagreement with Elizabeth Montagu over his critique of her friend Lord Lyttleton, Johnson remarks, "Mrs. Montagu has dropped me. Now, Sir, there are people one should like very well to drop, but would not want to be dropped by" (Williamson 93). Johnson astutely recognizes the position Montagu holds in society, and his statement testifies to their successful recognition as an intellectual force.

Unfortunately, many contemporary literary critics have failed to recognize the achievements of the Bluestockings, or have minimalized their accomplishments because of their conservative politics. In *First Feminists: British Women Writers 1578-1799*, Moira Ferguson allots one paragraph to the Bluestockings, locating their value in their opposition to "card-playing...and education in frivolous accomplishments," and in their "various models of independent womanhood...that mattered more in the long run than their salons and conversations combined" (21). She includes a chapter on the individual achievements of Elizabeth Carter; however, she undertheorizes the role that the Bluestocking community played in Carter's ability to produce such work. I have argued that Carter's text emerged out of financial and emotional support from the Bluestockings, as well as their complexly negotiated societal positioning. To treat Carter individually misses a crucial understanding about the production of her texts.

Marilyn Williamson criticizes them for not "translat[ing] their own achievements into fundamental social change for their sex" (98). Arguing that the Bluestockings' autonomous lifestyles were incongruous with codes of femininity that appear in their written texts, she wonders "how much more the Blues might have achieved if they had matched their works to their deeds" (100). However, I argue that the Bluestockings functioned as a reverse discourse, one that had as much stake in preserving certain tenets of the ideology of domesticity as in altering others. If viewed in this way, there is little incongruity between the written works and the lives of these women, and more importantly, the consistency between life and text is where they draw their power from. Even Sylvia Myers, who lauds the achievements of the Bluestockings, undertheorizes the investment the Bluestockings had in maintaining contemporary standards. All three critics recognize the Bluestockings' conservative politics but miss examining how an insistence on retaining class privilege prevents the Bluestockings from taking up the struggles of the majority of eighteenth-century women.

Certainly, the Bluestockings' strategy has limitations. For example, their protection of class privilege makes impossible the formation of broader feminist politics that could serve the needs of the majority of women. However, for the Bluestockings to attain such status during the eighteenth century is a remarkable achievement that should not go unacknowledged. By remaining solidly within the cult of domesticity, they were able to neutralize to some degree the forces that sought to discredit them. By negotiating the fissures inherent in Enlightenment ideology, they were able to evoke change, albeit in limited ways, in the construction of femininity. Contemporary feminist theory needs to reinvestigate the Bluestocking circle and their contribution to the history of feminism. I am arguing for a more complex reading of their achievement, one that recognizes their success (rather than marginalizing them as conservative), yet acknowledges the limitations implicit in their strategy of moderation.

Works Cited

Armstrong, Nancy. *Desire and Domestic Fiction*. New York: Oxford UP, 1987.

Chapone, Hester Mulso. *Letters on the Improvement of the Mind*. Portland, 1806.

Ferguson, Moira. *F.I.R.S.T. Feminists, British Women Writers 1578-1799*. Bloomington: Indiana UP, 1985.

Foucault, Michel. *The History of Sexuality*. Vol. 1. New York: Random House, 1978.

Meakin, Annette. *Hannah More*. London: John Murray, 1919.

Myers, Sylvia Harcstark. *The Bluestocking Circle, Women, Friendship, and the Life of the Mind in Eighteenth-Century England*. Oxford: Clarendon, 1990.

Nussbaum, Felicity. *The Autobiographical Subject*. Baltimore: Johns Hopkins UP, 1989.

Pennington, Montagu, ed. *Letters from Mrs. Elizabeth Carter to Mrs. Montagu between the Years 1755 and 1800*. London, 1817.

Poovey, Mary. *The Proper Lady and the Women Writer.* Chicago: U of Chicago P, 1984.

Rendall, Jane. *The Origins of Modern Feminism: Women in Britain, France, and the United States, 1780-1860.* New York: Schocken Books, 1984.

Staves, Susan. *Married Women's Separate Property in England 1660-1833.* Cambridge: Harvard UP, 1990.

Williamson, Marilyn L. "Who's Afraid of Mrs. Barbauld? The Bluestocking and Feminism." *International Journal of Women's Studies* 3 (Jan./Feb. 1980).

Wollstonecraft, Mary. *Vindication of the Rights of Woman.* 1792. London: Penguin Books, 1982.

Three Generations
of Radical Women's Man-Talk

Women across three generations of radical activity have baffled their male counterparts by the fact of their bonding with each other more firmly than with the mass movement they promised to support. More confounding still is that the locus of this bonding, the meat of their talk, is frequently the very male leaders who are exhorting them to look outward to the revolutionary process in general. By refusing the propaganda of their male leaders, by turning to each other for consolation when love goes awry in relationships with these self-same leaders, women radicals talking to one another about men cast a special light on the inner life of the radical movement and invite unique insights into the relationship between the personal and the political. Furthermore, the meaning of feminine friendship is enhanced when we see women in the context of discussing their lovers and masters, like slaves in the quarters, and adjusting their own relationships to accommodate heterosexual needs. Where does the loyalty lie in the conversations whose supposed subject is the men who dominate these women, when the attachments that seem strongest are among the women themselves? By examining women's man-talk in three novels by women radicals—Meridel Le Sueur's *The Girl*, placed in the 1930s; Doris Lessing's *The Golden Notebook*, set in the British left of the late 1950s; and Marge Piercy's American 1960s radical novel *Small Changes*—I hope to illuminate how man-talk among radical women has served to redefine both women's friendships with each other and women's particular relationship to radical politics.

Meridel Le Sueur's *The Girl* is not set in the radical movement, but Le Sueur was herself an active communist when she wrote the novel, and if she did not exactly follow the dictates of the proletarian realism injunctions prevalent in the party at the time she was writing, she at least listened to them and in her own way, out

133

of her own conscience, adapted an interest in the working class to the definitions of a uniquely feminine style. Le Sueur explained her methodology relating feminine lyricism to proletarian subject matter in an interview with Neala Schleuning:

> I think women have to really make their own language, use their own language. Language has been in the hands of the power structure. This language of women would probably be a subjective language, a language of lyricism, or a language of poetry—a language that will not be sterile. Analysis has become a way of seizing your mind. Now I'm not against analysis of power, but analysis is a way to trap you, to get you to think certain ways, to seduce you, or even rape you. Language has become a rape, a form of psychic rape...
>
> I also think women are afraid to use their language, I know I am! For a long time the woman language was excessive and hysterical. Somebody even told me the other day that I'm a "romantic." That's a put down because I've been called that by too many male editors. (Schleuning 138)

If *The Girl* is not the prime example of Le Sueur's lyrically feminine language that a story like "The Annunciation" may be, its significant aspect, both as a contribution to proletarian literature and for purposes of this discussion, is its emphasis on female bonding in a heterosexual context, even a political context. Unlike the Lessing and Piercy works, *The Girl* is not set in a specifically self-consciously radical milieu. Le Sueur, although herself a communist activist, was living in a women's collective in a warehouse in Minneapolis, much like the one in which the (unnamed) girl gives birth in the story. Naivete, almost painful at times, dominates the consciousness of the principals. They are waitresses and factory workers, hash-slingers and whores. The camaraderie of the women holds the novel together and becomes the locus around which the action revolves. Men enter the picture only in the first third of the novel, and thus their domination even of the women's talk is transitory. But clearly, right from the start, relations among the women, the Girl, Clara, and Belle, eclipse even the cohabitations with the tough guys, Butch and the roustabouts.

The time is the Depression in the Midwest, the 1930s. The Girl, so naive as to be virtually an existential tabula rasa, has gotten a job in a speakeasy with Clara and Belle, strong, knowing women who take her under their wing. The Girl immediately develops a crush on super-prol macho down-and-outer Butch, friend of Belle's husband Hoinck. Right at the beginning of *The Girl*, Le Sueur establishes the relationship between her protagonist and her friend Clara, in the Girl's voice:

> I was lucky to get the job after all the walking and hunting Clara and I had been doing. I was lucky to have Clara showing me how to wander on the street and not be picked up by plainclothesmen and police matrons. They will pick you up, Clara told me and give you tests and sterilize you or send you to the women's prison. I liked to be with Clara and hear about it and now with Belle, who with Hoinck her husband and Ack his brother ran the German Village. It wasn't German but lots of even stylish people came there after hours for the bootleg Belle and Hoinck made. (*The Girl* 1)

Clara, having taken the Girl under her wing, initiates her into the ways of the speakeasy and it is she who takes note of the Girl's infatuation with Butch and makes moves to get them together. Nonetheless, the Girl's infatuation with Butch remains problematical. Her essential relationship abides with Clara. Even smitten with Butch, the Girl comments, "I kept as close to Clara as I could. Something was in her so sure as if she knew everything I would never know" (*The Girl* 1).

Clara clearly mediates between the Girl and men who are interested in her or in whom she is interested. While this never gets to the overt point of conventional prostitutes engaging in lesbian activity, still the point forcibly hammers home that Clara is in charge of the Girl's sexuality, and even the Girl in her timidity recognizes this:

> I had to look at the doors opening in the cold steam and no Butch. You think something happened to him, I shouted to Clara, as we ran past each other with the mugs of beer. She shook her head laughing, her little mouth like a hungry rabbit's. Passing me, she yelled. No news is good news. He'll turn up the bad penny he is. (3)

At that point the Girl is noticed by the gangster/protector Ganz. The Girl turns to Clara in her quandary and again the two women share a bond through their exchange about the men they must deal with:

> I wished he'd ask for me, Clara said. I know, kid, you feel all lighted up if Butch should come in the door but you need butter on your bread and cream in your coffee. Butch can't give you anything but love, baby—here angel, take this to Ganz and she gave me the bowl of Booya [stew]. Look forward, baby, she said, look up. (3)

Slaves talking about their masters or whores about their johns could not be more eloquent about the essential relationship. When Butch does show up, he turns out to be a petty scab and would-be crook, much as Clara has indicated. Never does the Girl talk to Butch about Clara as she talks to Clara about Butch or about their life in general. In point of fact, Butch and the Girl hardly relate to each other meaningfully even in the act of getting together. Clara is the one who puts up the dollar for the hotel room once the sexual inclination drives Butch and the Girl to seek consummation. As Clara says when she intercedes:

> You sure are carrying the torch, she said. O.K. kids I think you ought to take it when it comes. You can remember it kids, stuff like this doesn't come everyday. You don't come to no good end but it'll be short and sweet.
>
> She dug in her sock and brought out a greenback.
>
> Here she blows, kids, and my blessing. She leaned over and I put my arms around her and put my face in her thin neck.
>
> Oh Clara honey, I said, should I?
>
> Go on, kid, she said, remember it.
>
> Come on, sweet, Butch said, you'll remember it. (50)

The upshot is the Girl gets pregnant, even while she acts as moll to Butch's misbegotten heist. Butch dies from a gunshot wound and the Girl places herself once again under Clara's protection. When the baby is born, a girl, Clara has died, leading the Girl to a warehouse sheltering a sort of women's collective. After Clara dies, the baby girl becomes the mascot for the commune, an emblem of the life-giving force in the face of near-starvation conditions that in a hobo-camp would be indicative of dissolution and despair. Sex, love, birth, community and just plain talk save the women in the end, the act of birth becoming an act of solidarity that supersedes male society.

The communist male pundits who accused Le Sueur of defeatism because her characters did not overtly see the necessity of revolution seem to have missed the point that in Le Sueur's work the emblem of birth and the solidarity of women become an even more positive measure of hope than the revolution has turned out to be. Perhaps those male party pundits missed the point because it came too close to home. While Le Sueur never writes about internal party life as do Lessing and Piercy, her work is deeply personally felt and surely relates to her radical experience. It doesn't take much stretching of the imagination to read in the character of Butch the prototype of the proletarian hero that Mike Gold, chief literary theorist, championed in the pages of the *New Masses*, for which Le Sueur sometimes wrote. Considering that the party's work was frequently illegal, often dangerous, and placed its organizers in the role of outsiders, one can easily draw the parallel between the naive happenstance gun moll Girl and the worldly wise Clara and the women who backed up the communist men in the front lines. These women worked to support their men when there were jobs, put out sexually, and frequently foiled the police and FBI, as well as overseeing mailings and painting placards.

Working-class women, they might often, by Le Sueur's own testimony, turn to each other for consolation and advice, sometimes not elegantly or eloquently. Clear in *The Girl* is the underlying sexuality latent in the relationship. Clara has paid the dollar for the Girl's sexual initiation, and Clara officiates at the final ensuing pregnancy. Clara guides, mentors; Butch is little more than a deus ex machina, a sperm bank. The fact is the political nature of Butch's activity, the strike he scabs at, the heist he pulls, even his dream of one day owning his own gas station pale beside the relationship between the Girl and Clara. The solidarity of the women battling starvation to preserve the baby in the end suggests the secondary nature of politic that permeates all three of the books I have chosen to discuss. Le Sueur never disowned the proletariat; indeed, it is my observation that to this day she has not disavowed hope for the proletarian revolution. She finds, however, in the proletariat, especially in the voice of proletarian women, a voice for the repressed, a source of solidarity stronger than the united force of men marching, stronger even than the force of heterosexual partnership.

The bonding and dualism of pairings in *The Golden Notebook* has been discussed by several critics. The very form of the novel itself has been described by those who follow French feminist definitions as distinctively feminine. Shunning linear narrative, Lessing explores the selfhood of her main character, Anna Wulf, in her late 30s, African born, coming of age in the context of the demise of the Communist Party, of which she has been a part. This exploration proceeds through a series of notebooks, which contain stories, dreams, novel fragments and diaries, and which are interspersed with sections, labeled Free Women, which more objectively chart Anna's relationship with her friends/doubles Molly and Saul and her daughter Janet and Molly's son, Tommy. All of them are suffering with the awareness that their god, the proletarian revolution as personified for them by Stalin, has failed, and they must now utilize friendship, therapy, love affairs, motherhood and fiction to sort out what has gone wrong with their world.

In her article "Women and Men in Doris Lessing's *Golden Notebook*: Divided Selves," Gayle Greene suggests that the relationships between men and women in the political milieu Lessing describes are notably more important than the political life of the movement itself. Obviously, considering that every other chapter heading in the Novel is "Free Women," the relations between Anna Wulf and her female friends Molly and Marion even supersede the male relations—as Charmaine Wellington has pointed out. Bearing in mind the context of radical politics, for the most part directed by men, the assertion of female solidarity is all the more startling.

Lessing's protagonist Anna has her mentors in the psychiatrists whose sessions she recounts. She and Molly are equals, more sophisticated and more self-conscious about their lives than Le Sueur's Girl and Clara, but quite possibly never more self-aware of the dynamics of their relationship than are the proletarian pair. They talk about themselves as parallels but the reader must draw conclusions for herself as to the importance to each of them of having the other. Claire Sprague calls attention to this doubling of characters:

> If Ann's other selves are called doubles, then another rich layer of meaning emerges. If these doubles are divided and examined by gender, the results are startling, for the central character conflicts are not between Anna and her female doubles but between Anna and her male doubles. Anna sees herself in her other female selves while she sees men as "others" for almost the entire novel. (Sprague 46)

Anna reflects this doubling among women early on when she says to Molly:

> Both of us are dedicated to the proposition that we're tough...I mean—a marriage breaks up, well, we say, our marriage was a failure, too bad. A man ditched us—too bad we say, it's not important. We bring up kids without men—nothing to it, we say, we can cope. We spend years in the communist party and then we say, Well, well, we made a mistake, too bad. (53)

Anna then shares with Molly her deep pain at being jilted by her lover Michael. But underlying this is the unstated expression that it is even more important to have Molly to share this with. Relationships with men may be transitory, even painfully so, but Anna and Molly are inviolable. Sprague discusses the fact that the women are, as are frequently the men for the women, doubles, as near to being reflections of each other as Poe's William Wilson:

> There is, in short, a complex layer of doubling in The Golden Notebook. That layer includes female/male as well as female/female doubles, mixed as well as same sex doubles. Like the more obvious Free Women/Notebooks overall patterning of the novel, this pattern has its disguises and ambiguities—its meaning is also slippery. But the pattern is there.... We might say that Anna/Saul represent the esoteric content of the novel and Anna/Molly its exoteric content, the content that satisfies the uninitiated. The separation of the two women represents a form of the doubletalk and doublestalk that pervades the novel. ("Doubletalk" 183)

The fact of this doubling aspect and the double talk quality of the dialogue between Anna and Molly, and the fact that the relationship between the two women is never an issue on its own terms make for a curious deflection in the tension of the novel. The inviolability of the relationship puts it out of the realm of the vicissitudes of life with men that Anna and Molly both agree must be shouldered. We know that no relationship will ever mean as much to Anna as the one she has with Molly and yet the coil of their interrelationship is not overtly sexual in terms of acts between themselves but manifests itself in the subliminal titillation of accounts of affairs with men. For all their self awareness about politics and love relationships, the characters do not ask themselves the question, why am I telling *her* this? It is as if Lessing were taking the solidarity of women for granted, even though it is the major subject of her narrative. When Marion tells Anna about her late relationship with Richard, knowing full well that Richard had once made a pass at Anna, she holds nothing back:

> "Anna, I wish I could explain it. It was really a revelation. I thought: I've been married to him for years and years, and all that time I've been—wrapped up in him. Well women are aren't they? I've thought of nothing else. I've cried myself to sleep night after night for years.... The point is, what for? I'm serious Anna." Anna smiled, and Marion went on: "Because the point is, he's not anything, is he? He's not even very good-looking. He's not even very intelligent—I don't care if he is ever so important and a captain of industry. Do you see what I mean?" Well and then: "I thought, My God, for that creature I've ruined my life.... It's humiliating, isn't it Anna?" (Lessing 398)

We have come to the modern linguistic awareness that more goes on with a text (or is it less?) than the surface narrative seems to indicate. By assuming Anna will understand her complaints, Marion implicates Anna as her ally. She seems to know in advance that Anna will not say, but you *should* care about your husband, for whom else do you live. It becomes almost an exasperating undecidable that all the women are on the same wavelength, understand each other perfectly, yet never discuss their own relationships to each other, connect to each other primarily through narration of their relationships with men.

Considering the monumental importance to Anna and her woman friends of their relationships to each other, it remains curious that none of them ever breaks out of the essential trap of attempting to connect to men. As Greene points out: "Anna and Molly admit that their real loyalties are to men and try repeatedly to fit themselves to conventional patterns rather than striking out to create new forms of relationships" (291). In point of fact, Lessing never submits the loyalty between Anna and Molly to the sort of test that would prove that they side with men rather than each other—never do two of the women fall in love with the same man at the same time. Instead, they know they can always count on each other to pick up the pieces when the men they do primarily long to identify with ultimately ditch them.

The women turn to each other as well for consolation after the betrayal of Stalinist politics. In that way they not only make the point that the personal is political and the political is personal, they also establish a communality of feminine personal feeling that replaces and supersedes party activism. In one of her early notebooks, Anna writes:

> Stalin died today. Molly and I sat in the kitchen, upset. I kept saying, "We are being inconsistent, we ought to be pleased. We've been saying for months he ought to be dead." She said: "Oh, I don't know, Anna, perhaps he never knew about all the terrible things that were happening." Then she laughed and said: "The real reason we're upset is that we're scared stiff. Better the evils we know." "Well, things can't be worse." "Why not? We all of us seem to have this belief that things are going to get better. Why should they? Sometimes I think we're moving into a new ice age of tyranny and terror, why not? Who's to stop it— us?" (Lessing 163)

The intrusion of another old comrade, Michael, points up that the problem of grief over the loss of belief can only be shared between the two women. Michael's concern is for the political facts of Stalin's betrayal. Anna and Molly empathize with each other for a personal crisis of faith. Anna and Molly talk to each other as "we"; Michael employs the impersonal passive. We further note in this context that Michael is Anna's man; there is no question of the two women competing for his attention or making points in his behalf to butter him up against each other. Anna may well wind up in his bed consoling him for the loss of faith, but the next time she says "we" she is more likely to refer to herself and Molly. Indeed, after Michael "ditches" her, Anna quite freely takes up primarily with ex-radicals, including an American blacklisted screenwriter, purportedly based on the writer Clancy Sigal. She is loyal to the disloyal, befuddled, betrayed radical men she identifies with—but never as loyal as she is to the women she befriends.

Never, strictly speaking, a feminist in the new generation's usage of that term, Lessing replaces the solidarity of the "Free Women," the loyalty and camaraderie and understanding of feminine relationships, for the belief in communality in a future world that, distorted by Stalinism, has betrayed her generation of ideologues. The "we" that had once been we the people, we the masses, we the party, becomes we free women, we friends. Although sisterhood

142 Communication and Women's Friendships

does not essentially overcome the isolation and fragmentation of the individual, or even the essential hurt of not being able to establish a stable romantic relationship with a man, the fact that these women can always talk to each other about this basic hurt balms the wound inflicted by failed gods. Sisterhood becomes the communality that one had come to believe would very likely never come to pass in the real world.

As the work of Meridel Le Sueur and many women writers of the left attests, there existed a distinction between proletarian realism as descriptive writing and proletarian propaganda or agit prop as writing with a social purpose. Both are the legacy of the new generation, including such femininist writers as Marge Piercy. Proletarian realism as descriptive writing traces its origins to the naturalism of Dreiser, Upton Sinclair, Zola and Gorky, writers who described the proletarian life in order to give it validity and acceptability. It has been felt—it continues to be argued in modern multicultural debates—that no writing can be revolutionary that does not give voice to the experience of the working class and those minorities traditionally excluded from upper-class effete intellectualism. While it is difficult for those with no education or cultural skills to express the variegations of their own lives in sophisticated artistic forms, the celebration of working-class life by sympathetic artists allowed the proletariat to find a point of contact in radical art and writing. The Communist Party, in taking over the journal New Masses, subtly shifted ground from mere expression of working-class life for the purposes of education to education and uplift for the purposes of motivation to action—the essence of propaganda as of advertising. Proletarian propaganda was supposed to show the light of revolution and the dawn of a new age of socialist man at the end of every mill strike depicted. Unity in action became a slogan to be enlivened with real characters, fleshed out with livid plot. Le Sueur herself, although she abandoned ties to her middle-class background to identify with workers and became a bona fide prol on real bread lines during the Depression, always wrote what she saw and knew, not what she felt people should learn to see. For this she may have been branded "defeatist," and because of this she may have taken a back seat and never vied for leadership in the Communist Party with which she may still sympathize. She was always her own woman, finding solidarity more often with other proletarian down-and-out women outside the party than with the front ranks within. It may be for that reason that one does not get from her work the insider's glimpse of party dynamic that one does in Lessing's Martha Quest series as well as *The Golden Notebook*, and from the 1960's work of Marge Piercy.

Piercy's early novel *Small Changes* shows an unexpected parallel to Le Sueur's *The Girl* in that it delineates a relationship between a neophyte, the working class Beth run away from a typically overbearing "good" husband, and the old hand Miriam, who plays the role of Le Sueur's Clara, introducing Beth to the ways of the free love commune in Boston where Beth turns up.

In his article "Are Three Generations of Radicals Enough?: Self-Critique in the Novels of Tess Slesinger, Mary McCarthy and Marge Piercy," Philip Abbott discusses Piercy's more recent, more overtly radical novel, *Vida*. He also, however, discusses the critique of radical politics from a feminist point of view, that is, "the failure of men to acknowledge the humanity of women despite their professions of radical imagination and, to a lesser extent, the failure of women to resist male domination" (613). In his discussion of Piercy, Abbott points out, "In the male-domination critique radical projects and organizations are the projections of male power fantasies and internal political conflict the result of male contests for domination and prestige. Men see women only tangentially or instrumentally related to these activities" (613).

It is true that in *Vida* these power plays come more to the fore than they do in *Small Changes* and, as Abbott points out, Vida herself engages in them, but even in *Vida*, which is a more overtly political novel than *Small Changes*, Abbott notes that Vida complains about meetings of SAW (SDS) that are dominated by sexual posturing and unstated personal concerns. Both Abbott and Vida herself would seem to be complaining in the novel about the femininizing of the male procedures—the intrusion of sexuality and female troubles. They do not question the rightness of the male-dominated procedures themselves, only their contamination by effeminate concerns. In *Small Changes*, which preceded *Vida*, those feminine concerns take the fore, making for a more convincing front stage, with the male rhetoric sounding unconvincingly in the wings.

In comparing *Small Changes* with Le Sueur's *The Girl*, we note that even the locale is similar. With its free love and free drugs, Piercy's commune is more speakeasy than radical enclave and the commune where Beth finally comes out as gay suggests the women's commune in the warehouse Le Sueur depicts during the Depression, where the Girl gives birth. That Piercy's novel is more political—her characters involved in demonstrations and defense committees—may be indicative of the times in which she lives. Piercy has been writing about the New Left since her early SDS days. (I trace her back to articles and poetry in the SDS journal *Leviathan*.) Her sympathetic connection to leading characters who are frequently second-generation radical may well be autobiographical. And yet, because her novels are placed in the fluid, cross-generational collectives of the counter-culture 1960s, they avoid the hothouse in-group exposes of 1930's writers Josephine Herbst and Tess Slesinger and even the hermetic introspection of Doris Lessing. To be sure, Piercy's characters talk a lot and are given to the self-conscious navel-gazing of the post-psychoanalytic generation. Still, when the women get together to talk about men, there is that old slave-quarter solidarity, however garbed in modern attempts at insight.

Beth's initiation to the commune, the scene that cinches her stay there, is actually a female talk-fest with overtones of languorous sensuality. Three women, two from the commune, Miriam and Dorine, along with the newcomer Beth, lie on a feather bed with the sun streaming in a Cambridge window in the collective's house. They talk about their families, their growing up; they are verbally feeling each other out, if not up, stroking each other with interest in each other's vulnerability. Beth keeps the talk going with her naive questioning. Finally Dorine asks Miriam:

Does your family know about Phil and Jackson?

Miriam: Not Jackson. But Phil. He was the scandal of my college years. I used to come running into New York every vacation to see him and my family would start screaming and yelling and carrying on. Oh, how they hated him!

Beth: I don't understand about him....

Miriam: Oh! (She shrugs, running her hand through her heavy hair, tugging on it. Then she smiles widely and sweetly, shaking her head.) It was all the doors in the world opening at once! (Piercy 82)

This last statement impacts double-fistedly. A certain braggadocio to Miriam's reply to Dorine's assertion of independence from her parents through choice of mate reminds us that the two experienced women are capable of rubbing Beth's nose

in her own naivete just as surely as two experienced men might lord
it over a freshman virgin by bragging about their sexual exploits.
Women in male conversations often become pawns of competitive
jockeying, tokens of sexual exchange between the men themselves,
extra-marital devices of titillation. Some of this jockeying underlies
the scene above. The three women in bed, sharing secrets about
their relationships with men, do not obviously suggest an
interpersonal dynamic. Ending as we do with Miriam's arousal
gesture, we see that the three women have been playing perhaps
unconscious games with one another almost as surely as if they had
been caught diddling. The clincher is that this is the last scene in
the Book of Beth; the scene will establish Beth's commitment to the
collective, make her want to stay. Nobody has talked about that,
but the haven from parental dominance, the free love with exciting
men, the offer of shared intimacy with the women will force her
hand and seal her decision.

Reading backwards, we can see foreshadowing in the repeated
women-talk about men of what will become Beth's overt lesbian
decision, a latent but unexpressed, perhaps inexpressible, factor in
both Le Sueur and Lessing. Later, as Beth is firmly established in the
house, Dorine curls up on her bed, with Beth at the foot:

> "Oh, my relationships with men..." she begins. "I don't know
> that I can say they're better. They're shorter. Yeah, you might
> say that now I have short miserable affairs instead of long
> miserable affairs. Sometimes I can see what's coming down in a
> couple of weeks and break it off, instead of letting it go on and
> on like a terminal disease, until the man gets nauseated and ends
> it. I suppose that's some kind of change." She made a face.
> "Nothing I would give a party to celebrate." (Piercy 331)

Dorine's complaint becomes a cautionary tale for Beth. Beth does
not have to go through the experience to the extent Dorine has. It is
enough to hear Dorine's plight, to sympathize from her perch on the
bed, to stroke Dorine verbally and to commiserate. This exchange
will become one of the factors leading Beth to embrace woman-
love.

In point of fact, Miriam's path and Beth's path intersect and
cross over, Miriam making a conventional marriage and leaving the
collective for a house and children where she promptly becomes
frowsy and miserable, Beth becoming more radical in life-style if
not in politics than any of her mentors. Early on in Miriam's

marriage, the two women talk about Miriam's new husband. Miriam says:

> "But I feel good as a woman now. Neil's done that for me. I don't feel like I'm battling all the time in every area of my life. For the first time in my whole life, somebody really loves me. I don't have to fight him, I don't have to be struggling on that front. I can enjoy being a woman. So I can do all kinds of things I never did, like cooking, like baking. And they give real pleasure to people and to me."

> "Why did you get married? Did you really want to?"

> "Yes!" Miriam clasped her hands on the table, leaning toward her. "Oh, yes, Beth, I did! I wanted so badly for some man finally to gamble on me as a woman.... Sometimes I dance around here by myself with joy, Thinking that I'm loved, finally I can love somebody without being charged my soul, without paying in blood." Miriam rose and came around the table to put her hands on Beth's shoulders. "I don't mean to sound egotistical, wrapped up and wallowing in comforts. It's just that it feels so nice to be happy for a change." (Piercy 335-36)

This annunciation reverberates with a double edge. First of all, it is clear, as with Lessing's characters, that Beth is not going to horn in. The relationship between the two women is sacrosanct, inviolable. Painfully enough, it is Beth's hesitation to believe in Miriam's unmitigated joy that is borne out. Moving farther and farther away from the movement politically, working in a defense industry, finally taking off to raise children as a homebody, Miriam will become slatternly around the house and lose Neil to a younger woman from the office in an ersatz soap opera scenario. At the same time, Beth, always sympathetic to Miriam, finds herself alone when it comes to talking about the older woman she falls in love with and with whom she has an affair.

In a final, ultimately poignant scene, Miriam is entirely taken up with asserting that everything is all right between her and Neil:

> "Growing up in a tight so-called happy family, he has fixed ideas about how wives are supposed to act, how I'm suppose to show I love him.... He needs, he wants a quiet, controlled,

contemplative life and that's been hard for me to provide because I'm not naturally that way...."

Beth rejoinders: "Why should anybody provide somebody else with a life? With Wanda—with the commune—we don't provide each other with a life—." (Piercy 501)

But Beth basically cannot get a word in edgewise about Wanda. Miriam herself has come to accept her own conventional marriage as the only relationship worth talking about. It has become her only means of relating to Beth. Men are for Miriam now husbands, as for so many of her new set, the only coin of the realm. Shutting out Beth in the exchange of talk about lovers entails shutting off the intimacy. Politics was never the central arena of conversation for any of these women that relationships had been, but now that Miriam has aligned herself conventionally with a Defense Department spouse, Beth is not even free or especially inclined to discuss her lover Wanda's court case (involving Wanda's Puerto Rican activist ex-husband).

The outcome every radical dreams of and fears is borne out. The working-class girl Beth has stuck to her origins and become a worker-Bolshevik intellectual, more loyal to her class interests than her own family. The middle-class intellectual Miriam has fallen for a line of conventionality, been bought off by toys for the children and new drapes for the living room, and will finally get her comeuppance when the husband who has captured her from the movement abandons her for a young rising starlet. I don't know to what degree Piercy intends such a class scenario, but she does definitely suggest that the relationships among the women are the most important ties, that these ties are ultimately more loyal, if not more binding, than ties to men, even when the primary sexual attachments are to men, and that these ties determine political affiliation more significantly than does establishing the right line in pamphlets and broadsides. In this way, Piercy joins Lessing and Le Sueur in circumventing, through woman-bonding, the fundamental isolation of modern defeatist alienation. Men may be shut out of the picture in the very act of their seeming inclusion; in being the objects of women's talks, they cease being the subjects: in becoming the means to the end of women's bonding, they cease being the ends themselves, they become the machines whereby women act together to effect a communality and loyalty among themselves, to forge a camaraderie to supersede alienation even in a context where the very struggle for collective solutions exacerbates the feeling of isolation of those who have been betrayed by political commitment.

Discussing Lacanian theories of subject/object relationships, Catherine Belsey offers the following observation:

> The displacement of subjectivity across a range of discourses implies a range of positions from which the subject grasps itself and its relations with the real, and these positions may be incompatible or contradictory. It is these incompatibilities and contradictions within what is taken for granted which exert a pressure on concrete individuals to seek new non-contradictory subject-positions. Women as a group in our society are both produced and inhibited by contradictory discourses. Very broadly, we participate both in the liberal-humanist discourse of freedom, self-determination and rationality and at the same time in the specifically feminine discourse offered by society of submission, relative inadequacy and irrational intuition. (598)

The context of Belsey's article is a discussion of ideology in Marxist terms, that is, of bourgeois ideology. In that context, women's retreat from masculine objectivity in a subjectivism that only feminine discourse can provide offers a unique escape from the dominant culture. Similarly, the subjectivism I have been discussing, that to radical women retreating from expected Marxist rhetoric to discuss their men as fair game for exchange among themselves, is a form of rebellion against and resistance to the patriarchal discourse of radical causes. Men as objects of women's talk serve to release women from the subject position that the dominance of masculine values in the radical movement would seem to subordinate them to. Women find their own communality and bonding, a solidarity of sisterhood without necessarily overt lesbianism in exchanging confidences about the men of their lives, and this bonding and solidarity function at a plane more real than all the rhetoric of class unity that bombards them from every male-generated source they are subjected to. Especially now in the shadow of the failure of male-dominated Marxist rhetoric to fulfill the promise of world peace and harmony it proffered, a failure that was becoming evident even at the time Le Sueur, Lessing and Piercy wrote, the reasons for that failure may profitably be examined by raising the question, who was left out? These women answer eloquently to their own men—you weren't listening to us.

Works Cited

Abbott, Philip. "Are Three Generations of Radicals Enough?: Self-Critique in the Novels of Tess Slesinger, Mary McCarthy and Marge Piercy." *The Review of Politics* 53 (1991).

Belsey, Catherine. "Constructing the Subject, Deconstructing the Text." *Feminisms*. Eds. Robyn R. Warhol and Diane Price Herndl. New Brunswick: Rutgers UP, 1991.

Green, Gayle. "Women and Men in Doris Lessing's *Golden Notebook*: Divided Selves." *The (M)other Tongue*. Eds. Shirley Nelson Garner, Claire Kahane and Madelon Sprengnether. Ithaca and London: Cornell UP, 1985.

Le Sueur, Meridel. *The Girl*. Cambridge, MA: West End P, 1978.

Lessing, Doris. *The Golden Notebook*. New York: Bantam, 1981.

Piercy, Marge. *Small Changes*. New York: Doubleday, 1973.

Schleuning, Neala. *America: Song We Sang Without Knowing*. Mankato, MN: Little Red Hen P, 1983.

Sprague, Claire. "Doubletalk and Double Talk in *The Golden Notebook*." *Papers on Language and Literature* 18 (1982).

_____. "Doubles Talk in *The Golden Notebook*." *Critical Essays on Doris Lessing*. Eds. Claire Sprague and Virginia Tiger. Boston: G.K. Hall, 1986.

Wellington, Charmaine E. "Female Friendship in Doris Lessing's Novels." Diss. U of Illinois, 1986.

Female Friendship
in the Contemporary *Bildungsroman*

KATHERINE B. PAYANT

In her review of *During the Reign of the Queen of Persia*, Margaret Atwood stated that the dominant motif in American literature has been the young, male loner leaving his matrix, "lighting out for the territory," having adventures. Atwood further asserts that had a novel like *Moby-Dick* been written from the point of view of Ishmael's mothers and sisters, it would not have been *Moby-Dick* at all, since for them images of Romanticism such as Captain Ahab and whales "have no place except over the mantelpiece" (9). As Atwood says, until the 1960s the novel of initiation in American letters was chiefly a male preserve and female adolescence largely unexplored territory. With a few notable exceptions such as Carson McCullers' *The Member of the Wedding* and Jessamyn West's *Cress Delahanty*, female rites of passage in literature were rare indeed.

Happily, however, since the advent of the women's movement, American literature has seen an outpouring of novels dealing with girlhood, female adolescence, and young adulthood. Some early examples are *Memoirs of an Ex-Prom Queen* by Alix Kates Shulman, *Fear of Flying* by Erica Jong, *Small Changes* by Marge Piercy and *Kinflicks* by Lisa Alther. Though different in superficial ways, all of these books had a common theme: the struggles of a young protagonist to overcome rigid sex roles and to find herself in a patriarchal society which devalues women. Sometimes overtly ideological and usually set in a white middle-class milieu, these feminist *Bildungsromans* explored in a literary format many of the issues of the women's movement.

Since those early days, the novel of initiation has moved in many directions, toward diverse themes. One of the most pervasive motifs in more recent *Bildungsromans* is the role of female friendship in the maturation of the central character. In three novels as disparate in setting as *During the Reign of the Queen of Persia* by Joan Chase, *Rumors of Peace* by Ella Leffland and *The Color Purple*

151

by Alice Walker, the protagonist's relationship with other women—friends, sisters and other female relatives—is a key force in shaping her. In fact, in Walker's novel female friendship or bonding is the key agent of "redemption" (Prescott 67), while in *During the Reign of the Queen of Persia* it is the novel's central theme.

Queen (1983) is set in the 1950s in a rural community in Ohio and has a unique vehicle as narrator(s): the collective vision of four adolescent girls who are sisters and cousins and live together in a female-dominated household. Though in this sense departing from the typical form of the novel of initiation, *Queen* indeed fits the genre because over a period of years from childhood to late adolescence, the girls confront many aspects of adult experience: sexual awakening, relationships between adults and, finally, the death of one of their mothers. The strong bonds between the girls and their aunts and mothers who comprise this extended female family provide the glue holding the family together.

The family is dominated by the grandmother (the Queen of Persia because she owns a Persian rug and acts like a queen). Gram was a rough, capable, yet sensitive farm girl who married for security and hoped for something more. When she receives only children (five girls), from her taciturn, brutish husband and, finally, in middle age, inherits some property to give her security, she spends the rest of her life going to bingo parties and movies. Gram is an unforgettable, indomitable old woman who licked life. Hardly a stereotyped "grandma" and bitter at much of what life dealt her, events in the big farm house revolve around her wishes because she owns the house and enough money to direct her own affairs.

Gram has five daughters, each quite different, whose lives and relationships with men provide the four girls with a blueprint to the adult world and give them an ample education. Aunt Elinor is a stylish New York advertising executive who descends on the farm with flashy clothes and later becomes converted to an optimistic Christian Science faith that Gram scorns. Aunt Rachel cracks dirty jokes and rides her horse across the fields. Aunt May mothers them all while soft Aunt Grace dies with dignity. Aunt Libby cautions the girls to "marry a man who loves you more than you love him." "Don't give it away," she says, like generations of mothers, teaching the girls to fear their sexuality:

> "There's nothing to be done about it," Aunt Libby said...She meant us...being female. She referred to it as...if it was both a miracle and a calamity, that vein of fertility, that mother lode of

passion buried within us, for joy and ruin. "None of us can no more than look at a man and we're having his baby." (35)

Libby speaks incessantly of betrayal, forsaken maidens, babies stabbed with scissors, teaching the girls that "sex was trouble and when a girl was in trouble, sex was the trouble."

Still, Libby is not entirely successful because the girls are fascinated by sex. When the oldest, Celia, turns into a ripe, blossoming beauty the summer of her 14th year, the younger girls watch her necking with her duck-tailed boyfriend:

> Tasting instead Corley's mouth on ours, its burning wild lathering sweetness. In the shaft of light we saw them pressed together, rolling in each other's arms Celia's flowery skirt pulled up around her thighs. His hand moving there.... Our hearts plunged and thudded. At that moment we were freed from Aunt Libby. We didn't care what it was called or the price to be paid; someday we would have it. (26)

Much later, the beautiful Celia, jilted by her doctor-to-be fiancé, sells herself lightly and at 18 marries the next boy who comes along. Near the end of the novel we learn that after moving to Texas she becomes pregnant and takes pills, one of the many casualties of the 1950s and the limited options these years held for young women. The final lesson learned by the girls is that a woman's sexuality can be her doom.

The relationships between the family women are not always warm and peaceful by any means; female bonding does not always mean sisterly love. Hostilities break out between Gram and her daughter Elinor during the pivotal event of the novel, the death of Aunt Grace from cancer. Through the eyes of Celia, Jenny, Anne and Katie, we witness the grinding down of Grace's life and the arguments between Aunt Elinor, the Christian Scientist, who prays for a miracle and Gram who shouts, "All's she wants is to go in peace. Why in God's name won't Ellie let her be?" When Libby asks, "What other hope is there, Momma?" Gram replies, "Sometimes there ain't no hope" (158). Here mother and daughter represent opposing points of views toward faith in God—a sort of sunny religious optimism and a pessimistic anti-religious realism. Nevertheless, despite their fundamental disagreement about life's ultimate questions, the closeness between these women is palpable, just as it is between the girls, who are also sometimes rivals. It is a closeness that the men in the story resent.

As in many recent novels where female bonding is important, the men in this story come off badly. They are mean and weak, like Grandad who spends most of the time in the barn with the cows, or sneering and weak like Uncle Neil, Grace's husband, who resents his wife's love of her family, or kindly and weak, like Uncle Dan, who would much rather be in California, but stays in Ohio in deference to his wife Libby's will. During the later part of his life, Grandad stays in the barn because it is away from the women, the only place on the farm he feels comfortable. At the time of his wife's death, Neil remarks that the trees in the orchard remind him of the family:

> ...some a little apart, on the fringes, a few little tots here and there, the gnarled old crone in the center, and then the five sisters, close together, their slender branches intertwined thrashing in any wind at all, making much ado about nothing. The sawn-off waterlogged stumps he compared to the few men who ever dared approach. (130)

Chase says that the traditional patriarchy was difficult for men as well as for women, because in their shared oppression and lack of power, women often excluded men, who found themselves on the fringes of the family unit. As we shall see, this idea is an important theme of *The Color Purple* as well.

Rosemary Booth says of *Queen*, "As in Eden [and this Ohio farm is a kind of Eden after the Fall], there is ordeal and education, trial and error but also opportunity for transcendence" (406). During Aunt Grace's illness, the girls are stirred to thoughts of immortality:

> We would often see Aunt Grace walking the back farm road, deeply concentrated. Once when we were coming come from the dairy with ice cream, we saw her from the highway against the backlight of the sky, there by the barn hill...and it seemed to us her figure was silhouetted, a shadow, indeed the visible incarnation of a present spiritual being. The newly cut grass was redolent of its raked crop and in the golden and purpling passage of evening light over it we perceived again the incorporeal origins of creation. Aunt Grace seemed to move across the edge of that vast stage as though she were already far beyond us on a quest which had already removed her from us as effectively as death. (141)

The girls share all of these stirring experiences of initiation together, which deepens their felt bonds and cement their emerging characters. Like other recent novels celebrating female bonding between relatives, these ties are, as Toni McNaron says in her study of sisters, pre-verbal and inexpressible, but nevertheless powerful (8). Though female relatives may often be rivals, their passionate bonds are central to their development.

Rumors of Peace (1979) by Ella Leffland confronts an important theme seldom treated by women writers—war, and it was this aspect upon which most contemporary reviewers commented. For example, Elinor Langer states that *Rumors* is one of the few recent women's novels to successfully combine the personal with a larger moral vision, an exploration of the morality of war (35). Set in a small California town, the novel opens with Pearl Harbor and closes with Hiroshima, focusing on the years from 11 to 14 in the life its protagonist, Suse. Through these years, we see Suse confront all the dilemmas of growing up—awakening sexuality, introduction to intellectual ideas and artistic beauty and death, along with the far away drama of World War II. Central to this maturation is her relationship with two friends, sisters and foils, who provide Suse contrasting values with which to develop her larger moral vision.

Until recently, perhaps because of a dearth of subject matter to study, there has been little of a critical nature written of women's friendships in literature. However, a 1981 debate between Elizabeth Abel and Judith Kegan Gardiner sheds some light on the way Leffland portrays female friendship. Abel argued that contemporary novels suggest that the dynamic of female friendship is "commonality" (415). Women are drawn together because of similar interests and values and, in some cases, recognize that despite surface differences they are much the same. In reply to Abel, Gardiner felt that "commonality/complementarity" alternate, with the writer stressing differences between the protagonist and her friend as well as similarities (436-37). The woman compares and contrasts herself with her friend, thereby gaining insights in her life choices. It is clear that in *Rumors* the sisters Peggy and Helena Maria function in this way for Suse.

A major issue confronted in the novel is racism—fear and hatred for those who are different. Suse's town has a sizeable Japanese-American population. At first Suse finds it hard to believe the gentle Nagais, who own the town's flower shop are spies, but soon she becomes infected with the hatred sweeping the community. When she hears the Japanese are being herded into detention centers, she feels such measures aren't enough:

> They had stuffed their wireless sets in the false bottoms of suitcases and baby buggies. They would escape from the camps and spread into the countryside to work from there. It was a measly, pointless move. Those who tried to kill you should be killed. (38)

Suse's friendship with Helena Maria eventually draws her out of her racist fears, but her friendship with Peggy, the younger sister, is also important in deciding the kind of person she wishes to be in her own milieu. Suse becomes close to Peggy first. They swim, play together, exchange confidences. However, as they enter junior high, Peggy becomes socially conscious, clothes conscious and disinterested in school work. She is one of the TOWKs, as Suse calls them (Those Who Count) and independent Suse rejects their values. The friendship of Peggy and Suse disintegrates as Leffland shows us how girls use their peers as guides to setting their own images for themselves. Fortunately, Suse rejects the adolescent herd instinct with few regrets.

Peggy's older sister, Helena Maria, on the other hand, is a bright young woman who encourages Suse to read and explore the world of ideas. She scornfully rejects the values of the TOWKs and points out to Suse the irrationality of her hatred for the Japanese. Helena Maria tells Suse that soldiers don't personally hate each other: on Christmas day during the Battle of Verdun the soldiers came out of the opposing trenches and played soccer with each other. Suse is flabbergasted. "You make it sound like a game," she says. Helena Maria replies that the hatred induced by war is "a scabby hysteria that attacks inferior souls. Cretins. Lynch mobs. Medieval witch hunters. Nonthinkers the lot. That's the company you're in." She gets Suse to admit that the California Japanese aren't really such bad people: "...you can't hate nations, they're only people" (141-42), she says. At this point, though Suse is willing to admit Helena Maria has bested her, she is not ready to give up the satisfying pleasure of her hatred. Symbolic of Suse's hatred is a photo of a dead Japanese soldier she clips from *Life* magazine:

> ...it showed a Jap soldier who had tried to crawl out of his tank and been burned to a crisp. His head stuck out of the turret, skull-like, and covered with tar or black molasses, a few wisps of singed hair hanging over the empty eye sockets. (34)

She treasures this photo for some time, taking it out and staring at it with "enravished loathing," her own private pornography. Suse's pleasure in contemplating the agony of the dead soldier and her objectification of him, represent what is most dark—even evil—in the human soul. The parallel between her reaction to the picture and the later discussion of the atrocities of the Nazi death camps is obvious.

Another important agent of Suse's growth is her first crush on a young German-Jewish man who is dating Helena Maria. Egon Krawitz is mysterious and dark, a refugee from Nazi persecution. Suse knows little of Jews: "But what was a Jew? From Sunday school they were mixed up with bulrushes and date palms, and that's where they were, the Bible" (192). On the advice of Helena Maria, she does some research on Jews and Judaism, which spurs her interest in history and social questions. Previously an indifferent student, she becomes stimulated by new ideas that are obviously connected to her own life, and her intellectual impulses are further stimulated by visiting Helena Maria at Berkeley. She can now see a reason for learning.

Near the end of the war Suse confronts what many would call the ultimate evil, newspaper photos of the Nazi death camps:

> ...on the front page was a mass of white tangled worms, extremely large, with a couple of people standing in them knee deep, each pulling a worm out. Then I saw it wasn't worms they were pulling, but a pair of long arms. (344)

The article continued to discuss prison camps and thousands of Jewish people killed: "Jews, then, that was why Egon had looked as he did yesterday. That was what he meant when he said he didn't think his brothers were in Berlin." This is what racial hatred, like her own hatred of the Japanese can lead to.

At the war's end with the coming of Hiroshima, Suse no longer gloats when she hears of thousands of enemy dead: "Gloating was human nature, there was too much about human nature that set your teeth on edge. Thank God it didn't have to be completely overhauled, an impossible job. Just draw the good out of each person." She welcomes the formation of the United Nations, but realizes that such an organization "smacked of good faith, hard work, and nothing more...it was the spirit behind those things that counted, and that was what we must put our hope in" (356). Though she does not yet realize it, Suse has solidified her own values by forging ties with humanity and rejecting racist ideologies that debase mankind. In large part these changes have come through her friendships with other girls, especially Helena Maria. Like *The Color Purple, Rumors of Peace* says that love redeems and hatred kills, and the love and guidance young women provide each other can provide that redemption.

Alice Walker in *The Color Purple* (1982), set in the rural South from around 1916-42, also uses female friendship as her central theme. The protagonist Celie, whom we follow from age 14 to middle age, finds independence, hope and finally transcendence through her love of women—a friend and lover, her sister and other women in the rural African-American community.

At age 14 Celie is raped by the man she believes to be her father (later we find he is her stepfather); she has two babies by him whom he gives away to a childless couple. Always told she is ugly and stupid—"You black, you pore, you ugly, you a woman, you nothing at all" (187)—she is married off to Albert, a widower with four children who looks at her as a sexual convenience and drudge. The only way Celie can endure her bleak situation is to numb herself to feeling: "You a tree," Celie says to herself as Albert beats her, "That's how I know trees fear men" (30).

Celie's first important friendship is with Sofia, a strong, feisty and independent-minded girl who marries Harpo, one of Albert's children. Although Sofia and Harpo love each other, Harpo has been imbued with the idea that a woman should mind her husband and, if she doesn't, he should beat her. Harpo tries several times to bend Sofia to his will but fails while Celie watches with wonderment at the unthinkable—a woman who fights back. Sofia and Celie form a close friendship as they work together on the farm, quilting or canning, exchanging ideas about marriage and the lot of women. With a role model like Sophie, Celie begins to believe that she need not accept her fate with such resignation. It seems that Celie sees the "complementarity" of her character with that of Sophie and begins to work toward having more in common with her. She too becomes feisty.

The situation changes rapidly with the coming of Albert's lover, Shug Avery (short for Sugar), a local blues singer, who is suffering from a "nasty women's disease." At first Celie meekly nurses Shug, impressed by her strength and glamour, but slowly a friendship grows between the women which completely shuts out Albert. Like Sofia, Shug is a strong woman who chooses her men and never lets them "mess with her." She treats Celie with love and respect, teaches her to love and respect herself and introduces her to sexuality, a feeling unknown to Celie. Eventually they become occasional lovers although the sexual relationship means more to Celie than it does to Shug. Shug protects Celie from Albert's beatings, showing how stronger women can help their weaker sisters and helps Celie muster the will to tell Albert off. This she finally does when she discovers he has been hiding her sister Nettie's letters: "You a lowdown dog....It's time to leave you and enter into the Creation. And your dead body just the welcome mat I need" (181).

As Leffland does in *Rumors of Peace*, Walker shows how women help each other in spiritual quests, certainly a new idea in our culture. Except for Helen Burns who helps Jane Eyre in her early spiritual development, one can think of few examples of female friendship in literature functioning in this way prior to recent times. In *The Color Purple* Shug's most important gift to Celie is to help her know God, who for Shug means all that is lovely and fun in life. When Celie tells her God is an old white man, Shug replies that God is everything, and God loves all human feelings that are joyful. "God loves admiration," Shug says, meaning admiration for the Creation. "I think it pisses God off if you walk by the color purple in a field somewhere and don't notice it" (178). At that point, Celie begins to notice "the color purple." There is further suffering in the story; sometimes having feelings is terribly painful, and Celie suffers greatly when Shug goes off for a last fling with a 19-year-old boy, but Celie's new maturity and strength help her to weather the unhappy times.

Equally important as her relationship with Shug Avery is Celie's tie with her sister, Nettie. During their childhood Celie must protect the younger and prettier Nettie from the sexual advances of their stepfather. Shortly after Celie's marriage the sisters become separated when Albert has his eye on Nettie. Nettie leaves the community and lives with the couple who have adopted Celie's two children. Eventually she leaves the country with this couple and becomes a missionary in Africa.

Nettie's letters from Africa and Celie's back to Nettie are an important avenue of growth for both women and hold them together until they are reunited at the end of the novel. This epistolary form, seldom used by contemporary writers, is an important and unusual feature of the novel and is particularly suitable for a novel of development. Celie's early letters are addressed to God, the only "man" Celie does not fear (and the only one she is unashamed to speak to). The letters between Celie and Nettie comprise the latter part of the novel. Through them, we can clearly see Celie's intellectual and emotional changes.

At the beginning Celie is naive and inarticulate, yet sensitive and observant; as her story progresses her voice becomes stronger and wiser, crackling with wry wit made more pointed by her black dialect. Nettie's letters are less arresting, written in standard English and full of preachy commentary on the fate of African blacks at the hands of the colonialists. With Nettie, we do not see, as we do with Celie, the emergence of a mature woman from a weak, shy adolescent.

Although these letters of Nettie's from Africa are the weakest part of the novel, they reinforce a theme treated in the section of the novel dealing with African-American women. Walker says that shared mistreatment of women at the hands of their men contributes to women's bonding, as does their shared work, another aspect of their oppression. In Africa, the wives who share a husband often become fast friends with their lives centered around work and their children and other women. Walker's point is obvious—women's friendships with each other are more important sources of warmth, human contact and avenues to growth than are their relationships with men.

For Walker, these close friendships of black rural Southern women, and indeed women around the world, are nothing short of redemptive. Through Sofia, Shug and Nettie's letters, Celie learns to love, to feel, to sense beauty, to transcend her everyday existence, even to forgive Albert who, by losing Shug and Celie, learns to love too. As Peter Prescott says of *The Color Purple* the novel contains a basic theme of most great literature: "love redeems, meanness kills" (67). The end of the novel finds Celie, Shug and Albert on the front porch back home waiting for Nettie to arrive with Celie's two grown children.

Since each of these novels stresses the importance of other girls and women to the maturation of the protagonist, examining the function of males in that maturation can provide further insights into each novel. Here we find striking differences: *Rumors of Peace* takes a decidedly positive view of the function of males, whereas in the feminist *The Color Purple* until the end of the novel the male sex (perhaps one could say the patriarchy) is a destructive force.

Unlike obviously feminist novels, *Rumors of Peace* does not concentrate on difficulties of growing up absurd and female in modern society, as does *Memoirs of an Ex-Prom Queen*. In fact,

Suse is an anomaly in the American literature of adolescence, quite unlike Holden Caulfield, Huck Finn or the heroines of early feminist novels (Hoffman 46). Their experiences highlight the corruption and insanity of adult society, whereas Suse's story "retrieves and illuminates the dappled variety of ordinary experience" (46). Life is essentially beautiful at its core, the possibilities for human happiness are great, and men are not agents of oppression, but simply human beings of various types whom Suse comes to know and sometimes to love. Similarly, traditional sexual roles are not seen as particularly burdensome.

The Color Purple also stresses the "dappled variety" of the pleasures of ordinary experience and the redeeming qualities of love, but these pleasures and redemption are achieved exclusively through love and friendships between women. Men in this novel are the enemy, "predators at worst, idle at best" (Prescott 67). When Celie separates from Albert she says, "One good thing bout the way he never do any work round the place, us never miss him when he gone." In its portrayal of the relationships between women and men, *The Color Purple* could be seen as a kind of African-American, rural *The Women's Room* albeit with more warmth, wit and optimism. Several critics have seen this portrayal of male characters as a serious failing of the novel, while otherwise praising its warmth and use of African-American dialect: "The humor, heroism, and endurance of the women are constantly extolled—and contrasted with the foolishness, selfishness, and often, the sheer brutality of the men" (Towers 36). On the other hand, other critics have praised Walker for her courage in raising the issue of the treatment of black women by black men, a topic few African-American writers have touched because of fear of reinforcing racial stereotypes (Watkins 7).

Joan Chase's attitude toward men in *During the Reign of the Queen of Persia* is harder to characterize. Although most of the male characters, as previously stated, are weak or even brutish, they aren't intrinsically bad. Their bad qualities seem more the result of the patriarchy which gives men physical and economic power over women, but in turn causes women to fight back with feminine wiles or by banding together to exclude their men from domestic matters. Thus we get the war between the sexes that is so obvious in the farmhouse—between Gram and Grandad and the five sisters and their husbands. Finally, though, in this house full of women, men simply don't matter very much. This is a story about female relationships, and the men occupy only the background of this theme.

Mary Gordon, another contemporary novelist who has written extensively of women's friendships, has stated that we have little romance or lore of female friendship in our culture (31). World literature since the tale of David and Jonathan has been full of tales of close male friendships, establishing a mythology which can be seen in our popular culture in the many "buddy" films from Hollywood. However, the women's movement seems to have wrought a change: Besides the novels discussed above and others like them, in recent years we have seen a number of popular films featuring women's friendships, among them *Beaches* and *Thelma and Louise*. Whereas in the past women were often portrayed in the culture as rivals, usually for the affections of a man, today we see themes emphasizing the gifts women give each other. One of the most exciting developments in contemporary literature by women has been this exploration of the bonds of enduring female friendship, especially its central importance in the development of a young protagonist. Such books have given thousands of women new insights into their experiences, as they ponder their own youths and come to realize how much they owe their friends.

Works Cited

Abel, Elizabeth. "(E)Merging Identities: The Dynamics of Female Friendship in Contemporary Fiction by Women." *Signs* 6 (1981).

Atwood, Margaret. "Romantic Idealism—Barnyard Realism." Rev. of *During the Reign of the Queen of Persia* by Joan Chase. *New York Times Book Review* 12 June 1983.

Booth, Rosemary. "The Presence of Grace." Rev. of *During the Reign of the Queen of Persia* by Joan Chase. *Commonweal* 15 July l983.

Chase, Joan. *During the Reign of the Queen of Persia*. New York: Harper, 1983.

Gardiner, Judith Kegan. "The (US)es of (I)dentity: A Response to Abel of '(E)Merging Identities.'" *Signs* 6 (1981).

Gordon, Mary. "Women's Friendships." *Redbook* July 1976.

Hoffman, Eva. "Growing Pains." Rev. of *Rumors of Peace* by Eva Leffland. *Saturday Review* 1 Sept. 1979.

Langer, Elinor. "Whatever Happened to Feminist Fiction?" *New York Times Book Review* 4 Mar. 1984.

Leffland, Ella. *Rumors of Peace*. New York: Harper, 1979.

McNaron, Toni. *The Sister Bond: A Feminist View of Timeless Connection*. New York: Pergamon, 1985.

Prescott, Peter. "A Long Road to Liberation." Rev. of *The Color Purple* by Alice Walker. *Newsweek* 21 June 1982.

Towers, Robert. "Good Men Are Hard to Find." Rev. of *The Color Purple* by Alice Walker. *New York Review of Books* 12 Aug. 1982.

Walker, Alice. *The Color Purple*. New York: Washington Square P, 1982.

Watkins, Mel. Rev. of *The Color Purple* by Alice Walker. *New York Times Book Review* 25 July 1982.

Women's Community and Survival in the Novels of Louise Erdrich

JULIE THARP

...The old women sit patiently in a circle, not speaking. Each set of eyes stares sharply into the air or the fire. Occasionally, a sigh is let loose from an open mouth. A Grandmother has a twitch in the corner of her eye. She rubs her nose, then smooths her hair.

The coffee is ready. Cups are brought from a wooden cupboard. Each woman is given the steaming brew. They blow on the swirling liquid, then slurp the drink into hungry mouths. It tastes good. Hot, dark, strong. A little bitter, but that is all to the good.

The women begin talking among themselves. They are together to perform a ceremony. Rituals of old women take time. There is no hurry. (Brant 15)

This excerpt from Beth Brant's *Mohawk Trail* sheds light on the traditional women's community of her Native origins. Within the old traditions of the Longhouse, Brant finds a spirituality grounded within the Grandmothers' gathering to honor life, to honor one another as sources of life and healing. The women speak very little, but smile, laugh and sing, kiss and hug one another during the ritual. They need few words because the significance of their gathering is understood. She ends "Native Origin" with this: "The Grandmothers gather inside the Longhouse. They tend the fire" (17). Female community signifies the life of the people, their survival in spirit as well as in body.

In *Mohawk Trail* this kind of community seems almost wholly a way of the past; Brant offers only one notable example of contemporary women's friendship, within a lesbian bar in Detroit, Michigan. The women there cling to one another as family because of legal and social difficulties in creating or maintaining other kinds of families. And, indeed, throughout Native American women's literature, the lack of women's gatherings like that depicted in

165

Brant's "Native Origin" is conspicuous. Within the novels of Louise Erdrich, friendships between women are rare, much less formalized or ritualized. In *Love Medicine* the two powerful grandmothers, Lulu Nanapush Lamartine and Marie Lazarre Kashpaw, are intense rivals throughout most of the novel. In *Tracks* Pauline and Fleur are divided by their contrasting loyalties to assimilation and tradition. *The Beet Queen*, alternatively, narrates the friendship between Mary Adare and Celestine James, a friendship that can, however, only exist because of the women's particular circumstances. As Erdrich carefully points out in all of her novels, the circumstances that made life felicitous for her ancestors have been disrupted and distorted in contemporary Native culture. There are clear historical reasons for the shift from the powerful women's groups depicted in Brant's story to the isolated women in Erdrich's novels.

Paula Gunn Allen connects the dispersal and dissolution of women's communal power to the waning of Native power, saying:

> ...the shift from gynecentric-egalitarian and ritual-based systems to phallocentric, hierarchical systems is not accomplished in only one dimension. As LeJeune understood, the assault on the system of woman power requires the replacing of a peaceful, nonpunitive, nonauthoritarian social system wherein women wield power by making social life easy and gentle with one based on child terrorization, male dominance, and submission of women to male authority. (40-41)

Allen locates four sites of change in the historical acculturation efforts of the federal government and of early missionaries: a change in religion that replaces female deities like White Buffalo Woman and Grandmother Spider with a male creator; a movement from egalitarian tribal government to hierarchical, male centered government; economic conversion from self-sufficiency to government dependency; and a shift from the clan system to the nuclear family system. The first change alters inner identity, cutting the individual loose from spiritual grounding within a matrifocal system and replacing that with the abstract notions of patriarchal dominance; individuals cease to recognize the "Grandmother powers that uphold and energize the universe" (Allen 203). The movement from tribal to hierarchical government discredits women's political alliances in favor of one representative who needs to be male to interact with the federal government. The spiritual basis for tribal government is erased.

Converting from familial self-sufficiency to wage labor further increases the perceived power of the men, since they frequently earn the money to support the family, while women remain at home with the children. This movement intersects with the breakup of clan units (often matrilocal) and the subsequent isolation within nuclear families which Nancy Bonvillain argues "results in the isolation of women within small households, exacerbated by their husbands' absence from home. Work which previously had been shared between spouses today falls exclusively to women" (11), and, Allen would add, to lone women rather than to groups of women laboring together. Marie Kashpaw, Lulu Lamartine and Zelda Kashpaw, for instance, all from *Love Medicine*, are depicted almost exclusively in their homes, often in their kitchens, husbands absent. Both the nuclear family household and wage labor isolate women from one another.

Acculturation to Anglo-American gender typing seems inevitable within these shifts. Citing both Patricia Albers and Paula Gunn Allen, Rebecca Tsosie argues that traditional Native gender roles were flexible and adaptive: "the ideal relationship between male and female [was] complementary and based on principles of individual autonomy and voluntary sharing. Because of this ethic, Albers claims that the concept of male 'dominance' was meaningless for the traditional Sioux" (Tsosie 5). Molding the man into patriarch, however, and further dividing chores more strictly between men and women, replicates Anglo notions of gender as differential and hierarchical, notions that have, further, bred institutionalized control of women. Allen notes that battered wives and "women who have been raped by Indian men" are no longer rare (Allen 50). Bonvillain's research concurs in this assessment and Erdrich illustrates it in *The Beet Queen* when Isabel Pillager marries a Sioux and moves to South Dakota:

> We hear she has died of beating, or in a car wreck, some way that's violent. But nothing else. We hear nothing from her husband, and if she had any children we never hear from them. Russell goes down there that weekend, but the funeral is long past. He comes home, telling me it's like she fell off the earth. There is no trace of her, no word. (BQ 100)

Although Isabel is a powerful woman, niece of Fleur Pillager and foster mother to her siblings after the death of their mother, she too can be swallowed up by domestic violence and utterly forgotten within a culture that once honored strong women. King Kashpaw of *Love Medicine* beats his wife with astounding regularity, emulating mainstream Anglo notions of male gender, as Nora Barry and Mary Prescott point out in their article on Native American gender identity.

Because of reservation land allotments, women have been and often are geographically distant from one another. Rather than living in closely knit villages with an interdependent network of kin and friends, people live miles apart and gather occasionally. The very struggle to keep land often tore families and friends apart. Erdrich dramatizes this in *Tracks* when Margaret and Nector Kashpaw use all of the money saved to pay for Fleur Pillager's land allotment to instead pay for their own. Once close friends, Margaret and Fleur are wedged apart over the struggle for newly limited resources.

Within all three of Erdrich's novels heterosexuality either threatens to or does divide women. Pauline's sexual jealousy of Fleur keeps the women wary of one another and creates a vindictive streak within Pauline. Marie and Lulu cannot speak to one another as long as Nector lives. In *The Beet Queen* Erdrich deconstructs the heterosexual unions that disrupt female community. Neither Mary Adare nor Celestine James fits the stereotypical gender notions formulated within American popular culture and they, therefore, have a difficult time attracting men (not that they seem to care much). Mary at one point considers a relationship with Russell Kashpaw. She invites him to dinner with less than lustrous results:

> He looked at me for the first time that night. I'd drawn my eyebrows on for the evening in brown pencil. I'd carefully pinned my braids up and worn a black chiffon scarf to set off my one remarkable feature, yellow cat eyes, which did their best to coax him. But I don't know coaxing from a box lunch. (65)

When Russell lets her know that he would be interested in Sita Kozka (blond, thin and pretty), if anyone, and then later makes a joke of her touching him, Mary concludes: "I was cured, as though a fever had burned off. One thought was clear. I would never go out of my way for romance again. Romance would have to go out of its way for me" (68). Because the experience is humiliating, from that point on Mary concentrates instead on her relationship with Celestine, one which affirms her "as is."

Celestine more obviously deconstructs the romantic ideology that influences both women when Karl Adare seduces her. It is quite possibly Celestine's non-stereotypical female beauty that attracts the bisexual Karl to her in the first place. She is taller than he and stronger; her face is "not pretty" (114). Celestine evaluates the encounter through reference to the romance magazines she has read. (She "never had a mother to tell [her] what came next" [115].) When Karl gives her a knife demonstration after their love-making, she ponders her expectations: "So, I think, this is what happens after the burning kiss, when the music roars. Imagine. The lovers are trapped together in a deserted mansion. His lips descend. She touches his magnificent thews. 'Cut anything,' he says..." (117). In a capitalist society the lover is ultimately a vendor looking for a quick sale. Karl does leave quickly, but he returns and this time Celestine asks him to leave: "In the love magazines when passion holds sway, men don't fall down and roll on the floor and lay there like dead. But Karl does that" (121). Rather than boldly declaring his love and ravishing Celestine in the true fashion of the male hero, Karl passes out. Celestine's worldly assessment reveals both self-irony for having read the "love magazines" and a cynicism about popular culture versions of reality.

Months later she thinks, "Something in this all has made me realize that Karl has read as many books as I, and that his fantasies have always stopped before the woman came home worn out from cutting beef into steaks with an electric saw" (122). Clearly the reason his fantasies and hers stopped short is because this reality defies the conventions of gender roles and romance. No heroine should be working as a butcher, and no hero should lie around the house all day. Celestine finds that heterosexual love does not live up to its reputation. It makes her feel like a "big, stupid heifer" (123). It is further made unattractive to her because it comes between her and Mary, who "talks around [her], delivers messages through others. I even hear through one of the men that she says I've turned against her" (122). Almost immediately after getting rid of Karl, Celestine calls to tell Mary.

When both women repudiate the expectations of romance and its attendant gender roles, they return with perhaps greater loyalty to their friendship and ultimately to themselves. In an interview with Joseph Bruchac, Erdrich speaks of writing for her daughters and sisters: "I have an urgent reason for thinking about women attuned to their power and their honest nature, not the socialized nature and the embarrassed nature and the nature that says, 'I can't possibly accomplish this'" (Bruchac 82). Neither obstinate, eccentric Mary nor fierce Celestine could be said to give up one ounce of their own power, except in their catering to Dot.

When Celestine gives birth to Dot, the two women find a mutual fixation. Mary continually tries to insinuate herself as a co-parent, although Celestine guards the right to herself. In the baby, Celestine finds a passion "even stronger than with Karl. She stole time to be with Dot as if they were lovers" (157). For Mary, Dot is a small version of herself. The two women quarrel over parenting issues, even behave as jealous rivals, but ultimately act as co-parents to the child. They create a family. Toward the end of the novel when they are both aging, they behave like an old married couple, sleeping together at Sita's house, conspiring together, griping at each other and even reading each other's thoughts.

The two women can also be close to one another because of their economic self-sufficiency. Mary owns and runs the "House of Meats" and Celestine works there, enabling them to set their own timetables and living arrangements. They need not depend on men for money. Instead they hire men. They also work very hard, however, perhaps resembling Celestine's grandmothers in their butchering of animals and preparation of foods. The infant Dot is propped in a shopping cart instead of a cradleboard. Their work literally feeds the community.

Their kinship network, while geographically apart, is interdependent—Sita Kozka, Russell Kashpaw, Wallace Pfeff, Karl Adare, Mary, Celestine and Dot all comprise a clan of sorts that is notable in its tenuous connection to larger communities like the town of Argus or Turtle Mountain Reservation. Karl—a drifter—has no family whatsoever beyond this group. Sita would like to claim the beau monde of the Midwest (if that's not oxymoronic), as her community, but even a Minneapolis department store clerk snubs her. Wallace, entrepreneurial spirit of Argus, is marginalized by his sexuality. His bogus deceased fiancee is a secret that forever thwarts genuine interaction with the other townspeople. Russell, though canonized by the local museum for his war exploits, would not be welcome within one of the local families. He only returns to the reservation permanently as an invalid. These characters cannot or will not conform to community expectations of gender, ethnicity or sexuality. Within this marginalized group, the two female parents and their child form a core, a familial center from which to grow. Their dual mothering is attractive to the many characters who lack a mother themselves. The lone child of the many adults is their "dot" of hope for the future.

Erdrich, in the interview with Bruchac, poses a question shortly after her comment about women's power that provides a useful entry into this dilemma and that has everything to do with women's community within her three novels. She says, "There's a quest for one's own background in a lot of this work...All of our searches involve trying to discover where we are from" (83). Although Erdrich does not specify here, background almost inevitably signifies "mother" for her characters. While many characters of *Love Medicine* and *Tracks* have lost their mothers through hardship or acculturation (I will say more on this later), the mothers of *The Beet Queen* are denied or renounced.

Both Karl and Mary renounce their mother for having left them stranded at the fairgrounds. Mary goes so far as to send word to her mother that her children starved to death. For Mary this solution seems plausible since she so readily plants herself within the new home in Argus. Karl, however, becomes completely unbalanced, helplessly relying upon any woman who will mother him as Fleur does when she finds him on the side of the railroad track and as Celestine does when she takes him in. He has no roots, only the branch he tears off the tree in Argus. Sita too renounces her own mother, identifying instead with her elusive aunt.

Mary and Celestine in fact first cement their friendship around their lack of parents. Asked about her mother and father, Mary responds, "They're dead," and Celestine answers, "Mine are dead too" (30). Sita observes that suddenly the two girls seemed very much alike, with "a common sort of fierceness" (30). The fierceness would seem to arise out of their motherless status. Forced to rely upon themselves, they develop an aggressive edge. In a sense, the two are grounded in their lack of a mother, perhaps the only coping strategy available to them and certainly better than Karl's strategy. Nonetheless, the ruling element of the novel is air, suggesting just how disconnected these characters are. Paula Gunn Allen develops the concept of grounding:

> Among the Keres, "context" and "matrix" are equivalent terms, and both refer to approximately the same thing as knowing your derivation and place. Failure to know your mother, that is, your position and its attendant traditions, history, and place in the scheme of things, is failure to remember your significance, your reality, your right relaionship to earth and society. It is the same as being lost...not confined to Keres Indians; all American Indian Nations place great value on traditionalism. (210)

Failure to know one's actual mother within Erdrich's novels is a metaphor for failure to grasp one's own significance within tribal traditions, within history. For women in particular, who lose all status within Anglo patriarchal traditions, it is a failure to embrace your own power. Celestine and Mary do not simply deny their mothers, however; they also create themselves in their own images of mother. Because Celestine did not know her mother well enough to carry on her traditions, and actually finds that her mother's heterosexual lifestyle does not suit her in any event, she becomes the mother she wanted. Mary rejects her distant self-centered mother and becomes an overprotective, indulgent mother. Both women are creating, from scratch, a family that can survive the harshness and sterility of Argus, North Dakota. Nevertheless, their lack of a women's tradition, of clan wisdom, leads to many mistakes in their mothering as Wallace Pfeff points out and as Celestine surmises.

In an article entitled "Adoptive Mothers and Thrown-Away Children in the Novels of Louise Erdrich," Hertha D. Wong describes in great detail the manner in which Erdrich develops complex mother/child relationships to dramatize the destruction of traditional family identities and the present need for maternal nurturance. That nurturance would not have been provided only by women in the past but rather by the entire tribe. Wong concludes that:

> Erdrich's novels, then, transcend easy categories of gender and ethnicity, reflect both Native American and Euroamerican influences, and extend Western notions of mothering. Mothering can indeed be a painful process of separation; it might be the necessarily insufficient dispensation of grace. But mothering can also be a communal responsibility for creating and maintaining personal identity. (191)

Whatever Celestine and Mary's faults, they maintain Dot's identity, try to mother Sita and create a familial context for the men in their kinship network, men who are otherwise isolated. They take on the responsibility of mothering that the other characters either ignored or lost. Without each other, however, it is doubtful if the two women could even sustain that.

As Wong points out, Nanapush, in *Tracks*, is a nurturing figure in the tribal tradition of communal parenting, but his nurturing is put to harsh tests when he loses his entire family one by one, his land and ultimately his way of life. Although both lyrical novels, *Tracks* and *Love Medicine* are firmly situated within historical events. Julie Maristuen-Rodakowski confirms the historical accuracy of Erdrich's depiction of the Turtle Mountain Reservation in North Dakota and their rapid assimilation to American culture. Maristuen-Rodakowski notes in particular the strong bicultural nature of this reservation, bred as it is from both Ojibwa and French trapper/traders. She also maps out a genealogical chart of the characters, illustrating how central family is within these works, that the reader should even be capable of drawing a detailed chart, and suggesting that such a chart is necessary for comprehension of the families' complex interrelationships (Wong's article contains a less detailed genealogical chart). The almost obsessive concern with family origins within *Love Medicine* and *Tracks* seems in part to arise from the characterization and status accorded to each family—largely the Kashpaws, Nanapushes and Pillagers on the clearly Chippewa side and the Lamartines, Lazarres and Morrisseys on the more French, mixed blood side, the latter holding far less worth in most characters' eyes.[1]

Another factor in this obsession is the mystery surrounding the parentage of many characters. Pauline, for example, hides her identity as Marie's mother after her liaisons with Napoleon Morissey result in the child's birth. Fleur is raped by three men, so literally does not know which man fathered Lulu. The destruction of Fleur's family leaves her orphaned; the removal of Lulu to a government boarding school divides her from her mother; because of Pauline's entrance into the Catholic order she leaves Marie with Sophie Lazarre. In *The Beet Queen* Adelaide Adare hides her children's father's identity until his death. For her, sexual license is not so much a choice made out of desire but rather one made out of economic necessity; her economic desperation leads to her abandonment of the children. Throughout all three novels families are both created and torn apart by economic, spiritual and social upheaval. Those same changes separate the women, who, together, could and eventually do resist their force.

The mothers of the two families most extensively portrayed within *Love Medicine* both obscure origin in their own ways, I would argue, because their own origins are problematic for them. Marie Lazarre Kashpaw raises, in addition to her own children, many stray and orphaned babies on the reservation, June Morrissey and Lipsha Morrissey to name two; to Lipsha she says only that his mother would have "drowned him in the slough" if she had not taken him in, a patent falsehood, as he learns later in the novel. Lulu Nanapush gives birth to eight sons and one daughter, all of different fathers and none fathered by the man she was married to the longest and whose name several bear. Both women redefine notions of the nuclear family. Marie's elastic household forms a kind of clan unit. In Lulu's many partners lies a deconstruction of the patriarchal family and Christian monogamy.

Nora Barry and Mary Prescott, in discussing the holistic vision of gender in *Love Medicine*, imply that Marie and Lulu act as facilitators to that holistic vision, Marie because she is "a blending of two complementary gender based traditions. Her life includes risk, transformation, householding, and medicine, as well as an integration of past and present" (127). Speaking of Lulu, they write that she is "a worthy adversary because she is as effective at complementarity as Marie is. The two characters mirror one another in their role as mother, in their ability to take risks, in their way of blending past and present, and in their wielding of power in old age" (129). Clearly it is because they resist gender bifurcation and emulate gender complementarity that they can become powerful in their old age, speaking as Grandmothers of their clans. Still, while separate, they are unable to create an empowering matrix for these children.

In the role of Grandmother they are able to mediate various Anglo institutions. Marie rejects the "deadliness of the convent" in favor of life (Barry 128) and Lulu remains mindful of the "conflict between old values and the influences of the white standard of economic success" (129). One mother serves as a mediator between her people and white religious ideology, answering a call to the convent and just as quickly rejecting it when she confronts the violence of Sister Leopolda. The other mother mediates commodity culture, calling the "tomahawk" factory proposed to be built on the site of her house "dreamstuff."

Marie and Lulu also unite the two family groupings—Chippewa and French—the historical discord between which has eased Anglo appropriation of land. Marie seeks to deny the French/Catholic side and embrace traditional Native culture. Even so, her healing powers are associated with Catholicism. She is truly a sister of mercy in caring for orphaned children and in attending to Lulu. Even though that power is not exclusive of Native identity by any means, here it carries Catholic overtones. Lulu seeks to deny her Native/traditionalist mother and ignore her Nanapush/father's teachings and marries the French Lamartine. Ironically she is only a good Catholic in her fecundity. The fact that her boys all have different fathers reveals her innate attachment to her rebellious mother.

These two women, however, who have so much in common and could become powerful allies, can only come together after Nector dies, suggesting that heterosexuality as it has been influenced by Anglo culture takes priority over women's community and therefore divides women and dissipates tribal strength.[2] Once the women have become fast friends Lipsha reports to Gerry Nanapush that Lulu had "started running things along with Grandma Kashpaw. I told him how she'd even testified for Chippewa claims and that people were starting to talk, now, about her knowledge as an old-time traditional" (268). Women's friendship here signifies tradition and resistance to acculturation, but Lulu and Marie's friendship also reunites the characters with their own pasts, with their mothers, ultimately with their tribal past.

Tracks takes up the subject of displaced origins from early in the novel when Fleur conceives Lulu. The complexity is well expressed in Nanapush's decision to give Fleur Pillager's daughter his and his deceased daughter's names, not knowing what to tell Father Damien since the father was unknown:

> There were so many tales, so many possibilities, so many lies.
> The waters were so muddy I thought I'd give them another stir.
> "Nanapush," I said. "And her name is Lulu." (61)

The muddy waters originate with speculation, particularly about Fleur's relationship to the water monster in Lake Matchimanito. Like her mother, Lulu is stigmatized for her unconventional sexuality, but they both see through the hypocrisy of others. When the townspeople jeer Lulu at a town meeting, she offers to enlighten everyone as to the fathers of her children, an offer the people decline.

Lulu's "wild and secret ways" are an obvious legacy from her mother Fleur Pillager, one of the last two surviving Pillagers, a wild and powerful family living far back in the bush. The Pillagers know the ways to "cure and kill." Lulu rejects her mother—Nanapush's narrative is in part his attempt to explain Fleur's actions to Lulu— but in fact Lulu greatly resembles her mother in her ability to stand up to the current notions of "progress" and in her steadfast defense of erotic integrity in the face of community opposition. That Lulu should come to be in her old age a bearer of the old traditions marks at least a symbolic reconciliation with her mother.

The young mixed-blood Pauline Puyat, who seeks to punish her body in any way imaginable in the effort to drive out the devil, also seeks sexual experience before becoming a nun. Her rendezvous with Napoleon Morrissey results in an unwanted pregnancy. Pauline's efforts to keep the child from being born in order to kill both her and the infant force the midwife, Bernadette, to tie Pauline down and remove the baby with iron spoons used as forceps. The dual surprise of the novel is that Pauline becomes, at the end of the novel, Sister Leopolda; and the girl she gives birth to and names Marie is eventually raised by the soft-witted Sophie Lazarre. Rather than the offspring of a "drunken woman" and a "dirty Lazarre," Marie is the child of Pauline and Napoleon Morrissey. Marie obviously has no clue to Sister Leopolda's identity in *Love Medicine*, but Leopolda recognizes Marie at least up to the end of *Tracks*. Marie and Sister Leopolda's mutual obsession, which leads to Leopolda's sponsoring Marie at the convent, is ostensibly religious and caring. That Leopolda should lock Marie in closets, scald her with hot water, brain her with an iron pole and skewer her hand with a meat fork suggests that, like Lulu, Marie has a difficult relationship with her mother. In retaliation for the scalding, Marie attempts to push Leopolda into a huge oven. Nonetheless, from her experience with Sister Leopolda, Marie learns pity, a gift that enables her to help her husband back to her side and that leads her to reconcile with Lulu. (Marie's compulsion to visit the dying nun many years later ironically leads to a battle over the iron spoon that Leopolda habitually bangs on her metal bedstead.)

Lulu's mother is deeply harmed in obviously material ways by Anglo encroachment—her parents and siblings are decimated by disease, her land is lost and her forest leveled, she and her family are starved, killing her second child. Still Fleur Pillager maintains her will to fight, crushing the wagons of the loggers when they come to throw her off her land. To keep Lulu safe from these circumstances Fleur has sent her to a boarding school, an act for which Lulu cannot forgive Fleur. Pauline/Leopolda is deeply harmed in more obviously psychological ways. An odd person from the outset, Pauline desires to move with the times, assimilating rather than "living in the old ways" as Fleur does. One critic describes Pauline as a trickster figure, but Nanapush, himself a trickster, confesses to being completely baffled by the girl. In several places Erdrich seems to suggest that it is Pauline's unattractiveness that drives her outside of the community. She cannot marry and so must find an occupation. In a community that has accepted Anglo definitions of use, value and gender roles, a woman like Pauline can find no recourse.

Marie and Lulu's friendship closes the circle as the daughters of Pauline—who rejects mothering from a distorted allegiance to Anglo culture—and Fleur—who gives up mothering the child upon whom she dotes in order to fight for Native culture—come together in the effort to nurture one another. In putting "the tears in [Lulu's] eyes," Marie helps Lulu to finally feel pity for her mother. Together the women have reconciled their own and their mothers' dilemmas, Marie by taking the good from Leopolda's venom and Lulu by claiming her mother's protective spirit. In that relationship lies the potential for community transformation that Lipsha notes. Wong writes, "It remains for those left behind, the adoptive mothers and thrown-away youngsters, to reweave the broken strands of family, totem, and community into a harmonious wholeness" (191).

The reconciliation takes place when Marie volunteers to help Lulu recover from cataract surgery. In the scene there is little dialogue and long periods in which the two women simply drink coffee and listen to music on the radio. Lulu thinks that "Too much might start the floodgates flowing and our moment would be lost. It was enough just to sit there without words" (236). The women understand that with a gulf as wide as the one they must cross, words will only divide them further. The benign music on the radio, the "music" of Marie's voice, and the soft touch of her hand provide the healing communication necessary to their alliance.

For Lulu this meeting provides a revelation: "For the first time I saw exactly how another woman felt, and it gave me deep comfort, surprising. It gave me the knowledge that whatever had happened the night before, and in the past, would finally be over once my bandages came off" (236). Marie indeed helps Lulu to "get [her] vision" as Lipsha testifies in the next chapter (235): "Insight. It was as though Lulu knew by looking at you what was the true bare-bones elements of your life. It wasn't like that before she had the operation on her eyes, but once the bandages came off she saw. She saw too clear for comfort" (241). Having seen "how another woman felt" Lulu is now capable of seeing into everyone; she is given a "near-divine" power of vision. Through imagery, however, Erdrich reveals that this connection is not simply one of friendship. Lulu imagines Marie, caring for her eyes, swaying "down like a dim mountain, huge and blurred, the way a mother must look to her just born child" (236).

In its coffee, contemplation and vision-seeking, this scene resembles the old women's ritual described at the outset and also depicted within Linda Hogan's short story "Meeting" about a contemporary women's ceremony:

> Mom was boiling coffee on the fire and serving it up. The women sipped it and warmed their palms over the fire. They were quiet but the lines of their faces spoke in the firelight, telling about stars that fell at night, the horses that died in the drought of 1930, and the pure and holy terror of gunshots fired into our houses.... Exhaustion had covered up all the mystery and beauty the women held inside.... I met myself that night and I walked in myself. I heard my own blood. I learned all secrets lie beneath even the straggliest of hair, and that in the long run of things dry skin and stiff backs don't mean as much as we give them credit for. (280)

In the meeting between Marie and Lulu rest the seeds for a return to powerful female political alliances, for necessary friendship that will signify not just caring, but survival, and not just survival, but prosperity. Significantly, it is in the nursing home, a communal dwelling place that ends the women's previous geographical isolation, that Marie and Lulu come together. Neither is their friendship strained, however, by familial or spousal demands.

Clearly the community can never again be what it was previous to the events of *Tracks*, but its very survival is at stake with the outside forces of capitalism and Anglo-American social, governmental and religious systems tearing at its fabric. That survival cannot take place without some kind of cohesive resistance. Since the traditionalist male figures—Old Man Pillager and Eli Kashpaw—have retreated into the bush and silence, it is left to the women in the novels to somehow save the children. Even though for some of those children the mothers may only be a shadowy presence, Lulu's sons idolize her and Marie's clan quickly materializes en masse for family gatherings. The two women's mutual grandson, Lipsha, as an old people's child and a caregiver to the old ones on the reservation, holds forth promise for a more powerful male presence. Although the desperation of some Turtle Mountain Reservation characters depicted in *Tracks* and *Love Medicine* may seem greater than of those characters living in Argus, the reservation also offers a portal to empowering traditions. Argus counts communal and personal strength only in dollar amounts.

Allen writes that in response to the "inhuman changes" wrought by Anglo colonization Indian women are trying to "reclaim their lives. Their power, their sense of direction and of self will soon be visible. It is the force of women who speak and work and write, and it is formidable" (50). Female friendship enables the women in Erdrich's novels to recreate an empowering matrix that was frequently lost or disrupted through colonization and acculturation. In turn the women are strengthened in their capacity to act as leaders for ensuing generations.

Notes

[1]Robert Silberman reads *Love Medicine* as largely a meditation on home, beginning as it does with June going "home" in a fatal blizzard. He writes: "Clearly, home in *Love Medicine* is an embattled concept, as ambiguous as June Kashpaw's motives in attempting her return" (108). The characters' loss of a satisfying home, while always functioning on a personal and familial level, surely carries echoes of their literal loss of homeland.

[2]Carolyn Neithammer argues that sexual jealousy in traditional Ojibwa communities could be intense: "Great shame was felt by any Ojibwa woman whose husband took another wife, and her wounded self-esteem was only aggravated by the talk of the rest of the villagers, who openly speculated on just what qualities the woman lacked that forced her husband to take another wife" (94). This underscores Marie's forgiveness of Nector and Lulu. The other community members, however, side with Marie and brand Lulu a Jezebel, calling her "the Lamartine." The aspersion may reflect French Catholic ideology.

Works Cited

Allen, Paula Gunn. *The Sacred Hoop*. Boston: Beacon, 1986.

Barry, Nora, and Mary Prescott. "The Triumph of the Brave: *Love Medicine's* Holistic Vision." *Critique* 30.2 (1989).

Bonvillain, Nancy. "Gender Relations in Native North America." *American Indian Culture and Research Journal* 13.2 (1989).

Brant, Beth. *Mohawk Trail*. New York: Firebrand Books, 1985.

Bruchac, Joseph. "Whatever is Really Yours: An Interview with Louise Erdrich." *Survival This Way: Interviews with American Indian Poets*. Tucson: U of Arizona P, 1987.

Erdrich, Louise. *Tracks*. New York: Harper, 1988.

_____. *The Beet Queen*. 1986. Rpt. New York: Bantam Books, 1987.

_____. *Love Medicine*. New York: Bantam Books, 1984.

Hogan, Linda. "Meeting." *The Stories We Hold Secret*. Eds. Carol Bruchac, Linda Hogan and Judith McDaniel. New York: Greenfield Review P, 1986.

Maristuen-Rodakowski, Julie. "The Turtle Mountain Reservation in North Dakota: Its History as Depicted in Louise Erdrich's *Love Medicine* and *The Beet Queen*." *American Indian Culture and Research Journal* 12.3 (1988).

Neithammer, Carolyn. *Daughters of the Earth: The Lives and Legends of American Indian Women*. New York: Macmillan, 1977.

Silberman, Robert. "Opening the Text: *Love Medicine* and the Return of the Native American Woman." *Narrative Chance*. Ed. Gerald Vizenor. Albuquerque: U of New Mexico P, 1989.

Tsosie, Rebecca. "Changing Women: The Cross-Currents of American Indian Feminine Identity." *American Indian Culture and Research Journal* 12.1 (1988).

Wong, Hertha D. "Adoptive Mothers and Thrown-Away Children in the Novels of Louise Erdrich." *Narrating Mothers: Theorizing Maternal Subjectivities*. Eds. Brenda O. Daly and Maureen T. Reddy. Knoxville: U of Tennessee P, 1991.

Inscriptions of Orality and Silence: Representations of Female Friendship in Francophone Africa and the Caribbean

RENÉE LARRIER

L'amitié se nourrit de
communication—Montaigne

African and Caribbean orature offer observations about friendship and communication. The Wolof of Senegal have a saying: *"Mbañ amul ñakk waxtaana am"* which means "hate does not exist, it's only the lack of dialogue" (Sylla 106). According to the Haitian proverb, "'Moun pa' sé dra," friends cover for each other (Jeanty 45). While these sayings acknowledge the importance of communication and mutual support, they do not take gender into consideration. Deborah Tannen's research in *You Just Don't Understand* shows that men and women communicate differently. Awa Thiam writes in *La Parole aux Négresses* that traditionally African women have been publicly silenced.[1] In *Black Feminist Thought: Knowledge, Consciousness, and the Politics of Empowerment*, Patricia Hill Collins identifies one of the three "safe spaces" where black women find a voice as being among other women (96). Female friendship, or to borrow Janice Raymond's term, "Gyn/affection" is one such locus; it entails commitment, bonding, sharing secrets and confidences, and listening to one another. The Hausa have a special word—"kawaye"—that designates a woman's best friend (Smith 56). Such a character is often found in women's narratives.

Most studies published in recent years on women's friendships in literature focus on English and American texts in which the friendships are somehow implicated in the marriage plot (Nestor, Knuth, Cosslett, George). An examination of female friendship in francophone African or Caribbean narratives has not yet been done. In my attempting such a study, the categories outlined by Janet Todd—sentimental, erotic, manipulative, political, social—and by

181

Charmaine Eileen Wellington—self-reflecting, otherness, heroic, mother-daughter—are based on novels by Western writers and, therefore, must be reformulated. As we shall see, different models emerge due to differences in cultures. For example, relationships between co-wives and intergenerational mentoring alliances are common in orature and literature in Africa and the Caribbean, respectively. In addition, because of history—specifically, slavery and colonialism—questions are raised about the possibility of interracial understanding and harmony. At the same time, however, women's friendships in Africa and the Caribbean are characterized by mutuality and reciprocity; in this way they resemble their American counterparts (Koppelman 280).

This study examines the specificity of female friendship in francophone African and Caribbean texts. We will see how differently male and female authors of oral and written texts represent women's friendships. Women writers especially are particularly concerned with communication. Their narratives are informed by oral, written, and silent discourses that characterize women's communication.

Friendship in orature

The link between oral and written narratives in Africa and the Caribbean has already been established (Irele, Julien); therefore a study of women's friendship in literature must begin with those kinds of texts. Birago Diop's *Les Contes d'Amadou Koumba* (1947) [*The Tales of Amadou Koumba*] and Werewere Liking and Marie-José Hourantier's *Contes d'initiation féminine* (1981) [*Female initiation tales*] are both collections of oral stories that were translated and transcribed from various African languages into French, but they provide distinctly different paradigms of traditional female friendship. The former, stories for a general audience, seems to suggest that women cannot get along with one another; the latter, consisting of two stories told *by* Bassa women exclusively *for* a female audience, shows otherwise. A genderized perspective is the case here.

Birago Diop collected stories from his grandmother, his and his brother's travels among various ethnic groups throughout West Africa, as well as from the family "griot," Amadou Koumba, for his *Les Contes d'Amadou Koumba*. In these stories the message seems to be that women are not to be trusted. For example, the moral *"Donne ton amour à la femme, mais non ta confiance"* (47) ["Give your love to a woman, but not your confidence" (trans. Larrier)]

closes "N'Gor Niébé," a story named for the title character who
refuses to eat string beans. His girlfriend N'Dèné is seduced by his
friends' promises of jewelry and clothing into agreeing to get him to
eat the vegetables. Moreover, this story comments on the
differences between male and female friendship. N'Gor has never
revealed to his male friends why he does not eat string beans. On
the other hand, N'Dèné's friends always share confidences. In fact,
the reason N'Gor gives for not explaining his dietary choices to
Dèné is precisely that she will tell her best friend Thioro, who will
tell her best friend N'Goné, who will tell her best friend Djégane.
Female friendship manifested through talk is represented in this
narrative not as a mutually supportive enterprise, but as a threat to
men.

A similar message is found in "Les Mamelles" [The Humps].
According to the narrator, two wives in the same household will
always be rivals:

> *Lorsqui'l s'agit d'épouses, deux n'est point un bon compte. Pour
> qui veut s'éviter souvent querelles, cris, reproches et allusions
> malveillantes, il faut trois femmes ou une seule et non pas deux.
> Deux femmes dans une même maison ont toujours avec elles
> une troisième compagne qui non seulement n'est bonne à rien,
> mais encore se trouve être la pire des mauvaises conseillères.
> Cette compagne c'est l'Envie à la voix aigre et acide comme du
> jus de tamarin.* (33)

> [In the matter of wives two is not a good number. The man who
> wants to avoid quarrels, shouting, grousing, reproaches, and
> nasty innuendos must have at least two wives, or else one, but
> never two. Two women in the same house always have with
> them a third companion, who is not only good for nothing, but
> also happens to be the worse of bad counsellors. This
> companion is shrill-voiced Envy, bitter as tamarind juice. (trans.
> Blair 2)]

The two wives in question are Khary, the jealous selfish first wife
and Koumba, the amiable generous second wife. Koumba shares
information with Khary that will make her hunchback disappear, but
Khary abuses the trust. Again, like in "N'Gor Niébé"
communication among women is stigmatized and leads to their
downfall. The message in "Petit mari" ("Little husband") is that
mother and daughters are rivals, too.

Mary Hunt's assertion that "in Western, especially Christian societies women's friendships have been downgraded, denied" (17) is relevant here. Although the culture in question is neither Western nor Christian, the issue of the maintenance of male dominance and control as reflected in orature is. Although critics Sonia Lee and Mohammadou Kane do not comment specifically on friendship, I agree with their conclusion that in general the stories contained in *Les Contes d'Amadou Koumba* are misogynist.

In Haiti female friendship is also stigmatized in the oral tradition. It is established at the outset of the story "Séraphine et Lilas" in *Contes et légendes d'Haïti* that the title characters' friendship is rare because two beautiful women are usually rivals. Their secret is that they enjoy doing different things: Séraphine reads and sews, Lilas prefers an active social life. The depth of their friendship is manifested when Lilas gets leprosy and Séraphine offers to let her borrow her skin to go dancing. Lilas, however, runs off and marries her favorite partner, leaving Séraphine with the unsightly skin. When Séraphine finally locates Lilas and demands her skin back, Lilas' husband, repelled by her appearance, abandons her. In addition to illustrating the importance of physical beauty in attracting and keeping a husband, it also very clearly indicates that women who are friends will eventually betray one another.

Contrary to the stories considered above, the ones Werewere Liking and Marie-José Hourantier collected and transcribed in *Contes d'initiation féminine* show that through cooperation and friendship women become empowered. The fact that these stories were originally told during Bassa girls' initiation ceremonies in Cameroon indicates that the storytellers as well as the target audience were exclusively female. Although the rituals are no longer performed, these surviving stories disclose traditional women's representation of friendship. In "Nguessi Ngonda" co-wives are not rivals as they are in Diop's "Les Mamelles," but get along very well. First, the title character accepts a young woman as a co-wife after she proves herself worthy by curing her husband's snake bite. Second, when Nguessi Ngonda, the new co-wife, and husband Johnny are held prisoner by the king, one of his wives liberates Nguessi Ngonda, and brings her to her home to talk and share a meal. It is significant that this meeting occurs in the particular place in the kitchen—"sous la claie"—where a woman keeps her private things and to which men are denied access.

The queen is so impressed that Nguessi Ngonda divides the food into equal portions for her co-wife, husband and host, that she offers to help find the answer to the king's riddles, which in turn will free the whole family. She then asks permission to join Nguessi Ngonda's household as the third wife. Nguessi Ngonda replies that she cannot give her consent without first consulting the co-wife who is responsible for initially saving their lives. The queen subsequently brings the co-wife "sous la claie" where all three women "concluaient l'affaire" (24). We can call the negotiations concerning their combined future a bonding scene. *Contes d'initiation féminine* illustrates that women in women's stories for women develop successful relationships with other women, and thereby subvert the message in stories for general audiences.

Friendship in literature

Ousmane Sembène, whom scholars such as Case, Linkhorn and Scharfman consider a feminist writer, rejects the male script offered by most oral stories. A close reading of his novel *Les Bouts de bois de Dieu* (1960) (*God's Bits of Wood*) illustrates that his representation of women resembles more closely that which is found in the women's oral stories. Not only do the women characters form alliances to support their striking railway worker husbands, but they make their own statement by marching from Thies to Dakar and confronting and successfully routing the police. While they collaborate for a political cause, they also relate to one another on a more personal basis. For example, the families survive the hardships due to the women's efforts to help each other. In addition, young Penda, who had been ostracized from the community, not only wins the respect of everyone because of her commitment, but also earns the friendship of Maïmouna. In this narrative even friendship between males and females is possible, but doomed. Bakayoko tells N'Dèye Touti that Penda *"était une vraie amie et elle a donné sa vie"* (342) ["was a real friend, and she lost her life because of it" (trans. Price 303)].

Simone Schwarz-Bart's *Pluie et vent sur Télumée Miracle (The Bridge of Beyond)* explores in more depth intergenerational friendships among rural Guadeloupean women who communicate orally. When Télumée's grandmother who raised her, dies, Man Cia, a healer, reputed witch and Toussine's best friend, takes her place. Every Sunday Télumée visits and sits under the mango tree where her grandmother had sat, and Man Cia prepares her a special bath. Together they garden and feed the chickens. More important,

Man Cia teaches Télumée the secrets of plants, initiating her through the spoken word. The mentoring relationship is reversed, however, when Man Cia changes into a dog. Every Sunday Télumée cooks the same meal—rice and beans—that Man Cia used to prepare for her which they eat under the mango tree. Later Télumée will earn a reputation as a healer and witch in her own right. After the dog disappears, another older woman forges a friendship with Télumée when she secretly leaves food on Télumée's doorstep. At their first meeting, bonding talks place as Olympia talks to Télumée about the neighbors. The mentoring process occurs as Olympia initiates Télumée into the intricacies of working in the cane fields—by putting bandages on one's hands to protect the skin, for example. That Télumée works behind Olympia in the fields—Télumée binds what Olympia cuts—is symbolic of this mentoring relationship. Télumée will also assume Olympia's habits of drinking alcohol and smoking a pipe.

While *Pluie et vent* privileges intergenerational relationships, friendships between females of the same age are not ignored. It is mentioned that Toussine and Man Cia were childhood friends and young Télumée, Tavie, and Laetitia (who will later betray Télumée by having an affair with her husband Elie) forge a bond while imitating the demeanor of women.

Women who do not read or write must rely on oral discourse to communicate. In order for friendship to flourish they must remain in close proximity to one another like Maïmouna and Penda, Télumée and Man Cia, Télumée and Olympia. When they lack close contact as in "La Noire de..." ("The Promised Land") by Ousmane Sembène, the results are tragic. Diouana from rural Casamance leaves Senegal to be a maid in the south of France. Separated from her family and friends, she is dependent on Madame, her employer, to write letters home. Separated from Madame by race, class and language, she is unable to confide in her. Diouana feels powerless, both linguistically and economically: "*Etait-ce possible de dire tout ce qui lui passait par la tête à Madame? Elle s'en voulait. Son ignorance la rendait muette. Elle écumait de rage, à son propos. Mademoiselle lui avait, en plus, pris les timbres*" (182) ["But was it possible to say to Madame all that went through her mind? She was angry with herself, for her ignorance silenced her. This impotence on her part made her foam with rage. Moreover, Mademoiselle had taken her stamps" (trans. Ortzen 98)]. Isolated, alienated, reduced to silence—in short, unable to communicate, Diouana commits suicide.

Written discourse between women provides that much needed support in Ousmane Sembène's short story "Lettres de France" ("Letters From France") and Mariama Bâ's novel *Une si longue lettre* (1979) (*So Long A Letter*). In both narratives—one by a male, the other by a female writer—female correspondents who were educated in Senegal at the French school now reside on different continents and thus communicate with their best friend through the mail. In each case the "destinataire's" letters are not represented, thereby the illusion of a listener or a sounding board is created.

In "Lettres de France" Nafi writes from her coffin-like attic room in Marseille to her old friend whom she refers to as "ma vieille, très vieille amie" back in Dakar. She discloses her disillusionment with her life in France and regret and disappointment in marrying 73-year-old Demba. Silence characterizes this marriage while open communication characterizes the friendship. For example, when Nafi becomes pregnant, she confides in her friend even before she tells her husband or other family members. Nafi recognizes that friendship sustained through writing has been her salvation:

> Que serais-je devenue sans toi? Toi, mon unique soutien, ma confidente! Tu ne sauras et ne pourras jamais savoir comment j'ai apprécié notre correspondance. Sans ce flux et reflux de lettres, j'aurais été sevrée de mon lait originel, une perdue, une égarée. Je ne suis pas une lyrique, mais, je voudrais pouvoir t'écrire pour te faire sentir toutes mes émotions. Nos tête-à-tête—malgré cette quantité d'eau qui nous sépare—furent pour moi, les joints qui solidifient notre amitié. (114)

> [What would have happened to me if it weren't for you? My one support, the only person I could confide in. You'll never know just how much our correspondence has meant to me. Without this coming and going of letters, I should have been cut off from my source, been lost, and gone astray. I'm not a poet, but I wish I could write and make you feel all my emotions. Despite all the water between us, our exchanges have put the seal on our friendship. (trans. Ortzen 76)]

The situation is similar for Ramatoulaye in *Une si longue lettre*; the act of writing to Aïssatou provides comfort and solidifies the friendship. This "very long letter" in fact, resembles a diary in that it consists of daily entries in a notebook and is never sent to Aïssatou who resides in Washington, D.C. where she is employed by the Senegalese embassy. The writing is prompted by the death of Ramatoulaye's husband of 30 years and her desire for closeness at a critical time in her life. It also allows her to reflect on her past and their relationship. For example, when Aïssatou gives Ramatoulaye a car to facilitate her getting around Dakar after Modou abandons her, Ramatoulaye writes: *"L'amitié a des grandeurs inconnues de l'amour. Elle se fortifie dans les difficultés, alors que les contraintes massacrent l'amour. Elle résiste au temps qui lasse et désunit les couples. Elle a des élévations inconnues de l'amour"* (79) ["Friendship has splendours that love knows not. It grows stronger when crossed, whereas obstacles kill love. Friendship resists time, which wearies and severs couples. It has heights unknown to love" (trans. Bode-Thomas 54)]. She confides only in Aïssatou when one of her unmarried daughters becomes pregnant.

One can say that this longstanding friendship—"wolĕre" in Wolof—was inherited. Ramatoulaye and Aïssatou's grandmothers and mothers exchanged messages daily over the fence separating their two compounds. Their own friendship, fondly recalled as the narrative opens, was solidified at a very young age when they buried their baby teeth in the same hole and shared mangoes. They were also students together at the Koranic school, French school and the Ecole Normale, became teachers, married friends Modou Fall and Mawdo Bâ, respectively, socialized and took vacations together. Ramatoulaye even named one of her daughters and one of her sons after Aïssatou and Mawdo. After many years of marriage, they both become single mothers when their husbands take a much younger second wife; Aïssatou chooses divorce, Ramatoulaye chooses to remain married but is abandoned by Modou.

In *Une si longue lettre* the women's friendship has outlasted their marriages and has been sustained over the years despite geographical distance: *"Tu m'as souvent prouvé la superiorité de l'amitié sur l'amour. Le temps, la distance autant que les souvenirs communs ont consolidé nos liens et font de nos enfants, des frères et des soeurs"* (104-05) ["You have often proven to me the superiority of friendship over love. Time, distance, as well as mutual memories have consolidated our ties and made our children brothers and sisters" (trans. Bode-Thomas 72)]. The two parties involved communicate through writing. Their mothers' and grandmothers' fence has been replaced by the Atlantic Ocean. The locus of this "modern" friendship is the blank page as writing replaces conversation. The unrepresented responses of Aïssatou are referred to as *"ces mots caressants qui me décrispent"* (104) ["Caressing words which relax me" (trans. Bode-Thomas 71)].

In the texts considered above, oral and written discourse strengthen ties between friends. When those forms of discourse are not available, a third form—silent discourse—is an adequate substitute. In Michèle Maillet's *L'Etoile noire* (1990) (*Black star*), speech and writing are forbidden in the concentration camp at Ravensbruck; consequently, prisoners Sidonie and Suzanne's friendship develops as they communicate using gestures.

Sidonie Hellénon, 25, mother of two, Martinican and Catholic, is arrested near Bordeaux and deported along with her Jewish employers, the Dubreuils, in December 1943. On the train to the concentration camp she notices a young French woman about her age who looks at her, smiles and then speaks softly, offering to watch the sleeping twins while Sidonie goes to the bathroom. She reassures Sidonie by introducing herself as Suzanne, a school teacher. This initial encounter causes Sidonie to want to establish a connection with Suzanne, to talk about their lives.

According to Ronald Sharp, "one of the crucial stages in the formation of most friendships is the long conversation in which one shares one's past with one's emerging friend" (16). Sidonie realizing they do not have the freedom nor the luxury of time, gives up: *"alors pourquoi se lier si vite et pour si peu de temps"* (51) ["Why forge a bond so quickly and for such a short amount of time?" (trans. Larrier)]. It is Suzanne, however, who pursues and cultivates the bond. Her strategy involves her body. As Sidonie and her young children embark from the train, Suzanne makes a path for them with her body; she uses it again to protect them during the bumpy bus ride. She holds Désiré's hand, and consoles a crying Nicaise. Sidonie and Suzanne do not speak, but a friendship blossoms anyway as they communicate without words. Sharp's "long conversation" has been replaced by gesture.

This silent discourse takes many forms in the narrative: a nod, a smile, a look, a movement of the eyelid, a hand gesture, a hand touching the shoulder, a nudge, an extended arm. These silent signals have meaning and more often than not replace speech: *"J'effleure la joue de Suzanne qui ouvre les yeux dans un sourire. Elle suit mon regard, mon geste. Elle a compris"* (78) ["I touch Suzanne's cheek. She opens her eyes in a smile. She follows my gaze, my gesture. She understood" (trans. Larrier)]. Sometimes Sidonie and Suzanne need not even look at one another: *"Nous n'échangeons plus un mot, plus un regard, mais je sens que nous sommes désormais quatre, deux enfants, deux femmes, une petite communauté dans la foule, un peu plus qu'une famille"* (56) [We do not exchange any more words or any glances, but I feel that we are henceforth four, two children, two women, a small community in the crowd, a little more than a family" (trans. Larrier)]. Sidonie eventually characterizes their relationship as a friendship, but one that must be hidden at all costs:

> *Mais Suzanne est devenue mon double, et moi le sien. Nous sommes comme Désiré et Nicaise, jumelles. Nous ne communiquons pas par mots, mais par signes, et le plus souvent par notre simple présence. Nous craignons la jalousie, l'envie des autres. L'amitié est une denrée rare; on ne peut pas la voler, mais on peut la détruire. Nous ne voulons pas non plus alerter nos gardiennes ni leurs supérieures: elles nous sépareraient ou nous feraient souffrir l'une par l'autre.* (180)

> [But Suzanne became my double, and I hers. We are like Desire and Nicaise, twins. We do not communicate with words, but with signals, and most often with our mere presence. We fear the jealousy and envy of others. Friendship is a rare commodity; it cannot be stolen, but it can be destroyed. We do not want to alert the guards nor their superiors. They would separate us or make us suffer. (trans. Larrier)]

Although Sidonie and Suzanne are both French citizens, their friendship crosses racial and religious boundaries. Being black, Sidonie is arrested and condemned by the Nazis along with her Jewish employers. Suzanne is arrested because of her religion. Thrown together for unjust reasons, they overcome their circumstances and provide support for one another.

This representation of a successful interracial friendship is unlike the one found in Ferdinand Oyono's *Une vie de boy* (*Houseboy*) and *Le Vieux nègre et la médaille* (*The Old Man and the Medal*) where friendship between white colonizer and black colonized is deemed impossible because of racism and inequality. Women writers, on the other hand, seem to be more positive about the possibility of interracial friendships—among women. In "La Voie du salut," a short story by Aminata Maïga Kâ, Rabiatou and Josette are friends but history provides a barrier. In Maryse Condé's *Moi, Tituba sorcière* (1986) (*I, Tituba, Black Witch of Salem* [1992]), both Tituba and Hester are accused of witchcraft, banished by

Puritan society, and brought together by circumstance. In Calixthe Beyala's *Tu t'appelleras Tanga* (1988) [*Your name will be Tanga*], Cameroonian Tanga relates her life story to French/Jewish Anna-Claude her cellmate. In spite of racial differences the friendship prevails.[2] Perhaps these women writers are more optimistic.

In *L'Etoile noire* not only does Sidonie form an alliance with Suzanne, but also with women of color: Carol, an African-American singer; Anastasie, a Martinican and daughter of Sidonie's former teacher; Aglaé, a Senegalese; Eloise, a Malagasy; and Nadine, a Chinese. Their common bond, a "solidarité de couleur" (198) separates them from the other women and subjects them to particular scientific experiments by the Nazis. In order to cope with such horrible conditions, they try to calm and comfort one another. Carol sings and teaches them spirituals. Anastasie helps deliver an unnamed black woman's baby. Sidonie entertains the idea of holding secret strategy meetings, including Suzanne whom she considers both black and white. All the women of color recognize the importance of the strong bond that they share.

In addition, they rely on silent discourse to communicate: Eloise questions Sidonie with a look and Sidonie in turns reads her eyes. Sidonie and Anastasie, who are compatriots, become especially close. Sidonie cares for Anastasie when she has a fever. While in different cells, they sing Creole songs to each other, and cry in silence and sing the spiritual they learned when Carol dies from the punishment she receives for resisting. Sidonie refers to Anastasie as not only her friend, but her memory. Perhaps the most convincing sign of their friendship is that when Sidonie learns that she will be transferred to yet another camp and certain death, she entrusts to Anastasie her three most important possessions for safekeeping: her medallion given to her by her mother, her journal in the hope that it will be read by someone after her death as a testimony to her suffering and her son Désiré if he is found. The close bond Sidonie had formed with Suzanne is replaced by the one with Anastasie. Although friendships with these women representing the African diaspora take up much less space in the novel than the relationship with Suzanne, they are not marginalized. Maillet has already established how the relationship functions.

Friendship is valorized and celebrated among women writers in the literature of French-speaking Africa and the Caribbean. These texts give the lie to the following sayings from Zaire and Cameroon, respectively: "The banana tree is felled by the wind; friendship is felled by a married woman. If friendship includes the wife, it will perish" (Schipper 80). Mary Helen Washington has identified a distinctly African-American women's literary tradition in which "women talk to other women...and their friendships with other women—mothers, sisters, grandmothers, friends, lovers—are vital to their growth and well-being" (xxi). Terry McMillan's *Waiting to Exhale* (1992), which privileges the close friendship of four Phoenix women, is the most recent example. Washington has also isolated what she calls a bonding scene in black women's narratives. Such a scene occurs frequently in texts by francophone African and Caribbean women. For example, in "Nguessi Ngonda" the title character, co-wife, and queen together decide their future in the space in the kitchen reserved for women. In *Une si longue lettre* Ramatoulaye and Aïssatou as children bury their baby teeth in the same hole and make the same wish. Bonding and confiding are in no way marginalized in these narratives. In fact, in *Une si longue lettre* and *Pluie et vent sur Télumée Miracle*, the friendship structures the text.

Whether communication takes place orally, in writing or by gesture is immaterial; it is essential to the survival of women in that it fosters growth and provides emotional support especially in difficult circumstances. Francophone African and Caribbean women writers recognize the importance of friendship in life and explore its dynamics in literature.

Notes

[1]For a discussion of the silencing and voicelessness of women writers in the Caribbean, see Carole Boyce Davies and Elaine Savory Fido, "Introduction: Women and Literature in the Caribbean: An Overview," *Out of the Kumba: Caribbean Women and Literature* (Trenton: Africa World Press, 1991) 1-22.

[2]In Ousmane Sembène's *Le Docker noir* (1956) (*Black Docker*) Bacari Sonko and Paul form a friendship. For a discussion of interracial friendship in American literature see Nancy Porter, "Women's Interracial Friendships and Visions of Community in *Meridian, The Salt Eaters, Civil Wars,* and *Dessa Rose,*" *Tradition and the Talents of Women.* Ed. Florence Howe (Urbana: University of Illinois, 1991) 251-67.

Works Cited

Bâ, Mariama. *So Long A Letter*. Trans. Modupe Bode-Thomas. London: Heinemann, 1989.

_____. *Une si longue lettre*. Dakar: Nouvelles Editions Africaines, 1980.

Case, Frederic. "Workers Movements: Revolution and Women's Consciousness." *Canadian Journal of African Studies* 15.2 (1981).

Collins, Patricia Hill. *Black Feminist Thought: Knowledge, Consciousness, and the Politics of Empowerment*. Perspectives on Gender. Vol. 2. Boston: Unwin Hyman, 1990.

Cosslett, Tess. *Woman to Woman: Female Friendship in Victorian Fiction*. Atlantic Highlands, NJ: Humanities Press International, 1988.

Dehon, Claire. "Les Influences du conte traditonnel dans le roman camerounais d'expression francaise." *Neohelicon* 16.2 (1989).

Diop, Birago. *Les Contes d'Amadou Koumba*. Paris: Presence Africaine, 1947.

_____. *Les Nouveaux contes d'Amadou Koumba*. Paris: Presence Africaine, 1961.

Faver, Susan Pauly. "The Narrative that Binds: Women's Friendship as Aesthetic and Political Strategy in Four Nineteenth Century Novels." *DAI* 50.7 (1990). U of Arkansas, 1988.

George, Susanne. "A Patchwork of Friends: The Female Community of Elinor Pruitt Stewart." *Platte Valley Review* 17.1 (1989).

Hunt, Mary E. *Fierce Tenderness: A Feminist Theology of Friendship*. New York: Crossroad, 1991.

Irele, Abiola. "The African Imagination." *Research in African Literatures* 21.1 (1990).

Jeanty, Edner A., and O. Carl Brown. *Parol Granmoun: Haitain Popular Wisdom*. Port-au-Prince: Editions Learning Center, 1976.

Julien, Eileen. *African Novels and the Question of Orality*. Bloomington: Indiana UP, 1992.

Ka, Aminata Maiga. *La Voie du salut*. Paris: Presence Africaine, 1985.

Kane, Mohamadou. *Essais sur les Contes d'Amadou Coumba*. Dakar: Nouvelles Editions Africaines, 1981.

Knuth, Deborah. "'We Fainted Alternatively on a Sofa': Female Friendship in Jane Austen's *Juvenilia*." *Persuasions* 9 (1987).

Koppelman, Susan. Afterword. *Women's Friendships: A Collection of Short Stories*. Norman: U of Oklahoma P, 1991.

Lee, Sonia. "The Image of the Woman in the African Folktale from the Sub-Saharan Francophone Area." *Yale French Studies* 53 (1976).

Liking, Werewere and Marie-Jose Hourantier. *Contes d'initiation feminine du pays Bassa*. Paris: Editions Saint-Paul, 1981.

Linkhorn, Renee. "L'Afrique de demain: femmes en marche dans l'oeuvre de Sembene Ousmane." *Modern Language Studies* 16.3 (1986).

Malliet, Michele. *L'Etoile noire*. Paris: Francois Bourin, 1990.

Nestor, Pauline. *Female Friendships and Communities: Charlotte Bronte, George Eliot, Elizabeth Gaskell*. Oxford: Clarendon P/New York: Oxford UP, 1985.

Raymond, Janice. "Female Friendships: Contra Chodorow and Dinnerstein." *Hypatia* 1.2 (1986).

Scharfman, Ronnie. "Fonction romanesque feminine: rencontre de la culture et de la structure dans *Les Bouts de bois de Dieu*." *Ethiopiques* 1.3-4 (1983).

Schipper, Mineke. *Source of All Evil: African Proverbs and Sayings on Women*. Chicago: Ivan R. Dee, 1991.

Schwarz-Bart, Simone. *The Bridge of Beyond*. Trans. Barbara Bray. New York: Atheneum, 1974.

_____. *Pluie et vent sur Telumee Miracle*. Paris: Seuil, 1972.

Sembene, Ousmane. *Les Bouts de bois de Dieu*. Paris: Le Livre Contemporain, 1960.

_____. *God's Bits of Wood*. Trans. Francis Price. Garden City: Doubleday, 1962.

_____. *Tribal Scars and Other Stories*. Trans. Len Ortzen. London: Heinemann, 1987.

_____. *Voltaique*. Paris: Presence Africaine, 1971.

Sharp, Ronald A. *Friendship and Literature: Spirit and Form*. Durham: Duke UP, 1986.

Smith, Mary. *Baba of Karo: A Woman of the Moslem Hausa*. London: Faber and Faber, 1954.

Sylla, Assane. *La Philosophie morale des Wolof*. Dakar: Sankore, 1978.

Tannen, Deborah. *You Just Don't Understand*. New York: Ballantine, 1991.

Thiam, Awa. *La Parole aux Negresses*. Paris: Denoel-Gonthiers, 1978.

Thoby-Marcelin, Philippe, and Pierre Marcelin. *Contes et legendes d'Haiti*. Paris: Fern and Nathan, 1967.

Todd, Janet. *Women's Friendship in Literature*. New York: Columbia UP, 1980.

Washington, Mary Helen, ed. Introduction. *Invented Lives: Narratives of Black Women 1860-1960*. New York: Anchor P, 1987.

Wellington, Charmaine Eileen. "Female Friendships in Doris Lessing's Novels." *DAI* 47.10 (1987). U of Illinois.

Primary Works Discussed or Mentioned

The Annunciation by Meridel Le Sueur
     Roberts
As We Are Now by May Sarton
     Waxman
At Seventy by May Sarton
     Waxman
Aurora Leigh by Elizabeth Barrett Browning
     Buchanan
The Beet Queen by Louise Erdrich
     Tharp
Between the Acts by Virginia Woolf
     Olano
Clarissa by Samuel Richardson
     Yadlon
The Color Purple by Alice Walker
     Payant
Contes d'initiation feminine du pays Bassa by Werewere Liking
  and Marie-Jose Hourantier
     Larrier
The Coquette by Hannah Foster
     Tassoni
Cress Delahanty by Jessamyn West
     Payant
Daniel Deronda by George Eliot
     Bunkers
The Diary of Emily Hawley Gillespie (unpublished manuscript)
     Bunkers
The Diary of Sarah Gillespie Huftalen (unpublished manuscript)
     Bunkers
The Diary of Ada L. James (unpublished manuscript)
     Bunkers
The Diary of Emily C. Quiner (unpublished manuscript)
     Bunkers
The Diary of Caroline Seabury, 1854-1863 by Caroline Seabury
     Bunkers
The Diaries of Jane Somers by Doris Lessing
     Waxman
The Diary of a Good Neighbor by Doris Lessing
     Waxman

During the Reign of the Queen of Persia by Joan Chase
    Payant
Fear of Flying by Erica Jong
    Payant
The Friendships Gallery by Virginia Woolf
    Olano
The Girl by Meridel Le Sueur
    Roberts
"Goblin Market" by Christina Rossetti
    Bunkers
The Golden Notebook by Doris Lessing
    Roberts
The House by the Sea by May Sarton
    Waxman
Jane Eyre by Charlotte Bronte
    Payant
Kinflicks by Lisa Alther
    Payant
"La Voie du salut" by Aminata Maiga Ka
    Larrier
Les Bouts de bois de Dieu by Ousmane Sembene
    Larrier
Les Contes d'Amadou Koumba by Birago Diop
    Larrier
L'Etoile noire by Michele Maillet
    Larrier
Letters on the Improvement of the Mind by Hester Chapone
    Yadlon
"Lettres de France" by Ousmane Sembene
    Larrier
Le Vieux negre et la medaille by Ferdinand Oyono
    Larrier
Love Medicine by Louise Erdrich
    Tharp
Maudie's Day by Doris Lessing
    Waxman
Meeting by Linda Hogan
    Tharp
The Member of the Wedding by Carson McCullers
    Payant
Memoirs of an Ex-Prom Queen by Alix Kates Shulman
    Payant
Moby Dick by Herman Melville
    Payant

Mohawk Trail by Beth Brant
  Tharp
Moi, Tituba Sorciere by Maryse Conde
  Larrier
Moments of Being by Virginia Woolf
  Cooley
  Olano
Mrs. Dalloway by Virginia Woolf
    Cooley
  Olano
Native Origin by Beth Brant
    Tharp
Night and Day by Virginia Woolf
  Cooley
Orlando by Virginia Woolf
  Cooley
  Olano
The Pargiters by Virginia Woolf
  Olano
Pluie et vent sur Telumee Miracle by Simone Schwarz-Bart
  Larrier
A Room of One's Own by Virginia Woolf
  Cooley
  Olano
Rumors of Peace by Ella Leffland
  Payant
Ruth by Elizabeth Gaskell
  Buchanan
Sense and Sensibility by Jane Austen
  Buchanan
Shirley by Charlotte Bronte
  Buchanan
Small Changes by Marge Piercy
  Payant
  Roberts
To the Lighthouse by Virginia Woolf
  Cooley
  Olano
Tracks by Louise Erdrich
  Tharp
Tu t'appelleras Tanga by Calixthe Beyala
  Larrier
Une si longue lettre by Mariama Ba
  Larrier

Contributors

Laurie Buchanan teaches parttime at both Marshall University and Ohio University Southern Branch. Her scholarship includes published papers and presentations on Victorian fiction, particularly women's fiction and Elizabeth Gaskell. She has published essays in *Joinings and Disjoinings: The Significance of Marital Status in Literature*, eds. JoAnna S. Mink and Janet D. Ward (1991) and *The Midwest Quarterly*.

Suzanne L. Bunkers is a professor of English at Mankato State University. Her research focuses on women's autobiography. Her edition of *The Diary of Caroline Seabury, 1854-1863* (1991) and her edition of *The Diary of Sarah Gillespie Huftalen, an Iowa Woman* (1993) reflect her research interest. Her articles have appeared in *Legacy: Journal of Nineteenth-Century Women Writers, Women's Studies International Forum; A/B: Auto/Biography Studies, Studies in Autobiography*, ed. James Olney (1988); *The Intimate Critique: Autobiographical Literary Criticism*, eds. Diane Freedman, Olivia Frey and Frances Zauhar (1992); *Muses; Minnesota English Journal*; and *Iowa Woman*.

Elizabeth Cooley is an assistant professor of English at Gonzaga University. She has presented papers and published articles on Virginia Woolf, Toni Morrison and other twentieth-century writers. She has also published short fiction.

Renée Larrier is associate professor of French and Women's Studies at Rutgers University. Her articles on francophone African and Caribbean literature have appeared in *French Review, CLA Journal, Studies in Twentieth Century Literature, Presence francophone, World Literature Today*, among others. She is currently working on a book-length manuscript on women writers from those regions and compiles the francophone Caribbean section of the annual *Callaloo* bibliography.

JoAnna Stephens Mink is an associate professor of English at Mankato State University. She is co-editor of *Joinings and Disjoinings: The Significance of Marital Status in Literature* (1991),

The Significance of Sibling Relationships in Literature (1993), and is currently working on an anthology on feminist collaboration. Her articles on nineteenth- and twentieth-century fiction and authors, as well as on aspects of the composing process, have appeared in *Heroines of Popular Culture*, ed. Pat Browne (1987), *Literature and Life: Making Connections in the Classroom*, ed. Patricia Phelan (1990), and *Teaching English in the Two-Year College*, among others. She has presented papers at annual conferences of the Midwest Modern Language Association and College Composition and Communication, among others. She is program director of a six-week summer course in Dorset, England, on the literature and landscape of Thomas Hardy.

Pamela J. Olano is a doctoral candidate at the University of Minnesota in the Department of English and the Center for Advanced Feminist Studies. She has presented papers on a variety of interdisciplinary topics at major national conferences including the International Virginia Woolf Conference, the Midwest Modern Language Association, the College Composition and Communication Conference, and the American Comparative Literature Association Annual Meeting. She has published articles in *Matrices: Lesbian Feminist Resource Network*, and a Summary of Scholarship and Research on Lesbian Feminist Literary Criticism in *Women's Studies Quarterly*. Currently, she is working on major essays that focus on Lesbian theory.

Katherine B. Payant is a professor of English at Northern Michigan University and Director of the Gender Studies Program. She has presented papers and published articles on contemporary women's literature, popular culture, and teaching composition, as well as her book *Woman Becoming: Contemporary Feminism and Popular Fiction by American Women Writers* (1993).

Nora Ruth Roberts is a lecturer in English at Medgar Evans College in Brooklyn, NY. She is a doctoral candidate at City University of New York, where she is preparing a dissertation on "Three Radical Women Writers: Meridel Le Sueur, Josephine Herbst and Tillie Olsen," contracted for publication by Garland Press. As a free-lance writer over the years she has published a travel memoir, a children's book, numerous essays and six short stories. She is a featured New York Council for the Humanities lecturer on Louisa May Alcott.

John Paul Tassoni is a lecturer in English at Francis Marion University. He has published articles in *Nineteenth Century Studies* and *Social Issues in the English Clasroom*, eds. C. Mark Hurlbert and Samuel Totten (1992). He has presented papers on American women writers at the Pennsylvania College English Association Conference and the Pennsylvania State System of Higher Education Graduate Colloquim.

Julie Tharp is an assistant professor of English at the University of Wisconsin Centers—Marshfield. Her articles and essays have appeared in the *West Virginia University Philological Papers, Prairie Women's Journal* and *Hurricane Alice*. She has presented papers and published articles on twentieth-century literature by women of color as well as published her own creative non-fiction. She has given several presentations at the Midwest Modern Language Association annual meetings. She is currently working on an oral history project focusing on Native American women quilters.

Janet Doubler Ward teaches composition and literature at Illinois Central College. She is co-editor of *Joinings and Disjoinings: The Significance of Marital Status in Literature* (1991) and *The Significance of Sibling Relationships in Literature* (1993). She has presented papers on women in literature and on composition studies at the annual conferences of College Composition and Communication, Midwest Modern Language Association and Philological Association of Louisiana.

Barbara Frey Waxman is a professor of English at the University of North Carolina—Wilmington. She has published a book on the literature of aging, *From the Hearth to the Open Road: A Feminist Study of Aging in Contemporary Literature* (1990) and articles on nineteenth-century British writers, twentieth-century American ethnic writers and feminist pedagogy. She is currently editing a collection of feminist/poststructuralist essays entitled *Multicultural Literatures through Feminist/Poststructuralist Lenses* (forthcoming) on multicultural literatures, for which she has written an essay on Toni Morrison's *Beloved*.

Susan M. Yadlon received her M.A. from Syracuse University and is currently a doctoral candidate at Ohio State University. She has presented papers on feminist theory and contemporary fiction. Her latest project is an essay focusing on power relations between students which will be published in *Political Moments in the Classroom: Teachers Talking Towards Knowledge and Action*.

DATE DUE

AUG 2 6 2002 ILL # 8728633 DRB			
AUG 3 1 2003 ILL # 8153470 NHM			
MAR 1 8 2010			
GAYLORD			PRINTED IN U.S.A